(continued from front flap)

governmental institutions (See back cover), *The Miami Metropolitan Experiment* illustrates what is probably the most unique and most interesting of these efforts in America to date. City planning officials, legislators, administrators and students of government will welcome the data and sound analysis which it presents.

EDWARD SOFEN is a professor of Government, and a member of the Committee on Municipal Research at the University of Miami. He has written extensively on the Miami-Dade experience, as well as on other problems of government and civil liberties, in articles which have appeared in the *National Civic Review*, the *Midwest Journal of Political Science*, the *Miami Law Quarterly*, and the *Wayne Law Review*.

# THE MIAMI METROPOLITAN EXPERIMENT

METROPOLITAN ACTION
STUDIES NO. 2

EDWARD SOFEN

# THE
# MIAMI
# METROPOLITAN
# EXPERIMENT

METROPOLITAN ACTION
STUDIES NO. 2

INDIANA UNIVERSITY PRESS
BLOOMINGTON

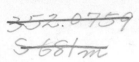
This book has been published with the assistance of a grant from the
Ford Foundation.

# Foreword

TIIE CITY AND metropolitan area of Miami present one of the most spectacular examples of a set of processes and problems that are occurring in practically all the urban areas of this country and, in great measure, other countries as well. Impelled by multiple forces and pressures, thousands and thousands of new citizens have moved to the area in recent years, from near and far, and the tide of in-migration and population increase shows no signs of coming to a halt. Some of the newcomers come into the existing cities, but some of them, along with many of those previously living in these cities, have moved out in restless surges over what were previously great expanses of rural countryside. Supplied with automobiles, these populations are highly mobile, criss-crossing the expanding urban area in journeys to work and school and recreation.

Although there have been some stresses and strains, the economic structure of the area has adapted to the population changes rather well—houses are built, stores are opened, goods are distributed, employment opportunities develop and workers are found to fill jobs. Per capita incomes, both in dollars and in real terms, have continued to be higher in these growing metropolitan areas than in the remainder of the country. Since most people are able to afford new facilities in new sections of the community, the chief economic problems occasioned by these shifts ordinarily turn around the deterioration and decay of older facilities—houses, central business districts, older transportation methods.

Political institutions and processes have not adjusted as well. The traditional units have been designed to fit tight, compact urban communities on the one hand or loose, rural areas, with little need for intensive public services, on the other. Neither the cities nor the counties nor the multiplying special districts have been able to adapt rapidly enough to the new situations. The provision of roads, new schools, and good water, the disposal of garbage and sewage, the control of land use and building—all these and many other public functions have been provided late and inadequately, and the allocation of responsibility for the services themselves and the financial support of them has been confused and inequitable.

In the hope that something useful can be learned through careful inspection of the processes through which some particular communities have tried to adjust to some of their metropolitan governmental problems, the Ford Foundation made a series of grants to help support case studies of these processes in several different communities. These case studies are being made, ordinarily, by groups of social scientists at a university in or near the metropolitan community involved. A grant was also made to Indiana University to enable it to attempt some coordination of the individual case studies.

Miami was almost inevitably the subject of one of these case studies. Its effort to create a major metropolitan-wide unit to address itself to the problems of provision and coordination of governmental services was unique in this country (a somewhat different and perhaps even more sweeping attempt to provide metropolitan governmental unity has been recently approved by the voters of the Nashville area), and the recurring struggles to set it up and then to modify it have attracted national attention. Several political scientists and economists at the University of Miami, with the Ford Foundation support and through their own efforts, have been engaged in continuous study and observation of these developments through the many years of discussion and argument. Professors Ross C. Beiler of the Department of Government and Reinhold P. Wolff of the Bureau of Business and Economic Research were in charge of the foundation-financed studies; Professors Gustave Serino and Thomas J. Wood, of the Department of Government; and several staff members of the Bureau of Business and Economic Research, as well as the author of this volume, have also been engaged in this research. This book, with its primary focus on political and governmental history of the movement for metropolitan government, reports only a portion of their observations. Professor Wolff analyzed some of the ecological and economic aspects of Miami metropolitan developments in *Miami Metro,* published by the Bureau of Business and Economic Research of the University of Miami in 1960; other results have been and will probably continue to be published in various journals. Miss Laverne Burchfield, of Public Administration Service, assisted in editing this manuscript.

This is the second of these studies of metropolitan action programs to be published in this series. The first, *Decisions in Syracuse,* described the adjustments and attempts at adjustment made in that older, smaller, and more stable metropolitan community over a period of years. In other cities, with which later volumes of the series will deal, there are both significant similarities to and significant differences from the situations and actions in Miami and Syracuse.

Through this and the other volumes of the series, we hope that a better understanding of the processes of governmental adaptation to social change, and of community decision-making in general, will be promoted.

YORK WILLBERN

*Professor of Government*
*Indiana University*

# Preface

*The Miami Metropolitan Experiment* is a study of the background, initiation, and first achievements of Miami's metropolitan government. This study traces the history and development of the movements leading to the creation of a metropolitan government and describes the struggle for power between the municipalities and the new metropolitan county government. Other related matters are discussed only as they shed light upon the main concerns of the study.

The nature of the study necessitates both a chronological and a topical organization of the material. While evaluation may be found on many pages, some chapters are devoted entirely to inquiring into the meaning of some of the more important questions of political behavior.

Several devices have been used to assist the reader in coping with the enormous amount of detail presented in the study. Chronologies appear at the beginning of most chapters. A number of appendices make available documents, statistics, and other basic facts.

This study was made possible by a Ford Foundation grant to the University of Miami's Department of Government and to the University of Miami's Bureau of Business and Economic Research for a joint study of the politico-governmental and economic aspects of metropolitan government in Dade County. Ross C. Beiler, Professor of Government, and Reinhold P. Wolff, Director of the Bureau of Business and Economic Research, were cochairmen of the project. Other participating members included Professors Gustave R. Serino and

Thomas J. Wood of the Government Department, Research Analysts
Uriel Manheim and Robert W. Benner of the Bureau, and the author. Professor York Willbern of Indiana University was coordinator
of the Miami metropolitan study and other similar studies sponsored
by the Ford Foundation.

The cooperation of many persons helped to make this study possible. Dr. Wood and the writer interviewed many persons who were
active in the consolidation and home rule movements, all of whom
were helpful and gracious. Because of the nature of the inquiries the
interviewees are not identified, but they include former legislators,
city and county officials and employees, representatives of interest
groups, members of the Metropolitan Miami Municipal (3M) Board
and the first and second Charter Boards, newsmen, and community
leaders.

The author would be remiss if he failed to acknowledge the gen-
erous assistance of former County Manager O. W. Campbell, County
Manager Irving C. McNayr, County Attorney Darrey A. Davis,
Thomas C. Britton, first assistant to the county attorney, former Metro
Budget Director Harry T. Toulmin, and such members of the county
staff as Mrs. Beverly B. Phillips and Don Petit, and former members
Charles R. Davis and Louis Malley, all of whom made many sources
of information available.

He also is indebted to the Dade County League of Municipalities,
the Miami-Dade Chamber of Commerce, and the Dade League of
Women Voters. The *Miami Herald* and the *Miami News* generously
made their library facilities available to the research group.

Dr. Wolff and Analysts Manheim and Benner of the Bureau of
Business and Economic Research were very cooperative in providing
pertinent data. They also provided significant insights on many matters.

The author is grateful to Professors Beiler, Wood, and Serino, his
colleagues in the Government Department, for their generous advice
and assistance. In particular, Dr. Wood's statistics on key elections
proved most useful and Dr. Beiler's criticism of a first draft of the
manuscript was most helpful. Findings from political behavior surveys
conducted by Dr. Beiler were utilized when available. Student assistants Michael C. Slotnick and Miss Charis C. Schubert helped
ease the burden of the innumerable chores associated with the study.

Miss Mary A. Hayes and Mrs. Marjorie Sander did yeoman work in the typing of the manuscript.

The author is profoundly grateful to Dr. Frank Wilhoit of the Government Department, who, although not associated with the Ford Foundation study, encouraged, inspired, and assisted him throughout the preparation of this report. Dr. Vergil Shipley, another colleague in the Government Department, rendered invaluable assistance on the final draft of the study.

Professor Wallace S. Sayre of Columbia University, as counselor and critic, has given generously of his time and ideas, inspiring the author to seek constantly to improve the study through greater clarity, scholarship, and meaningful analysis. The keen, incisive comments of Professor David B. Truman, also of Columbia University, made the author aware of many sins of omission and commission. To both of these scholars, I am deeply indebted.

Professors Edward C. Banfield of Harvard University, John C. Bollens of the University of California, Peter B. Clark, formerly of Yale University and presently with the *Detroit News,* and Scott Greer and Norton E. Long of Northwestern University were extremely gracious in making available to the author some tentative findings regarding leadership in such metropolitan areas as Cleveland, Boston, Chicago, and St. Louis.

For all conclusions and for any errors and shortcomings, the author assumes full responsibility.

EDWARD SOFEN

*University of Miami*
*Coral Gables, Florida*

# Contents

# THE MIAMI METROPOLITAN EXPERIMENT

METROPOLITAN ACTION
STUDIES NO. 2

# CITY OF MIAMI AND ADJACENT AREAS

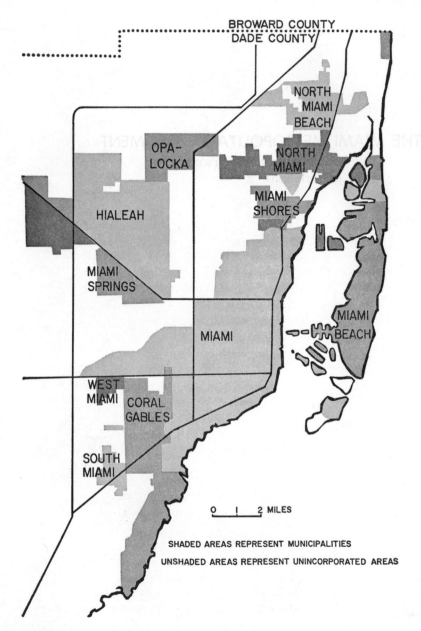

BROWARD COUNTY
DADE COUNTY

NORTH MIAMI BEACH

OPA-LOCKA

NORTH MIAMI

HIALEAH

MIAMI SHORES

MIAMI SPRINGS

MIAMI

MIAMI BEACH

WEST MIAMI

CORAL GABLES

SOUTH MIAMI

0    1    2 MILES

SHADED AREAS REPRESENT MUNICIPALITIES

UNSHADED AREAS REPRESENT UNINCORPORATED AREAS

# Introduction

THE POLITICS OF Greater Miami can be understood best in the broader perspective of state and regional politics.

Florida's "Old South" is composed of the counties of north and west Florida. These counties, which were economically conservative during the pre-Civil War days, had undergone a sufficient change by the 1880's and 1890's to become ardent supporters of the Populist party and the National Farmers' Alliance. Yet, despite their economic liberalism, which some observers say still prevails, these areas continue ultra-conservative on questions of race relations. On the other hand, the areas of present-day economic conservatism, located in south Florida both on the east coast and in the resort counties of the west coast, have a much heavier percentage of white population and consequently are far less concerned with the Negro question. Their economic conservatism is reflected in elections in the heavy votes cast for Republicans and for conservative Democrats. Wealth appears to be a key factor in this conservatism, for in these areas are found the huge citrus groves of the Indian River region, the great cattle ranches of the Kissimee Valley, the truck farms of the Everglades, and large numbers of well-to-do in-migrants from the North.

For the purpose of ascertaining the nature of voter cleavage in Florida, Professor Herbert J. Doherty has examined the record of a number of elections: the Hoover-Smith presidential election of 1928, the state gubernatorial vote of 1948, the Truman-Dewey-Thurmond presidential election of 1948, and the Pepper-Smathers senatorial vote of 1950.[1] He concluded that in each instance voters in north and west Florida tended to favor candidates with liberal economic views, whereas voters in south Florida showed an affinity for candidates with a conservative economic philosophy.

The Democratic party in Florida, the dominant party since the end of Reconstruction in 1876, has been composed of two factions— the liberal and the conservative. Since 1948 the party has been dominated by moderate conservatives. Florida officeholders on both the national and state level overwhelmingly endorsed the conservative Senator Richard B. Russell as a Democratic presidential nominee in 1952. Of the 24 Florida delegates to the Democratic National Convention in 1952, 19 voted for Russell and 5 for Estes Kefauver. After the liberal Adlai E. Stevenson was nominated for the presidency, most officials of Florida's Democratic party made it plain that they were adopting a "do-nothing" policy. In 1960, a number of prominent Florida Democrats, although initially favoring the nomination of Lyndon B. Johnson, actively supported John F. Kennedy in his campaign against Nixon.

Despite the alignment of voters who might be classified as liberal or conservative in presidential and congressional elections, most students of the Florida scene would concede that there are no organized liberal or conservative factions in the Democratic party when it comes to selecting a gubernatorial candidate in a primary election. Alignments of any constancy in this regard are such rare phenomena in Florida politics that V. O. Key, Jr., writing on *Southern Politics*,[2] was moved to entitle his chapter on Florida, "Every Man for Himself." This thought will be explored subsequently.

Although the Democratic party continues to dominate Florida politics, recent developments make it necessary to examine the status of the Republican party in Florida. In five presidential elections Florida has cast a majority vote for a Republican: Rutherford B. Hayes in 1876, Herbert Hoover in 1928, Dwight D. Eisenhower in 1952 and 1956, and Richard M. Nixon in 1960. The only other time a Democratic nominee for president failed to receive a majority vote in Florida was in 1948 when the Republicans, States' Righters, and Progressives together captured 51 per cent of the popular vote. (However, Harry Truman did carry a plurality of the 1948 vote.)

In the 1952 election, 544,036 Florida voters cast their ballots for Eisenhower as against 444,950 for Stevenson.[3] Eisenhower made even a stronger showing in 1956 by receiving 643,849 votes to Stevenson's 480,371.[4] In 1960, however, John F. Kennedy received 748,700 votes to Richard M. Nixon's 795,476, a difference of only 46,776 votes.

In 1954, for the first time since Reconstruction, a Republican Congressman was elected in Florida. In that year William C. Cramer was chosen to represent Pinellas County, and he has been returned to office three times. At the state level, out of a total of 133 members in the 1961 state legislature, there were only 7 Republicans—6 in the House and 1 in the Senate.

The Republican leadership in Florida and in Dade County has not been effective either in building a strong party organization or in getting out the vote in state and local contests. Republican politics in Dade County has been characterized by organizational schisms and factions, as is common with a permanent minority party. Not even the overwhelming victories of President Eisenhower in two elections have operated to change the general ineffectiveness of the Republican organization in Greater Miami. Some cynics contend that a group or groups of Republicans have deliberately chosen to maintain the status of exclusive in-groups. Thus, a relatively small number of adherents in Dade County, having contact with the national Republican organization, has reaped a rich harvest of Republican rewards and patronage during two national Republican administrations.

While the Eisenhower elections have been explained as a personal victory, the authors of a recent study of two-party voting in the South have concluded that the 1952 and 1956 Republican votes in the South must be understood "in terms of 'natural' class-related forces which a popular personality permitted to come into operation. . . ."[5] The Southerners who voted Republican were high in the socio-economic scale and tended to respond to class and personality rather than to traditional party loyalty.

Although it would seem that Florida is willing to reflect a two-party orientation in presidential elections, the same cannot be said for the elections of Congressmen and members of the state legislature. As long as the Florida Democratic party is dominated by the moderate conservatives, there is no real pressure to seriously consider establishing a two-party system. Nor, indeed, can many Florida Republicans be distinguished from Southern Democrats, even when the race issue is involved. It is interesting that the only Florida Congressman refusing to sign the 1956 Southern Manifesto in criticism of the United States Supreme Court's integration decision was not the Republican representative from Pinellas County but Democrat Dante Fascell, who represents the rather socially liberal Dade County area. As of the fall of 1962, the Republican organization in Florida not only had learned to live with its minority status but actually seemed to enjoy it. Only in the event of a rather severe economic depression and the ousting of the moderate conservatives from Democratic leadership by a more liberal group could one expect the emergence of a more formalized two-party system.

In commenting on the Florida scene, Key attributed the amorphous quality of Florida politics to the great geographical distances between the different parts of the state, heavy urbanization, inmigration from other states, and the state's highly diversified economy.[6] These elements, however, are meaningful only to the extent that they are interlocked. For example, urbanization cannot explain the lack of organized factions unless one considers such additional factors as the tremendous influx of newcomers from outside the state and the diversified nature of the state's economy. The lack of deep-rootedness in Florida's population and the many-sided nature of the state's economy are unquestionably factors that have tended to prevent the establishment of strong political organizations within the state.

The provisions of the Florida Constitution pertaining to the executive branch help to compound the difficulties of building a unified political organization on the state level. The constitution, which was adopted in 1885, provides for a collegial executive composed of the Governor and the elected cabinet members—the Secretary of State, the Attorney General, the Comptroller, the State Treasurer, the Superintendent of Public Instruction, and the Commissioner of Agriculture. The governor and members of the cabinet, each have a four-year term of office. Although the governor may not succeed himself, there is no such restriction on cabinet members and generally they are re-elected. The cabinet members, in addition to supervising their respective departments, serve with the governor as ex-officio members of several state boards and commissions. Thus, for example, all the cabinet members serve on the Budget Commission, the Board of Conservation, the Executive Board of the Department of Public Safety, and the Board of Commissioners of State Institutions. Other agencies, such as the Board of Education, the Pardon Board, and the Trustees of the Internal Fund, include the governor and designated members of the cabinet. Each member is entitled to an equal vote on the decisions of the agencies upon which he serves.

Former governors of Florida have, for the most part, applauded what some observers have described as the most obsolete and anachronistic state executive system in the United States. Their generous appraisal of "the cabinet system" may be explained in part by the rather benevolent type of assistance and advice rendered by the cabinet to neophyte executives and, in part, by the desire of the former governors to maintain cordial relations with these Florida officials subsequent to holding office. The cabinet also provides whatever political stability exists in the state. In the words of V. O. Key, "It may not be mere coincidence that such an institution [the cabinet system] developed in the southern state with the most disintegrated and least-stable structure of political organization." [7]

While the individual cabinet members, with their long tenure, may build personal followings or factions among departmental personnel and clientele groups, they have not developed any kind of institutional machinery that is generally associated with organized politics. As a result of Florida's failure to develop strong political organizations, election campaigns have become popularity contests. To be sure, candidates must turn for financial support to such special interests as insurance companies, loan groups, supermarket owners, farm bureaus, labor unions, organized cattlemen, fruit-growers, lumber dealers, and phosphate companies. There is not, however, any consistent alliance of these interest groups and, indeed, one might parody Key by describing the role of these groups as "Every Interest for Itself." Combinations are fortuitous and tend to change from candidate to candidate and election to election—no candidate can hope to achieve victory if he comes to be permanently identified with any one or a combination of special interests.

In the absence of any organized groups sufficiently powerful to

8 INTRODUCTION

elect a governor, candidates necessarily have had to appeal to a wide variety of interests. Serious contenders for the office advocate middle-of-the-road policies and try to avoid controversial issues. Sincerity, personableness and articulateness; political record; and size of campaign "kitty" tend to be the important factors in deciding elections. To the extent that a candidate receives adequate financial support, one may consider the interest groups to be the initial screening bodies.

Upon attaining office, the governor is in a position to influence public opinion, bring pressure to bear upon the legislators, and influence the distribution of monies by the politically important State Road Board, whose members he appoints. Yet Florida governors, because of future political aspirations or the occupational hazards of officeholding in the chaotic setting of Florida politics, tend to avoid conflict and are loath to make full use of the few powers they possess. Thus a psychic handicap reinforces the weakness of the state's political structure.

The same type of atomization that is found at the state level also prevails in the counties. Aside from a few closely knit factions in north and west Florida and the existence on occasion of courthouse "gangs" in urban counties, the general situation seems to be "Each County Official for Himself." One student of the Miami scene has maintained that the nearest approach to an effective political organization in Greater Miami came in the 1930's under the tutelage of Daniel J. Mahoney, publisher of the *Miami Daily News*, and State Senator Ernest G. Graham.[8] By obtaining control of most of the political patronage in the City of Miami and in the county, the Mahoney-Graham combination exerted a strong influence on local elections in the populous northwest section of the city and, for a short time, functioned as a "Little Tammany." Since the 1930's, however, Dade County has lacked a political machine that could deliver the vote. Somewhat of an anomaly in the last few years was Abe Aronovitz, former mayor of the City of Miami, who, because he was a symbol of political honesty and integrity, exercised a significant impact on public opinion. Aronovitz was able to influence the election of a number of city and county officials, with whom he maintained rather close contact.[9] In recent times, the nearest thing to a leader or political "boss" in Greater Miami has been Associate

Editor John Pennekamp of the *Miami Herald*. His position will be more fully examined later in the study.

The government of Dade County prior to Metro was a conglomeration of a Board of County Commissioners elected under a commission form of government and a number of other elected officers, most of whom also exercised administrative authority. The commission form of government in Dade County was in many respects analogous to the cabinet system on the state level. Like the cabinet members, the commissioners were able through patronage and the letting of contracts to build up personal followings. Some of them held office for 20 years or more. Other elected officers, such as the Tax Assessor, Tax Collector, Sheriff, Surveyor, Clerk of the Circuit Court, Purchasing Agent, and Supervisor of Registration, also developed their own retinues. Dade County voters were expected to elect no fewer than 39 officers—5 county commissioners, 10 heads of independent county departments, 14 judges, 5 constables, and 5 justices of the peace. Each ran independently, and the electorate voted for candidates on the basis of personality and record rather than on the basis of organized political affiliation.

The cities in the Greater Miami area also lack political leadership and organized political factions; although, as in many other cities throughout the nation, specialized interests reflected by Chambers of Commerce and other business groups generally are influential with the city commissions. Structurally, city government in the area for most city residents is of the council-manager type. Despite the supposedly noncontroversial nature of this type of administration, the cities of Miami and Miami Beach have long been characterized by political dissension.

It was in this political setting that the forces of the Greater Miami community in 1957 aligned themselves for or against metropolitan government. Those favoring Metro included the Dade delegation to the Florida Legislature, the Dade County Research Foundation, the Miami-Dade Chamber of Commerce, the Miami Junior Chamber of Commerce, the League of Women Voters, the *Miami Herald*, and the *Miami News*.[10] Opposing Metro were the majority of county and municipal officials and employees, the Dade League of Municipalities, the economic beneficiaries of city business and city contracts, most of the municipal chambers of commerce, a number of local newspapers with circulations confined to particular cities and their adjacent areas, and certain municipal civic and citizen organizations. The activities and influence of these groups are detailed in subsequent chapters.

In this study the terms Metropolitan Miami, Greater Miami, the Miami area, and Dade County are used interchangeably to describe the entire area involved in the Miami metropolitan experiment. This area includes 26 municipalities and the unincorporated areas of Dade County, Florida. The government of Dade County was not, however, the metropolitan government until after the adoption of the charter. The core city of Miami, the largest of Dade's municipalities, will be designated as the City of Miami.

PART ONE: BACKGROUND AND SETTING

1

# Metropolitan Miami

WHEN ONE THINKS of Metropolitan Miami,[1] the fabulous resort area of Florida's Gold Coast, the images that come to mind are sun and sand, bathing beauties, glamorous hotels, palatial homes, night clubs, race tracks, and a certain dash of sin. Although Miami is this concatenation, it is far more. It is one of the fastest growing metropolitan areas in the nation. At the turn of the century it was populated primarily by Indians and alligators; the total non-Indian population was only 5,000.[2] In 1960 Metropolitan Miami had a population of approximately 935,000, almost triple its population near the end of World War II and twenty-one times greater than its population at the end of World War I.[3]

While tourism is the backbone of the economy, Metropolitan Miami is a classic example of an area whose growth has been nurtured by the basic needs of its own residents. Migrants settled in the area because of the climate, not because of economic opportunities. The increasing population created the need for new industries to supply expanding local markets; the new industries, in turn, attracted other auxiliary industries. The declining growth rate of tourism in recent years has been more than compensated by an increase in manufacturing, the service industries, real estate business, and finance.

Nevertheless, a significant number of people, who settle in the Miami area because of its special attractions, are forced to leave either because of their inability to find suitable employment or because of unsuccessful business ventures. Consequently, Miami has a fairly large turnover in its population.[4] While like all tourist areas Miami is apprehensive about the smoke and dirt of heavy industry, community leaders hope to attract more high-skill and precision industries and the regional and home offices of insurance companies, publishing firms, and other commercial houses. "Far from being a 'sinner,' industry in South Florida may well be a 'savior'—for it can provide the answer to the problems that are rapidly increasing as a result of Miami's tremendous growth in permanent population."[5]

Like most other metropolitan areas, Miami is concerned with the everyday problems of traffic, transportation, sewage disposal, water supply, and the like. It is also faced with the problem of an expanding metropolitan frontier, for it is anticipated in the not too distant future that Dade County, together with Broward and Palm Beach counties to the north, will constitute a single coherent metropolitan area of some two million inhabitants.[6]

In 1957 Greater Miami had but 31 local units[7] while the nation's other 18 metropolitan areas of comparable size[8] averaged over 120 local governmental units each. This study will deal primarily with Dade's 26 municipalities and the Dade County government.[9]

Greater Miami's habitable area is confined to a narrow strip of high-lying land between the ocean and the Everglades swamplands. In recent years the most significant change in the composition of the area has been the tremendous population growth of the unincorporated areas. Since 1950 these areas have tripled in population and in 1960 they accounted for some 38 per cent of Dade's total population. The City of Miami, the central city and the largest municipality in Dade County, had 63 per cent of the population in 1943; 50 per cent in 1950; and approximately 31 per cent in 1960. The other 25 municipalities contained the remaining 31 per cent of Dade's population in 1960 (Appendix A).

Hialeah, Dade's second largest city with 66,972 residents, has tripled its population since 1950. Miami Beach (63,145), Coral Gables (34,793), and North Miami (28,708) hold third, fourth, and fifth positions, respectively. The next 7 largest cities range in size from 21,405 to 5,296, and the 14 remaining municipalities have fewer than 4,200 persons each (Appendix A).

Miami's suburbs do not appear to be typical of suburbs in most other metropolitan areas. In Greater Miami the population is constantly shifting and growing, not with the overspill from the central city but with in-migration from all over the United States. Crisp Yankee accents mingle with the more dulcet tones of Georgians, the nasal twang of Midwesterners, and the somewhat harsh intonations of New Yorkers. Even in communities where there is a common background of education and economic status, a good deal of "living together" is needed to create a sense of oneness. Miami's year-round tourism poses a special obstacle to such a development.

Notwithstanding the differences in background noted above, the citizens in a number of Dade's municipalities do appear to have a strong sense of loyalty to their newly adopted home towns. Coral Gables, a dormitory community with a fairly high income level, takes particular pride in its garden-club setting and its high caliber of government services. To reside in Coral Gables carries a certain amount of prestige—as well as the burden of relatively high costs of homeownership.[10] The "snob appeal" characteristic of Coral Gables also prevails in Miami Shores, a city of somewhat similar socioeconomic background. In fact, Miami Shores, completely surrounded by poorer neighbors, is even more desirous than Coral Gables of maintaining its distinctiveness.

Miami Beach, despite its cosmopolitanism, evidences a surprising provincialism which is based, in part, on its unique tourist position and, possibly, also on its ethnic composition. The Jewish population of this community is economically, politically, and numerically dominant, and it does not want to risk changing the status quo for any unknown and unproved form of government.

Similarly, the Negro precincts in the City of Miami have invariably opposed governmental change, for they too have been able to establish a *modus vivendi* with municipal authorities. As evidence, they point to a separate Negro police force and a separate Negro court within the city,[11] a somewhat sympathetic consideration of their housing needs by city administrators, and, in general, a cooperative relationship between city officials and Negro leaders. On the less meritorious side, however, there exists a rather lax enforcement within the Negro area of the laws against bolita, a numbers game.

Hialeah, with a substantial degree of industrial development, numbers some 67,000 residents, of a fairly uniform lower middle class status. This city with its Tammany-like political setting has developed a certain clannishness that sets it off from the rest of the county.

Another community that has developed an identity of its own is the agricultural but urban-transitional Homestead area. This area, which lies 25 miles from the county seat, has been alienated from the county government. Geographical distance alone does not explain this situation; there exists also the psychological gap between the urban-oriented county commissioners and the agricultural-oriented population of Homestead. Moreover, there is a large contingent of Homestead residents who migrated from the Old South and who give a Southern flavoring to the politics of the city.

There are also a number of smaller cities that have developed a strong community consciousness, i.e., Miami Springs (population, 11,229); West Miami (population, 5,296); and several other cities with less than 3,500 population such as Golden Beach, Surfside, North Bay Village, Bal Harbour, Bay Harbor Islands, El Portal, and Biscayne Park, but the total population of these areas amounts to only 31,067 or 3.3 per cent of the persons residing in Dade County. The population of all the "self-conscious" communities,[12] excluding Coral Gables, is 183,315 persons, or 20 per cent of the entire Dade population.

Most of the incorporated areas in Dade County were first established under the general laws of the state of Florida, but later their incorporation was reaffirmed by special acts of the Florida Legislature[13] for the purpose of precluding judicial attack. Actually, incorporation could have been accomplished by general law or special act. The latter method, in effect, meant receiving approval from the Dade County delegation in the legislature. In the absence of home rule, custom decreed that local bills sponsored by each county delegation, so long as the delegation's action was unanimous, would be approved automatically by the state legislature. Before 1949, under the general laws of Florida, the method of incorporation within Dade County allowed 25 or more persons of any hamlet, village, or town who were both freeholders and registered voters to establish a municipal government with corporate powers and privileges.[14] If, after the public notice required by law, two-thirds of the group, but not fewer than 25 persons, met and agreed to form a municipality, they could select a corporate name, choose their officials, and possess those powers granted by the general laws of Florida to municipal corporations.[15]

The earliest municipalities to be incorporated in Dade County— the City of Miami (1896), Homestead (1913), and Florida City (1914)—were developed along the Florida East Coast Railroad tracks. However, the real impetus to the development of the cities came from energetic real estate promoters. Their extensive activities led to the development of Miami Beach (1915), Coral Gables (1925), Opa-locka (1926), Miami Springs (1926), and North Miami (1927).

Because of the devastating effects of the Great Depression and a severe hurricane, a number of cities in the 1930's were forced to reduce their services and contract their boundaries. The City of Miami, for example, gave up jurisdiction over a good deal of land north of the city which it had annexed in 1925; and subsequently three new cities—Miami Shores (1931), Biscayne Park (1931), and El Portal (1937)—were created from this area. Across the bay from the City of Miami, a number of island areas, also gained their independence and later were incorporated.[16] The newly formed cities were Surfside (1935), Indian Creek Village (1939)—more of a country club than a city—Bal Harbour (1946), and Bay Harbor Islands (1947). Other cities—Florida City (1914), South Miami (1926), and West Miami (1947)—were incorporated in order to prevent annexation by the neighboring cities of Homestead, Coral Gables, and Miami, respectively.[17]

In addition to Bal Harbour, Bay Harbor Islands, and West Miami, the 1940's saw the establishment of Sweetwater (1941), Virginia Gardens (1947), Hialeah Gardens (1948), Medley (1949), and Pennsuco (1949). Medley, Pennsuco, Sweetwater, and Hialeah Gardens, with a total population in 1960 of approximately 1,000, were established in rather undesirable geographical areas subject to severe flooding.

In 1949, after the incorporation of the aforementioned cities and a number of attempts by developers to create still others, the Dade legislative delegation secured the enactment of a measure that foreclosed further incorporations in Dade County under the general laws of Florida; [18] then in 1953 the delegates arrived at an informal agreement to create no additional cities through special acts.[19] One may hazard a guess that had the legislature failed to take the necessary actions to forestall the creation of additional cities from the unincorporated areas, there would have been far greater opposition to the formation of Miami's metropolitan government.

A variety of factors contributed to the establishment of the cities of Dade County. They included the "imperialism" of the land promoters, the expectation of escaping zoning restrictions, the quest for inexpensive land, and the desire to obtain liquor licenses and other benefits. The initial reasons for creating each municipality have had a bearing on its development, but it is the geographic, educational, and socio-economic background of the many thousands of newcomers that is primarily responsible for shaping the character of the various cities and towns.

It was within this Greater Miami setting, with its 26 municipalities and its extensive unincorporated areas, that a metropolitan government was created. "Metro," as the Miami metropolitan government came to be known, was officially launched on July 21, 1957. Since that date the municipalities and Metro have engaged in a struggle for power that has largely shaped the Miami metropolitan experiment. To understand the ramifications of the struggle and other problems involved in establishing a metropolitan government, it would be helpful to examine the history of the decade and a half preceding Metro's launching—particularly the movements for functional and geographical consolidation.

2

# Functional Cooperation and Consolidation

| | |
|---|---|
| 1943, May 27 | A county-wide public health system was created pursuant to an enabling act of the state legislature. |
| 1943, June 10 | The state legislature approved a proposed amendment to the Florida Constitution providing for consolidation of all tax assessing and collecting offices and of certain court offices in Dade County as well as in Orange County. |
| 1943, June 14 | The Greater Miami Port Authority was created pursuant to a special act of the state legislature. |
| 1944, August 22 | The Dade County Coordinating Planning Council was organized. |
| 1944, October 5 | The Florida Supreme Court declared unconstitutional the proposed amendment of June 10, 1943. |
| 1945, June 11 | The Greater Miami Port Authority was abolished and the Dade County Port Authority created. |
| 1945, October 2 | Dade County voters approved the consolidation of the area's 10 school districts into a single county-wide school system. |
| 1949, January 1 | Jackson Memorial Hospital, the main hospital in the Greater Miami area, was transferred by the City of Miami to Dade County. |
| 1957, October 3 | A Mutual Aid Agreement was adopted by the county and most of the cities of Greater Miami in order to provide better emergency fire protection in the unincorporated areas and the several municipalities. |

1957, October 29    The County Commission by ordinance adopted the
                    South Florida Building Code.

## INFORMAL FUNCTIONAL AGREEMENTS

The virtual autonomy of Dade's municipalities did not result in each
city becoming an island unto itself. Over the years informal functional cooperation in the Greater Miami area developed in a number
of spheres.* One interesting arrangement, developed in pre-Metro
days, is the sale of water by the City of Miami to a private utility
(Consumers Water Company) and to the cities of Hialeah, Miami
Springs, West Miami, and Miami Beach.[1] Miami Beach, in turn, supplies water to its own residents and in addition sells water to neighboring communities. The City of Miami directly serves its own
residents and the residents of a number of nearby areas. All in all
the Department of Water and Sewers of the City of Miami directly
or indirectly supplies water to 13 municipalities and to parts of the
unincorporated areas.[2]

In the pre-Metro period, Dade County and the cities of Miami,
North Miami, Coral Gables, Hialeah and Miami Beach, each had
its own police communication system. The largest system, that of the
City of Miami, not only served the police departments of its own
city and eleven other cities but also served a variety of non-police
groups. The second largest police communication system belonged
to North Miami, which serviced its own department and the police
departments of eight other municipalities. Coral Gables, in addition
to caring for its own needs, also serviced West Miami. Hialeah,
Miami Beach, and Dade County (serving the unincorporated areas),
each had its independent communication system. The major criticism of these separate and independent systems was their failure to
provide machinery for immediately alerting all police cars throughout Greater Miami in case of an emergency. However, an Emergency
Radio Network maintained by the City of Miami provided a radio
police system through which any one of some twenty dispatchers

---

* Since flood control and surface drainage in Dade County are primarily
the responsibility of the Central and Southern Florida Flood Control District and the United States Corps of Engineers, rather than of the
county, they are not discussed in this chapter.

both within and without Dade County could contact the other nineteen dispatchers, who in turn could relay the message to their respective mobile units.[3]

There was cooperation, also, in other areas of public safety which still exists today. One example, the training of police for all local Dade jurisdictions, is handled by the Dade County and the City of Miami police training academies.[4] The City of Miami academy rates among the best in the nation. Again, smaller communities that cannot afford to maintain their own jails lodge their prisoners in the Dade County jail or in the jails of adjacent municipalities.

Since a number of cities and much of the unincorporated area are without adequate fire-fighting facilities, the county and all cities but Coral Gables, Miami Beach, and South Miami entered into a Mutual Aid Agreement whereby each jurisdiction pledges itself to respond to a request for assistance from neighboring fire departments. The agreement was not formalized until October, 1957. Under the terms of this agreement the responsibility for providing fire protection for an area left unattended shifted to another jurisdiction. This plan is referred to as a "sliding zone" or "belt" system, with definite areas and belts established throughout the county. Because of its emergency character, the communities were able to establish the plan without running into insurance problems; complete disregard of normal boundaries by the cities' fire departments would have encountered opposition from the insurance companies. Under the agreement, a call to the City of Miami fire department from a citizen of West Miami will normally be referred to the West Miami fire department unless a life is in danger or the circumstances are such that it would be considered derelict to refuse to respond.[5] The more adequate fire departments of the larger cities necessarily have to bear the burden of fire fighting under the Mutual Aid Agreement.

One of the major criticisms of the governmental structure in Dade County before the creation of Metro was the lack of any agency responsible for area-wide, long-range planning. There were no master plans for welfare, recreation, and other social services or for the economic and physical development of the county.[6] Problems of capital improvements, such as high-level bridges, tunnels, causeways, civic centers, international trade centers, and other matters of vital concern to the area as a whole, were decided on the basis of the needs of the moment and the desires of particular areas. The planning that was undertaken by the Dade County Planning Board was confined primarily to the unincorporated areas; and city planning boards, for their part, were concerned only with their own municipalities. In most instances the planning boards lacked trained technical staffs, adequate financial support, and official and public understanding of the nature of the planning function. The Dade County Coordinating Planning Council was created in 1944 in an effort to meet these shortcomings. It was composed of members of the County Planning Board as well as representatives from various municipalities. However, the deliberations of this council failed to yield any significant results, as the members continued to be primarily concerned with local issues.[7]

Before World War II three jurisdictions in the Greater Miami area promulgated building codes—Miami Beach, Coral Gables, and the City of Miami. The entire unincorporated area of Dade County and all municipalities lying west of Biscayne Bay followed the City of Miami code; those east of the Bay followed the code of Miami Beach. The Coral Gables building code was applied only in the sponsoring city.

The obsolescence of the building codes by the end of the war resulted in a strong demand, both by building interests and by public officials in the Greater Miami area, for the formulation of a single uniform building code that would serve as a model for all of South Florida, an area that arbitrarily may be assumed to include Broward, Collier, Dade, Hendry, Lee, Monroe, and Palm Beach counties. Attempts by Dade's builders and officials, in 1949 and again in 1951, to rewrite the City of Miami building code to meet the needs of South Florida met with failure. In 1953, a Steering Committee for a Uniform Building Code of South Florida was established. The committee received the support of the building officials of south Florida, the Dade County Commission, and the Dade League of Municipalities; it received financial contributions from the county and from each municipality in Dade County except Indian Creek Village and Golden Beach. Eventually, a uniform building code, designated the South Florida Building Code, was adopted by the County Commission and became effective in Dade County on December 31, 1957.[8] By that time a metropolitan government had been established, and the implementation of the code became the responsibility of the new government.

## FORMAL CONSOLIDATION MOVEMENTS

The beginnings of formal consolidation movements in Dade County, both functional and geographical, can be traced to the early 1940's. At the outset it should be noted that no move for functional consolidation has ever failed to gain approval, whether presented to the legislature or to the people, although in one instance a decision of the Florida Supreme Court prohibited a functional consolidation measure from being placed on the ballot.[9]

The year 1943 saw the creation of a county-wide health department as a result of enabling legislation adopted by the state legislature.[10] The future pattern of opposition to consolidation began to emerge at this time as health employees of the City of Miami, prompted by fear of losing their jobs and pension rights, organized to oppose the bill. There was also some resistance from the restaurant and hotel owners of Miami Beach.

At the 1945 session the Florida Legislature enacted a school consolidation bill, subject to the approval of the people of Dade County at a referendum election.[11] The act provided for a single unified county-wide school system and authorized the County Board of Public Instruction under the powers conferred by the Florida Constitution to levy for school purposes a county-wide property tax up to 10 mills. The option of imposing up to 10 additional mills was granted to the board if this were approved by the qualified electors of the county.[12]

At the time the school legislation was introduced, Greater Miami was divided into 10 school districts, the boundaries of which corresponded with municipal boundaries only in the case of Miami Beach. The Dade County Board of Public Instruction had the authority to levy a general county-wide tax of from 3 to 10 mills,[13] and each school district with the voters' approval could levy up to 10 additional mills for its own needs.[14] Every two years the voters of the respective districts went to the polls to determine the amount of their levy. Although a minimum standards program had been established, wide differences existed in the school programs of the several districts—differences reflecting economic disparities in the Greater Miami area. Schools generally were inadequate throughout Dade County except for the area of Miami Beach and an affluent area in the City of Miami.

The need for school consolidation was dramatized by the *Miami Herald* with stories revealing the confusion rampant in the school system. A typical illustration was the maintenance of 28 separate school bank accounts to be drawn on with checks of 28 different colors.[15] The school consolidation bill met with overwhelming support except in Miami Beach, which had a superior and well-supported school system. Many Miami Beach voters were reluctant to assume the costs of county equalization and the vote here split exactly even in the election.[16]

It might be appropriate at this point to note the anomalous position of Miami Beach in Dade County, a position analogous to that of the county in the state. Dade County spokesmen never tire of exploiting the fact that the county receives so little money from the state in proportion to the vast amounts of state taxes collected from local residents and tourists.[17] Miami Beach misses no opportunity to raise a similar plaint in its own behalf. In 1959, with less than 7 per cent of the population of Dade County, Miami Beach carried 20 per cent of the tax load of the county and received a less proportionate return from the county than the latter did from the state.[18] The same hue and cry of disproportionate taxation is raised by well-to-do areas throughout the country and by wealthier states in relation to federal aid programs.

A third functional consolidation arose out of the new air age. The location of airfields in Miami by the United States Air Force during World War II made the area air-conscious, and the expectation that the federal government would dispose of these airfields at the end of the war was the principal reason for the creation of the Greater Miami Port Authority. The Port Authority, an agency of the City of Miami established in 1943 by a special act of the legislature, was given jurisdiction over harbors, ports, airport facilities, and tunnels, causeways, and bridges incident to the maintenance of the airports and the seaports "either within or without or partly within and partly without the territorial boundaries of the city." The governing board of the Port Authority was composed of four representatives from the City of Miami, and one member each from Coral Gables, Miami Beach, and that portion of Dade County outside the corporate boundaries of these three cities.[19] Representatives from outside the City of Miami were included to meet objections from other Dade areas to exclusive control of a Port Authority by the central city.

In 1945 the legislature abolished the Greater Miami Port Authority and created the Dade County Port Authority in its stead, with the Board of County Commissioners designated the governing board of the Authority. Its jurisdiction extended to Dade County and to territory beyond the county in order to allow Port Authority facilities to expand beyond Dade County boundaries.[20]

The transfer of the Port Authority from the City of Miami to the county received support from several sources. As a whole the airline companies and the City of Miami businessmen preferred county to city control of the airport because of the greater prestige and better financial standing of the county government.[21] Unlike the City of Miami, the county was not plagued by long-term debts. Certain local oil companies, which were more concerned with a seaport than with an airport, took an active part in promoting the transfer, apparently believing that a large seaport could be attained only through the efforts of the county. The oil companies looked forward to the establishment of Virginia Key, an island to the south of Miami Beach, as a site for both an airport and a seaport; [22] however, the Dade County Coordinating Planning Council recommended against this site in a report released in September, 1945.[23] The council took this position because of its belief that, at the end of the war, the Port Authority would obtain the federal airfield in the northwest part of the county.

Still another issue involving the Port Authority was the question of control by either the County Commission or an independent board. The *Miami Herald* favored an independent board modeled after the City of Miami Water and Sewer Board,[24] a self-perpetuating body "free from politics." The Water Board exercises complete responsibility for the Department of Water and Sewers other than for the determination of rates and the issuance of bonds, which are the responsibility of the City Commission. The City Commission, however, generally follows the advice of the board. Unlike the Water and Sewer Board, the County-Commission-directed Port Authority has never become a semiautonomous agency, although efforts continue in this direction.

The fourth successful functional consolidation involved the acquisition by Dade County of the City of Miami's Jackson Memorial Hospital, the principal hospital in the Greater Miami area. As early as 1939 a grand jury had recommended the transfer because of the hospital's financial inability to maintain either suitable facilities or the necessary equipment to discharge its functions properly.[25] The grand jury also noted that the hospital was used by persons from all over the county.

The Dade delegation was moved by these considerations to introduce legislation in 1945 which authorized the Dade County Commission "to construct, erect, maintain, operate, equip and improve hospitals" and issue bonds for payment thereof when approved by the electorate.[26] A second special act of the same session of the legislature authorized the City of Miami to lease or sell Jackson Memorial Hospital. The preamble to the act read: "A consolidation under one management of all public hospital facilities in Dade County would create greater economy and efficiency in the medical care and treatment of the public and of indigent patients in the City of Miami and the County of Dade." [27]

On May 7, 1946, when freeholders throughout the county were given an opportunity in a special election to express their opinion on the suggested hospital transfer, 28,205 voted for the measure and 3,843 against.[28] The vote both in the City of Miami and in the remaining areas of the county was preponderantly in favor of the transfer. A grand jury report in 1947 estimated that the hospital was costing city taxpayers $600,000 a year; and the hospital trustees, in a public statement in 1948, estimated that the operation of the hospital was then costing the city more than a million dollars a year.[29]

Despite the findings of two grand juries and the expressed sentiments of City of Miami voters, the officials of that city refused to turn the hospital over to the county, stating that they were unwilling to dissipate the assets of the city by transferring them to the county. Some observers, however, were of the opinion that the city politicians were really motivated by fears of losing patronage and political favors.

At a meeting on June 6, 1946, between city and county commissioners, County Commissioner Preston B. Bird stated that the county would be willing to assume the obligations of the hospital if a two-million-dollar bond issue for the expansion of the hospital were approved by Dade County freeholders.[30] City Commissioner R. C. Gardner expressed determination to fight the transfer unless the county "paid off" the city for its investment, and he charged the county would staff the hospital with "political heels" if the city relinquished control. He also used the occasion to accuse County Commissioners Preston B. Bird and Hugh Peters, Sr., of lobbying at the preceding session of the state legislature to have their salaries increased; his remarks provoked these commissioners to withdraw abruptly from the meeting.

As a result of a diarrhea epidemic at Jackson Memorial Hospital in the early part of 1948, during which a number of infants died, the City of Miami created a special committee to investigate the hospital.[31] The information elicited from the staff indicated a desperate need for funds and for an increase in hospital facilities. In April, 1948, the Dade County and City of Miami commissions again met to explore the possibility, so often discussed over the years, of turning the hospital over to the county. On June 2, 1948, the City Commission voted 3–2 to approve the transfer,[32] and in November of that year the freeholders of Dade County overwhelmingly approved a bond issue of $2,250,000 to expand the hospital.[33] The hospital was officially transferred on January 1, 1949. Thus, the operation of Jackson Memorial Hospital became a county function some 10 years after a grand jury first recommended the transfer.

## CONCLUSION

A variety of factors contributed to informal cooperative action and to the several functional consolidations in the Greater Miami area. In the field of education, consolidation was urged as a means of providing a particularly vital service to the area at a higher over-all level than was possible when educational standards were dictated by the economic ability of each local school district. In the case of Jackson Memorial Hospital, consolidation was desired in order to relieve the City of Miami of the heavy costs of supporting a hospital which was used by all of Dade County, and in order to obtain funds from the county sufficient to care for the needs of the entire Miami community. In the cases of police communications and health, division of responsibility among many jurisdictions jeopardized the provision of adequate services; criminals and disease have no respect for geographical boundaries. A uniform building code was forthcoming primarily because the builders in the Miami area were an important pressure group which would not tolerate the expense and inconvenience of a number of separate building codes. The Dade County Port Authority, a self-supporting governmental agency, was created for a more effective financing of capital projects of a county-wide nature and for placing the responsibility of such projects under the jurisdiction of the well-respected County Commission. The Mutual Aid Agreement was an attempt to systematize cooperation among municipal fire departments for emergency purposes.

The accomplishments resulting from these various actions, however, could hardly satisfy the desires of the leaders of the consolidation movement, who looked upon such moves as preliminary steps to more ambitious undertakings. The forces that were later to lead in the struggle over total city-county consolidation had already emerged. The central city businessmen, the Miami Chamber of Commerce, and the *Miami Herald* assumed the leading roles they were later to play in support of future consolidation movements. On the other hand, city officials, municipal employees, and certain business groups in the satellite cities emerged as the archfoes of consolidation of any kind.

The opposing positions on functional consolidation can be explained only in part as maneuvers for advantage on the part of various power groups. Functional consolidation in the cases of health, hospitals, and education indicated an awareness, both by the Dade County legislative delegation and by the voters of Greater Miami, in those instances where referendums were held, that certain functions required county-wide management in the interest of the general welfare. Although the Port Authority acts may be attributed primarily to economic pressures, consolidations in the areas of health, hospitals, and education were motivated largely by the desire for improved services. It could be argued that large taxpayers in the City of Miami were eager to rid themselves of the responsibility of the hospital, but for the county freeholders who voted to approve the hospital bond issue, it was a question of providing adequate hospital facilities. Far more reflective of economic and power motivations was the opposition of both municipal employees and officials to the health and hospital measures and the opposition of Miami Beach groups to a consolidated educational system.

The developing community sentiment favoring functional consolidation represented an evolutionary prelude to later demands for the creation of a new governmental entity that could effectively deal with the over-all problems of the Greater Miami metropolitan complex.

# 3

# Moves for Governmental Consolidation

1945, April 3     The Dade delegation refused to submit to the state legislature the plan of City of Miami Mayor Leonard K. Thomson for consolidation of all governmental units in Dade County.

1948, May 25     The voters of Dade County, Florida, rejected a proposed amendment to the Florida Constitution which would have consolidated Dade County, the City of Miami, and four small cities, and would have provided for optional consolidation of other municipalities.

1952, November 4     A permissive state-wide home rule amendment was rejected by the voters of the state. The vote in Dade County, however, was favorable.

1953, June 9     In a city-wide referendum City of Miami voters rejected a proposal which would have abolished the city and transferred its functions to Dade County.

Several moves toward the consolidation of governmental units in the period from 1945 to 1957 were unsuccessful, although at times missing victory by rather narrow margins. The first Greater Miami consolidation effort came in 1945 when Mayor Leonard K. Thomson of the City of Miami suggested a plan whereby the county and all of Dade's cities would be combined into a single "City and County of Miami." [1] This consolidation would take effect immediately upon the approval of an amendment to the Florida Constitution by the voters of the state. A charter, to be drafted by a charter convention, would subsequently be submitted to the Dade County voters. During the interim period, the consolidated government would be administered by the County Commission under the existing laws.

An examination of Mayor Thomson's correspondence reveals that some City of Miami businessmen had begun to complain of the inequity of saddling the city with the costs of maintaining facilities enjoyed by all of Dade County,[2] a theme that recurred in every subsequent consolidation movement. The proponents of the 1945 plan believed that consolidation would remedy this situation and predicted that taxpayer costs would decrease as a result of reducing duplication and overlapping in governmental services. The *Miami Herald*, which first publicized the Thomson plan with a front-page headline and a subsequent summary of its contents,[3] said editorially that consolidation would produce "a governmental unit that would be adequate, effective, progressive, scientific, and with assured sources of revenue." [4] The *Herald* enthusiastically supported the measure throughout the period of its consideration. Other proponents of the Thomson proposal were the Miami Junior Chamber of Commerce and the Dade County Taxpayers Association.

The opponents of the consolidation plan argued that it would abolish small communities in which the residents had a deep sense of pride and would inconvenience the public by the elimination of local law enforcement agencies. There was also some question of the legality of eliminating certain offices established by the Florida Constitution before the terms of the officeholders had expired. A protest meeting attended by the mayors and other official representatives of 13 of the 18 then existing municipalities unanimously condemned the consolidation plan.[5] Coral Gables leaders emerged as the chief spokesmen for the opposition forces. Miami Beach was also strongly anticonsolidationist, and its representatives vehemently denounced the Thomson proposal.

Despite newspaper pressure, the Dade delegation refused to introduce the Thomson consolidation proposal in the state legislature.[6] Dade Representative C. W. Peters voiced disapproval of the proposed consolidation measure on the ground that the voters of the City of

Miami and Dade County had not been sufficiently educated to accept so drastic a change.[7] He reported that he would introduce a compromise bill for consolidation of the tax-collecting agencies of the City of Miami and Dade County as a first step toward a consolidation of governmental functions. Some observers were of the opinion that in this period the delegates were influenced primarily by the officials of communities other than the City of Miami.

The *Herald* denounced the delegates for their stand and demanded that they reverse themselves so as to afford the people an opportunity to accept or reject the plan.[8] As the result of these protests, Representative George S. Okell, Sr. of Dade County joined with Representative Jerry Collins of Sarasota County to introduce a bill providing for an amendment to the Florida Constitution to permit consolidation of city and county governments or of their agencies and departments.[9] If the bill had been passed and if the amendment had been approved in the 1946 general election, a referendum election on the question of consolidation could have been called by the governing bodies of the governmental units affected, or would have had to have been called upon a petition signed by not less than 25 per cent of the qualified voters of the affected area. However, the compromise was damned by the proponents of the Thomson plan, and the Okell-Collins Bill, though passed by the House, was killed in the Senate.[10]

In 1947 the Dade delegation proposed an amendment to the Florida Constitution that would have authorized the consolidation of Dade County, the City of Miami, and the four small, recently created municipalities of North Bay Village, Virginia Gardens, West Miami, and Flagler City [11] into a new city-county government to be called the County of Miami.[12] Under the proposal other Dade municipalities had the option to enter into the arrangement at a later date. If the Dade County electorate cast a favorable vote on the proposal in the May, 1948, primary, the amendment would then be submitted to a state-wide vote.[13] The particular form that the new government would take was to be left to a charter board.[14]

The city of Coral Gables once again emerged as the chief center of opposition to consolidation. Both businessmen and officials feared that the amendment, though aimed primarily at meeting the problems of the City of Miami, would, if adopted, eventually jeopardize the existence of all municipalities in the county. Their fears were not allayed by a provision in the amendment which required that any subsequent merger had to be approved by the voters of the affected city.[15] The opponents also objected to the fact that the plan did not reveal the form that consolidation would take or the extent to which the merger would affect county taxes. The anticonsolidationists claimed that the merger would lead to an increase in county taxes of 40 per cent or more without any corresponding benefits to the municipalities which remained independent.[16] Loss of municipal autonomy in zoning, liquor licensing, and law enforcement (particularly in regard to gambling), were alleged as some of the consequences of consolidation.

Early in 1948 representatives of 21 of the 24 Dade County municipalities attended a number of meetings at the behest of Coral Gables and formed an organization called the Taxpayers Vigilance Association of Dade.[17] Only the City of Miami failed to receive an invitation to join. A February report unanimously endorsed by 18 attending representatives of the municipalities recommended court action to prevent the proposed consolidation amendment from appearing on the ballot in the May primaries.[18] At a subsequent meeting a plan was adopted to assess the 21 municipalities in the amount of $10,000 for the purpose of initiating legal action; [19] 17 municipalities were to contribute $400 each, Hialeah and North Miami $500 each, Coral Gables $750, and Miami Beach $1,500. Edward L. Semple, Coral Gables city attorney, was named chief counsel. Three separate attempts to rule the amendment off the ballot by challenging either the constitutionality of the amendment or the validity of the county referendum were defeated in the courts.[20]

The proponents of the amendment included the Dade legislative delegation, the Dade County Research Foundation, the Miami-Dade Chamber of Commerce, the Miami Junior Chamber of Commerce, many individual members of the League of Women Voters, the *Miami News*, the *Miami Herald*, and the Dade County Consolidation Committee.[21] This last group, composed of some rather prominent persons, planned to underwrite an education program to promote the proposed consolidation through contributions solicited from civic organizations, business groups, and interested individuals. It also had somewhat grandiose plans for the creation of 9 committees, the organization of a corps of "doorbell ringers and button-holers," and the publication of question-and-answer booklets for general distribution [22]—plans that only partially materialized.[23]

The proposed amendment, which required county approval before it was submitted to the state, was rejected in Dade County on May 25, 1948, by a vote of 27,821 to 23,513 (Appendix D). At this time, the population of the City of Miami represented somewhat more than 50 per cent of the total population of Dade County.[24] Of all the votes cast in favor of the amendment, 16,853 came from the City of Miami, where 58.5 per cent of those voting cast favorable ballots.[25] Actually a little less than one-third of Dade's registered voters turned out for the election. Ironically, the total vote on the issue of consolidation was some 5,000 fewer than on the question of changing to daylight saving time.[26] Whatever else may be said of voter reaction to consolidation movements in Dade County, numerically the electorate displayed relatively little concern over the matter.

John F. Willmott, executive director of the Dade County Research Foundation at the time, attributed the voters' apathy to the relatively weak campaign conducted by both sides.[27] He directed attention to the difficulty experienced by the League of Women Voters in finding a speaker to present the anticonsolidation point of view. Neither the Dade County Consolidation Committee nor the opposition organization, the Taxpayers Vigilance Association of Dade, ever gained real momentum. Willmott believed that an active campaign would have turned out more of the voters who had a distinct interest in public affairs and that generally the majority of such voters would have tended to favor consolidation. He concluded, however, that considering the circumstances the end result should have been highly encouraging to the advocates of consolidation.

In 1951 a permissive state-wide home rule amendment to the Florida Constitution was proposed by the state legislature.[28] This amendment, if adopted by the voters of the state, would have provided for two methods of creating a home rule charter. The first would have given the legislature power to grant a charter to any county. Under the provisions of such a charter the county could govern itself in respect to any local and internal functions not directly related to any state function or responsibility of the legislature;

however, the charter would become effective only upon ratification by a majority of the electors of the county. The second method granted authority to the legislature to specify the manner in which a county itself might draft a charter. Any such charter could deal with the powers, duties, and jurisdictions of most county officers, and their compensation and method of selection. No county charter, however, could impair the powers and jurisdiction of the County Board of Public Instruction or of any court created by the Florida Constitution. The charter could in no way affect the levy, imposition, or collection of any taxes prescribed by general law for state purposes. After a charter was drafted, the legislature could authorize a vote on its adoption at a primary, general, or special election; the charter, in this instance, too, would have to be approved by a majority of the county's qualified electors.

In Dade County the proposed home rule amendment met with opposition from the city councils of Coral Gables, Opa-locka, North Miami, the City of Miami, Miami Shores, and Miami Beach.[29] Voters in the last-named city received letters from the City Council urging them to reject the amendment.[30] Despite this opposition, the home rule amendment, although defeated in the state, was approved in Dade County by 54.7 per cent of those voting on it (Appendix D). While it is true that home rule is not comparable with consolidation, the adoption of this amendment would have facilitated consolidation.

A consolidation attempt in 1953 came so close to victory its proponents could almost taste success. A bill to abolish the City of Miami and transfer its functions to the county without a referendum, was ostensibly agreed upon by the four members of the Dade delegation, prior to the assembling of the state legislature.[31] The Dade delegation apparently was convinced that the favorable vote in the City of Miami for the 1948 consolidation amendment was to be interpreted as a mandate for the outright abolition of the city. Yet they excluded a provision for a referendum because they feared that the opponents of the consolidation measure, particularly city officials and municipal employees who believed their positions were in jeopardy, could generate more votes than its proponents.[32]

When the consolidation proposal was publicly announced, it met with vigorous opposition from several groups: officials and employees of the City of Miami, those doing business with the city government, the bolita interests, and the Dade League of Municipalities. More important, however, was the public's vigorous opposition to the arbitrary abolition of a city without the consent of its people. Feeling on this point became so intense that the *Miami Herald* and the *Miami News* deemed it advisable to get on the bandwagon and demand a referendum.[33] A petition of 55,555 signatures gathered by the Young Democrats was subsequently presented to the Dade delegation.[34]

Robert L. Floyd, a former popular mayor of the City of Miami and a member of the Dade delegation, endorsed a referendum [35] despite accusations by the three other Dade delegates that he had reneged on a tacit agreement with them to oppose any referendum provision. Mr. Floyd denied that any such agreement had been made and emphasized that he favored a referendum because of the import of the question to the voters of the City of Miami. Despite the opposition of the majority of the delegation, the city referendum was approved by the legislature.[36] This marked one of the few occasions in Florida history that the state legislature overruled the wishes on a local bill of a majority of a county delegation.[37] The action is difficult to explain. It was not simply a remarkable feat of persuasion by Representative Floyd or purely an act of enlightenment on the part of Florida's legislators or even a calculated move by more ambitious representatives intending to seek state-wide office. In all probability, it may well have been a combination of these factors. Moreover, an examination of the votes cast by the legislature shows that the small counties gave Mr. Floyd his victory. The large counties generally sided with the majority of the Dade delegation by opposing the referendum. Those who opposed the referendum hinted also at the nefarious influence upon the legislature by the illegitimate bolita groups.

The delegation was compelled to accept the referendum provision.[38] The forces urging the voters of the City of Miami to approve consolidation were generally the same as those in earlier consolidation movements: the Miami-Dade Chamber of Commerce; the Miami Junior Chamber of Commerce; the *Miami Herald* and the *Miami News*, the only two area-wide newspapers; many individual members of the League of Women Voters; the County Commission; and, with some qualifications, the Dade County Research Foundation. The opposition consisted of officials and employees of the City of Miami, certain beneficiaries of business transactions with the city, and the officials, employees, and chambers of commerce of other municipalities—an alignment typical of Dade anticonsolidation groups. Also, a small group of knowledgeable citizens was averse to turning the City of Miami over to Dade County's rather disorganized system of government.[39] The Dade County Research Foundation, although supporting consolidation, expressed similar qualms.[40]

In a referendum on June 9, 1953, the voters of the City of Miami defeated the consolidation proposal by a mere 908 votes—26,692 voting for the abolition of the city and 27,600 voting against (Appendix D). A Dade representative predicted that the consolidation movement was "dead perhaps for twenty to thirty years."[41] Such an observation, however, failed to take into account the phenomenal growth of Dade's population; the fears of the City of Miami fathers that the near-victory of the abolition election might presage future success; and the growing feeling of the *Miami Herald*, the *Miami News*, the Miami-Dade Chamber of Commerce, and members of the League of Women Voters that consolidation was the trend of the future.

4

# Opening the Way
# for Metropolitan Government

| | |
|---|---|
| 1953, July 1 | The City of Miami created the 3M (Metropolitan Miami Municipal) Board. |
| 1954, March 9 | Under a 3M Board contract, the University of Miami's Department of Government agreed to supervise a fact-finding survey of the governments in the metropolitan area. |
| 1954, March 24 | The University of Miami's Committee on Municipal Research recommended that Public Administration Service be engaged to prepare a study of metropolitan Dade County. |
| 1954, December 31 | The PAS report recommended a federal form of metropolitan government. |
| 1955, January 14 | The 3M Board approved the PAS report. |
| 1955, June 23 | The first Charter Board was created by the state legislature. |
| | The Florida Legislature approved a Senate joint resolution providing for a Dade County home rule amendment to the Florida Constitution. |
| 1956, August 9 | At an extraordinary session of the legislature, a second Charter Board was created. It superseded the first Charter Board. |
| 1956, September 7 | The Florida Supreme Court upheld the constitutionality of the proposed home rule amendment. |
| 1956, November 6 | The home rule amendment was adopted in a statewide election. |

The closeness of the 1953 consolidation vote led to serious consideration of the need for further study and analysis of the underlying issues implicit in the whole concept of consolidation. City officials were convinced that they had better devise an acceptable alternative plan or risk extinction of their cities as separate governmental units.

Immediately following the 1953 election, William L. Pallot, an attorney active in civic affairs, addressed a letter to the mayors of 18 cities and to the chairman of the County Commission in which he stressed the need for a comprehensive study of Miami's metropolitan problems. Mr. Pallot also discussed the subject with three members of the City of Miami Commission and with John D. Pennekamp, associate editor of the *Miami Herald*, who publicized Pallot's letter in his column the following day.[1] Some two weeks later County Commissioner Jesse H. Yarborough proposed that a 10-member planning commission composed of "public-spirited, nonpolitical citizens" draft a consolidation plan for Greater Miami.[2]

## THE 3M BOARD

Apparently inspired by these moves, as well as by a deep-seated interest in the problem, City of Miami Commissioner Robert H. Givens, Jr. introduced a resolution on July 2, 1953, calling for the creation of a Metropolitan Miami Municipal Board.[3] The City of Miami Commission adopted the resolution by a vote of three to two and allocated the sum of $50,000 to the board to study the municipal and county governments in Dade County and to draft a plan for their "consolidation, merger, federation, or reorganization."

In this same period W. C. Herrell, president of the Dade League of Municipalities, visited Toronto, Canada, at his own expense to study the well-known metropolitan "Toronto Plan." Upon his return he recommended that the league form an independent study group to consider the feasibility of creating a metropolitan plan for the Miami area similar to that of Toronto's.[4] The league, intent on making its own study, urged its members on July 25, 1953, to boycott the 3M Board.[5] Eventually, upon the promise of substantial representation on the board, the league was persuaded to join forces with the board.

The 3M Board was composed of the 11 persons named in the

resolution creating the board, 8 members named by the Dade County League of Municipalities, and 1 member appointed by the Board of Public Instruction. The County Commissioners, because of their sensitivity to a "power-grab" charge hurled at them in the 1953 election, rejected the City of Miami's invitation to appoint a member to the 3M Board. An Advisory Committee to the board, consisting of a chairman and 3 other members, was very active in determining board policy.[6] The board authorized the Government Department of the University of Miami to supervise "a fundamental fact-finding survey" of local government in the Greater Miami area; and upon the advice of the Government Department's Committee on Municipal Research,[7] Public Administration Service was chosen to prepare the study.

An interesting question is the extent to which a mission set for a research group predetermines its conclusions. Public Administration Service, although reflecting some of the provincialisms of "local government" research, approached the question of the division of powers between the municipalities and the county in a politically realistic manner. PAS was searching for a viable solution which would be acceptable to the members of the 3M Board and to the voters at large.

The principal recommendations of the PAS report, entitled *The Government of Metropolitan Miami*, embodied the idea of a federal system of government.[8] Each of the cities in Dade County would continue to be responsible for its local functions, with minimum standards determined by the county government. A reorganized and expanded county government headed by a county manager would take over such area-wide functions as tax assessing, tax collecting, sewerage, transportation, water, waste disposal, traffic planning, and over-all metropolitan planning.

The 3M Board accepted these recommendations in principle and proceeded to draft a home rule amendment to the Florida Constitution in cooperation with the Dade delegation. The board representatives held three meetings with the delegation prior to the legislative session, and subsequently visited the state capital on three occasions. The delegation objected to the board's insistence upon eliminating the existing county government[9] and the inclusion of a provision guaranteeing the continuance of the cities.[10] Daniel P. S. Paul, an attorney who had been active in the law firm that drafted the 1953 consolidation act, was retained by the delegation to draw up an acceptable home rule amendment.

Mr. Paul's draft centered around the County Commission as an old and revered institution; it also left to the discretion of a charter board, to be created by the state legislature, the determination of whether the cities should be retained or abolished.[11] However, the 3M Board contended that the latter provision by alienating the cities would cause the defeat the home rule amendment.[12] The board insisted that, in order to refute a charge that the voters were being asked to buy a "pig in a poke," a home rule charter must appear on the ballot with the amendment.

The difference of opinion between the 3M Board and the Dade delegation is understandable. The 3M Board included localists who realized that they would have to come up with some form of metropolitan government or face the possibility of a completely consolidated government. A metropolitan framework was acceptable to this board only if preservation of the cities was guaranteed. The Dade delegation, on the other hand, leaned toward consolidation.

The Dade delegation rejected a request by the 3M Board to be named as the charter board. The delegation contended that the 3M Board was "loaded" with members who had a strong "municipal flavoring" and that the members of the charter board should be persons with an area-wide outlook.[13] Nevertheless, 7 members of the 3M Board were designated to a 19-member Charter Board in order to maintain a certain amount of continuity and possibly to insure the future support of both the federalists and the pro-city factions.

The 3M Board's contribution to the creation of Metro was significant. The fact that it induced the stalwarts of the Dade League of Municipalities to cooperate was a major achievement. Moreover, it succeeded in maintaining harmonious relationships among all its members and in developing a workable plan, thus paving the way for the first and second Charter Boards. Its final task was to conduct a state-wide campaign for adoption of the home rule amendment.

## THE CHARTER BOARDS

The 1955 act of the Florida Legislature that created the Metropolitan Charter Board also named the 19 members who were to serve on it. Under provisions of the act, the board was to deliver, no later than October 1, 1956, a home rule charter to the Dade County Commissioners, who, in turn, were to submit it to the voters of the county at the general election in November, 1956. The electorate would then have an opportunity to vote on this question: "Do you approve the Dade County Home Rule Charter as prepared and certified by the Metropolitan Charter Board?"

Under the 1955 act the home rule amendment and the home rule charter were to be submitted together in the November, 1956, election. The adoption of the amendment required the approval of the voters of the entire state; the charter needed only the assent of the Dade County voters. The linking of the home rule charter to the home rule amendment could have caused difficulties similar to those encountered in the 1952 election, when a permissive home rule amendment was defeated. In Dade County the amendment might also have been jeopardized by opposition to some terms of the charter. It was for this reason that the Dade delegation, in a special legislative session in 1956, sponsored legislation to divorce the charter from the amendment, repeal the legislation on the Charter Board, and establish a new Charter Board. If the people of Florida approved the home rule amendment in the November, 1956, election, a referendum on the charter would subsequently be held in Dade County.[14]

A slightly altered Metropolitan Charter Board, consisting of 17 members appointed by the governor, was the successor to the old 19-member board. There had been a question of the legality of designating the members in the statute, since under the Florida Constitution the legislature may not both create an office and name its appointees.[15] There was also a question whether an officer of the state (which has been interpreted to mean state or county [16]) could hold more than one public office.[17] Five members of the first Charter Board who also held other public offices [18] and 2 members who had previously resigned were not reappointed by the governor.

Twelve members of the first Charter Board (four of whom were also 3M Board members) and 5 new nominees were recommended by the Dade delegation and appointed by the governor to the new 17-member Metropolitan Charter board (Appendix F); they were to serve until June 30, 1957, and subsequent appointments, except for filling vacancies, were to be for two years each. The Metropolitan Charter Board would continue until a charter was adopted, and an appropriation of $50,000 a year was to be made by the county to the Charter Board until the board's mission was accomplished.

The 1955 bill had permitted the Charter Board to select its own attorney; however, the 1956 bill included a provision, inserted by Senator R. Bunn Gautier, that gave this power to the Governor. The Senator and the Governor were close political allies. Since the Governor's appointments were in most cases those recommended by the delegation, the Senator from Dade was able to designate as the Charter Board attorney the consolidationist-minded Daniel Paul, who had originally been hired by the Dade delegation to draft the home rule resolution that was the basis for the home rule amendment. The consolidationists hoped, by obtaining Paul's appointment, to secure a charter that would reflect their centralist views rather than the pro-city or federalist views of some of the Charter Board members.

## THE HOME RULE AMENDMENT

Since the home rule amendment (Appendix E), approved by the legislature in the closing days of the 1955 session, is the constitutional basis for the Miami metropolitan government, it is appropriate to analyze its provisions.[19] In essence, the amendment declared it to be the intent of the legislators and of the electors of Florida to provide home rule for the people of Dade County in local affairs and thus free both the county and the municipalities from having to turn to the legislature for the enactment of local laws. The amendment also enabled the voters of Dade County to establish a metropolitan government.

The home rule amendment provided that under the home rule charter the right to create, merge, consolidate, and abolish municipal corporations, special taxing districts, boards, and other governmental units or offices whose jurisdiction lay totally within Dade County could be transferred from the state to the local level. Only the County Commission, as it might be reorganized,[20] the Board of Public Instruction, the superintendent of public instruction, and the state court system within the county were exempt from such transfer. The charter could grant full power to the Board of County Commissioners to do everything necessary to carry on a central metropolitan government in Dade County, including the creation of local courts to try all offenses against county ordinances. The charter had to specify the number, terms, compensation, and methods of electing the commissioners, lay out the boundaries of commission districts and establish a procedure for changing them from time to time. The amendment was explicit about the power of the charter-makers to provide a method by which any or all of the functions or powers of any municipal corporation or any other governmental unit in Dade County could be transferred to the Board of County Commissioners.

The charter had to provide a method whereby municipalities could make, amend, or repeal their own charters. Provisions also were required for initiative and referendum relating to county ordinances, charter amendments, and the recall of county commissioners. The recall power could not, however, impair the power of the governor and the senate to suspend and remove any officer specified in the Florida Constitution. The usual provisions were to be inserted in the charter for the protection of the creditors of any governmental unit that might be affected by changes provided in the charter. Another section, which specifically prohibited the Charter Board from tampering with the jurisdiction and powers of any state agency, bureau, or commission, preserved the status quo for the Florida Power and Light Company and other utility companies. Utility rates would remain under the control of the Florida Railroad and Public Utilities Commission whose members are elected by the voters of the state.

A number of concessions were made by the Dade delegation before the home rule resolution was accepted by the Florida Legislature. The resolution as adopted embodied the more restrictive views of the legislature in each of the following matters:

1. The County Commission could levy and collect only such taxes as might be authorized by general law. This provision was intended to maintain state control over any additional taxes that the county might want to levy and to safeguard the distribution of race-track taxes. Although a major portion of race-track revenue is derived from Dade County, total parimutuel revenues are divided equally among Florida's 67 counties.[21]

2. Dade County would continue to receive its pro rata share of

all state revenues and the equivalent of revenues paid to any Dade municipality that might be abolished under the home rule charter. The resolution did not, however, confer upon the unincorporated areas the privilege of receiving a pro rata share of the cigarette sales tax.[22] The return on these taxes in the fiscal year 1960 ranged in Dade County from $557 for Pennsuco (population 117) to $2,562,-286 for the City of Miami.[23] An equivalent return for the unincorporated areas in Dade County would have amounted to approximately $2 million.

3. To assure itself of adequate controls over Dade County, the legislature included a number of other restricting provisions. Neither charters nor ordinances of either the county or the municipalities could conflict with the state constitution or any general laws that applied to Dade and at least one other county, except as expressly authorized by the home rule amendment itself. The resolution emphasized the power of the legislature to pass general laws pertaining to Dade County and its municipalities; all general laws would apply to Dade County jurisdictions as if the amendment had not been adopted and would supersede any conflicting provisions of the home rule and municipal charters and county and city ordinances.

The resolution added, however, that the home rule provisions of the amendment were to be liberally construed to carry out the principle of home rule in local affairs for the people of Dade County. Thus the charter and county ordinances might modify or nullify any local, special, or general law applicable only to Dade County.

The home rule amendment did not bestow upon Dade County all the powers granted to municipalities by state law.[24] Moreover, the legislature was, in effect, given concurrent powers with Dade County so long as such powers were exercised through the general laws that applied to Dade and at least one other county.[25] Certain confusions inherent in the amendment, particularly in regard to the concurrent powers of the state and county and to the relationship of the municipalities and the county, would need to be clarified by the courts.

The proposed home rule amendment was held by a Florida Circuit Court on May 28, 1956, to contravene Article XVII, section 1 of the Florida Constitution, which provides that "an amendment may relate to one subject or any number of subjects, but no amendment shall consist of more than one revised article of the constitution." [26] The court was also of the opinion that the provisions of the amendment were inconsistent, contradictory, and conflicting and hence were not reasonably intelligible to the voter.

The Circuit Court decision was set aside by the Florida Supreme Court, however, on September 7, 1956.[27] The opinion, written by Chief Justice Glenn Terrell, declared that the purpose of the proposed amendment was to provide the people of Dade County with home rule in local affairs. To effectuate this latter purpose, the legislature might construct the amendment so as to limit or modify articles in the Florida Constitution other than the article to be amended. To hold otherwise would, in effect, nullify the power of the people to amend the Constitution. Justice Terrell also held that, although the provisions of the amendment when viewed separately might appear conflicting, this was not so when they were related to each other in terms of the common purpose of the amendment.

## ADOPTION OF THE AMENDMENT

The people of the state voted on the home rule amendment on November 6, 1956, following an extensive state-wide campaign conducted by both the Charter Board and the 3M Board. The campaign was aimed at rallying persons and organizations throughout the state; a public relations firm was employed. Dade organizations worked to persuade affiliated groups throughout the state to support the amendment. Rotarians wrote to Rotary groups; members of the League of Women Voters to sister leagues; builders to building associations; and members of the Jaycees, chambers of commerce, and other groups to associate organizations. The following letter from the Charter Board files, signed by representatives of the Dade League of Municipalities, was sent to 3,200 members of the State League of Municipalities and to county officials throughout the state:

Dear League Member:

We ask your support for Amendment 2, to permit Home Rule in Dade County. As you doubtlessly know, the undersigned were appointed to the Metropolitan Miami Municipal (3M) Board by the Dade League of Municipalities three years ago, to officially represent the League, to assure that League principles and aims are upheld in this movement to solve the urgent local governmental problems of our area.

Following extensive study, our 3M Board sponsored the Dade Home Rule Amendment, and we are working diligently for its passage.

We will appreciate your best efforts in encouraging a favorable vote on this Amendment.

The amendment was also endorsed by the Dade County Bar Association, the Dade County Research Foundation, the Miami-Dade Chamber of Commerce, the Miami Beach Taxpayers Association, the Miami Junior Chamber of Commerce, the Florida League of Women Voters, and the Florida Citizens Constitutional Committee.

The League of Women Voters, the Dade County Research Foundation, and the Miami-Dade Chamber of Commerce were the only citizen groups that did extensive campaigning both locally and statewide in support of the home rule amendment. Members of the Chamber and the Dade County Research Foundation appeared on television and radio programs and visited the principal population centers of the state to meet with mayors, newspaper editors, and other community leaders. Because of the persuasiveness of Associate Editor John D. Pennekamp of the *Miami Herald* and Thomas W. Hagan, then editor of the *Miami Daily News*, every major newspaper in the state endorsed the amendment. The Dade League of Women Voters did yeoman work to win converts by distributing brochures, postcards, and bumper strips and by conducting an extensive telephone campaign. Its own rather meager budget for campaign expenditures was supplemented by a $500 contribution from the 3M Board. The league worked closely with the Dade County Research Foundation and often used the foundation's newsletter as a study guide.

The state-wide vote on the amendment was 322,839 (69.99 per cent) for and 138,430 (30.01 per cent) against; in Dade County the vote was 86,612 (71.55 per cent) for and 34,437 (28.45 per cent) against. A division of all of the residences in the county into four categories based on assessed valuation showed that residents in all four categories supported the home rule amendment. Miami Shores,

El Portal, Homestead, and Florida City were the only Dade munici-palities that voted against the amendment.

The voters of the state construed the amendment strictly in terms of home rule—the right of Dade County to enact local measures without approval from the state legislature. At least, that was the emphasis placed upon the amendment by the local Dade people who campaigned throughout the state. A fairly typical pitch was that made in *Your Vote*, a brochure put out by the League of Women Voters in Dade County: "The 'local bill evil' is probably the most im-portant single reason for the lack of effective functioning of our state legislature. . . . The Home Rule Amendment makes it pos-sible for residents of Dade County to decide for themselves the kind of local government they want."

To reassure the voters outside the county, the pamphlet also stated: "This amendment does not change the tax assessing power of the state legislature. Dade County must continue to pay into the state treasury all taxes and funds which are now considered state revenue." This particular brochure did not describe the powers granted by the home rule amendment in the formation of a metropolitan govern-ment. Nor was the county voter alerted to the fact that the amend-ment vested no additional taxing powers in any prospective met-ropolitan government.[28] Cities in Dade County, however, were assured that: "The Home Rule Amendment does not abolish the al-ready existing municipalities. It establishes that the charter: 'Shall provide a method by which each municipal corporation in Dade County shall have the power to make, amend, or repeal its own charter.' "

The implications of the home rule amendment for the develop-ment of a metropolitan government probably were not appreciated by most of those voting on it or, for that matter, by most city officials.

# 5

# Allocation
# of Powers by the Charter

| | |
|---|---|
| 1955, June 27 | The first Charter Board met for organizational purposes. |
| 1955, August 26 | The first Charter Board adopted a policy decision that guaranteed autonomy of the municipalities. |
| 1956, June 26, 27, 28 | The first Charter Board conducted public hearings on a proposed home rule charter. |
| 1956, December 6 | The second Charter Board held its first meeting. |
| 1957, January 10 | The second Charter Board reaffirmed the principle of municipal autonomy for purely local matters. |
| 1957, April 2, 3, 4 | The second Charter Board conducted public hearings on a proposed home rule charter. |
| 1957, April 15 | The final draft of the home rule charter was officially signed by the members of the second Charter Board. |

With the adoption of the home rule amendment, a Charter Board could draft a home rule charter that would authorize metropolitan government in Dade County.

## CHARTER BOARD ACTIONS

Public Administration Service, which made the initial study for the 3M Board, also prepared a preliminary charter draft, which was submitted to the first Charter Board on December 1, 1955,[1] and constituted the basis of the finished product. Interestingly, there was no real controversy within either the first or the second Charter Board over the division of powers between Metro and the cities. An inspection of the minutes of Charter Board meetings shows that this potential powder keg did not explode.

The first Charter Board, in a policy decision adopted in August, 1955, declared that it had unanimously voted to guarantee the "autonomy" of the municipalities.[2] In furtherance of the declaration, the board passed the following resolution: "We shall not abolish any municipality in Dade County nor jeopardize its autonomy."

On December 2, 1955, during a discussion by the Charter Board of the PAS charter proposal, Donald R. Larson, a leading board member, observed that two of the most significant issues confronting the board were (1) the division of powers between the county and the cities and (2) the limitations to be imposed upon the powers of the county government. The consensus of the group at that time appeared to favor creation of a central government with a limited number of functions.

A few days later, at a meeting of the executive committee of the Charter Board with its consultants, Herman G. Pope, executive director of Public Administration Service, indicated that the board might have difficulty in creating an effective county government and at the same time preserving all those local units of government desired by Dade citizens. Mr. Pope, when asked by Dr. Larson whether it was preferable to compromise on the form or on the powers of the metropolitan government, replied there were "fleas and elephants" in both choices. He believed, however, that the form was less important than the powers; metropolitan government had to have adequate powers or it would fail. Dr. Larson, on the other hand, was inclined to sacrifice some powers but not structure; he was hopeful that the operation of the metropolitan government would earn the trust of the voters so that in time they would willingly expand Metro functions.

Concern over the division of powers between the cities and the county was also apparent from a list of questions drawn by the first Charter Board for consideration at public hearings on the charter. Of the 10 questions drafted by the board, 5 dealt with city-county relations. The hearings produced little discussion on the subject, however.

The members of the second Charter Board, in a meeting on January 10, 1957, reaffirmed the board's commitment to protect the purely local powers of the cities. One member, William L. Pallot, expressed his belief that the services performed solely within the boundaries of a municipality and meeting minimum requirements set by the county should remain the responsibility of the cities. If a service went beyond municipal boundaries, however, he believed it should be a function of the metropolitan government. The interstate and intrastate concepts prevailing in federal-state relations appeared to Mr. Pallot to be a good example for Metro-city relations.

Other Charter Board members favored broader powers for the county government, although some concern was expressed over such proposals as the creation of a single tax assessor's office for the county and cities, the elimination of city police and fire communications systems, and the abrogation of any municipal control of utilities. At a meeting on March 21, 1957, PAS consultant John D. Corcoran observed that one of the most difficult problems was that of equipping the county with adequate powers while at the same time protecting the local functions of the cities.

On April 12, 1957, after public hearings on the charter draft, which produced little that differed from the earlier hearings, the second Charter Board completed its work. All the members of the board voted to endorse this final draft of the home rule charter with the exception of George S. Okell, Sr. Mr. Okell was the board member perhaps most concerned about the cities' loss of powers, but even he raised relatively few major objections. Three days later, at a formal ceremony, the Charter Board officially signed the charter. Later, as a good-will gesture, Mr. Okell also signed it.

While it is somewhat difficult to compare the PAS working draft of the home rule charter with the final product, it appears that the charter that emerged (Appendix G) was a more powerful instrument for metropolitan government than that suggested by Public Administration Service.[3] Daniel Paul, the attorney for the second Charter Board, maintains that the charter as enacted did, in fact, create a strong central government with sufficient power eventually to take over all the functions of the cities. Despite this contention, the members of the Charter Board, unlike their attorney, were not consolidationists; and without the peg of federalism, the formula proposed by PAS, they would have found no place to hang their views.

## POWERS OF THE COUNTY

While no serious difficulties developed within the Charter Board over the division of powers between the county and the cities, the issue was destined to plague the new metropolitan government. The provisions of the charter relating to the powers of the county—provisions that were important in subsequent events—can be divided into four categories:

A. "Municipal-type functions" that the county can carry out directly or indirectly.[4]
B. Responsibilities in unincorporated areas.
C. Responsibility for minimum standards.
D. "Elastic" powers.

### Responsibility for Municipal-Type Functions

The first category consists of powers that are granted exclusively to the county; or that may be exercised by the county without any distinction as to municipalities or unincorporated areas; or that give the county the prerogative of assuming a function if it so desires. Section 1.01 A grants the Board of County Commissioners the "power to carry on a central metropolitan government." It enumerates 24 powers, 12 of which are in this first category:

1.01 A    1. Provide and regulate arterial, toll and other roads, bridges, tunnels, and related facilities; eliminate grade crossings; provide and regulate parking facilities; and develop and enforce master plans for the control of traffic and parking.

2. Provide and operate air, water, rail, and bus terminals, port facilities, and public transportation systems.

. . . . . . . . . . . . . . . . . . . . . .

4. Provide central records, training, and communications for fire and police protection; provide traffic control and central

crime investigation; provide fire stations, jails, and related facilities. . . .

5. Prepare and enforce comprehensive plans for the development of the county.
6. Provide hospitals and uniform health and welfare programs.
7. Provide parks, preserves, playgrounds, recreation areas, libraries, museums, and other recreational and cultural facilities and programs.
8. Establish and administer housing, slum clearance, urban renewal, conservation, flood and beach erosion control, air pollution control, and drainage programs, and cooperate with governmental agencies and private enterprises in the development and operation of these programs.
9. Provide and regulate or permit municipalities to provide and regulate waste and sewage collection and disposal and water supply and conservation programs.

. . . . . . . . . . . . . . . . . . . . . . . .

12. Establish, coordinate, and enforce zoning and such business regulations as are necessary for the protection of the public.
13. Adopt and enforce uniform building and related technical codes and regulations for both the incorporated and unincorporated areas of the county; provide for examinations for contractors and all parties engaged in the building trades and for the issuance of certificates of competency and their revocation after hearing. Such certificates shall be recognized and required for the issuance of a license in all municipalities in the county. No municipality shall be entitled to require examinations or any additional certificate of competency or impose any other conditions for the issuance of a municipal license. . . .
14. Regulate, control, take over, and grant franchises to, or itself operate gas, light, power, telephone, and other utilities, sanitary and sewage collection and disposal systems, water supply, treatment, and service systems, and public transportation systems, provided, however, that:
(a) Franchises under this subsection may only be granted by a two-thirds vote of the members of the Board present and approved by a majority vote of those qualified electors voting at either a special or general election.
(b) The county shall not operate a light, power, or tele-

phone utility to serve any territory in the county which is being supplied with similar service except by a majority vote of those qualified electors voting in an election held not less than six months after the Board has passed an ordinance to that effect by a two-thirds vote of the members of the Board present. Such ordinance shall contain information on cost, method of financing, agency to regulate rates, agency to operate, location, and other information necessary to inform the general public of the feasibility and practicability of the proposed operation.

15. Use public funds for the purposes of promoting the development of the county, including advertising the area's advantages.

The County Commission also has the authority to determine the size of the Metropolitan Court established by the charter and to appoint the judges and remove them for cause. This court "shall have jurisdiction to try all cases arising under ordinances adopted by the Board" (Sections 6.01 and 6.02). Further, Section 4.04 of the charter provides that "beginning with the tax year 1961, the county tax rolls prepared by the county shall be the only legal tax rolls in this county for the assessment and collection of county and municipal taxes," except in hardship cases as provided in Section 9.03 D, under which the Board may grant exemptions from year to year, but not beyond January 1, 1966. Section 4.04 also provides that "no municipality shall have an assessor or prepare an ad valorem tax roll." [5] Nothing in the charter, however, limits the power of the municipalities to levy taxes upon property within their own boundaries.

### Responsibilities in Unincorporated Areas

In addition to being the legislative and governing body for the unincorporated areas, the Board has specific responsibilities in these areas set out in the charter:

1.01 A   3. License and regulate taxis, jitneys, limousines for hire, rental cars, and other passenger vehicles for hire operating in the unincorporated areas of the county. [6]

1.01 A 16.  Establish and enforce regulations for the sale of alcoholic beverages. . . .

1.01 D      . . . levy . . . all taxes authorized to be levied by municipalities and *to receive from the state any revenues collected in the unincorporated areas on the same basis as municipalities.* [Emphasis added.] [7]

5.05        . . . only the Board may authorize the creation of new municipalities in the unincorporated areas of the county after hearing the recommendations of the Planning Advisory Board, after a public hearing, and after an affirmative vote of the majority of the electors voting and residing within the proposed boundaries.

## Responsibility for Minimum Standards

Section 1.01 A 18 of the charter gives the County Commission power to set minimum standards for governmental services and to take over services from other governmental units under certain conditions:

1.01 A 18.  [The County Commission has the power to] set reasonable minimum standards for all governmental units in the county for the performance of any service or function. The standards shall not be discriminatory as between similar areas. If a governmental unit fails to comply with such standards, and does not correct such failure after reasonable notice by the Board, then the Board may take over and perform, regulate, or grant franchises to operate any such service. The Board may also take over and operate, or grant franchises to operate any municipal service if:
(a) In an election called by the Board of County Commissioners within the municipality a majority of those voting vote in favor of turning the service over to the county; or
(b) The governing body of the municipality requests the county to take over the service by a two-thirds vote of its members, or by referendum.

The county is authorized to "approve municipal regulations on the hours of the sale of alcoholic beverages" (Section 1.01 A 16). Since this requirement differs specifically from the county's power to establish and enforce regulations for the sale of alcoholic beverages in the unincorporated areas, it would seem that the county has the power only to set reasonable regulations or "reasonable minimum standards" for the municipalities, as described in Section 1.01 A 18. Minimum standards however, would not necessarily have to be the same for dissimilar sections of the county. Miami Beach, for example, might find that its extensive tourist trade required a later curfew hour for the sale of alcoholic beverages than was necessary for a primarily residential community.

Section 1.01 A 3 authorizes the county to license and regulate taxis, jitneys, and rental vehicles in the unincorporated areas. Since there is no section dealing with the control of these vehicles within incorporated areas, it may be assumed that such authority remains with the municipalities.[8]

Section 1.01 A 4 specifically authorizes the county to "provide a uniform system for fire and police protection," subject to the minimum standards provision of Section 1.01 A 18. Thus the county may not pre-empt the authority of the municipalities in providing these services unless they fail to meet minimum standards or request the county to provide them.

### Elastic Powers

"Elastic" powers are those rather broad and inclusive powers granted to the county which permit the commission to go beyond its specifically stated powers. Section 1.01 A of the charter also sets forth the following "elastic"-type powers of the County Commissioners.

21. Exercise all powers and privileges granted to municipalities, counties and county officers by the Constitution and laws of the state, and all powers not prohibited by the Constitution or by this Charter.

22. Adopt such ordinances and resolutions as may be required in the exercise of its powers, and prescribe fines and penalties for the violation of ordinances.

23. Perform any other acts consistent with law which are required by this charter or which are in the common interest of the people of the county.

24. Supersede, nullify, or amend any special law applying to

this county, or any general law applying only to this county, or any general law where specifically authorized by the Constitution.

Not only is there no equivalent in the home rule charter to the Tenth Amendment of the United States Constitution; but Section 1.01 B may be considered a Tenth Amendment in reverse:

> No enumeration of powers in this Charter shall be deemed exclusive or restrictive and the foregoing powers shall be deemed to include all implied powers necessary and proper to carrying out such powers. All of these powers may be exercised in the incorporated and unincorporated areas, subject to the procedures herein provided in certain cases relating to municipalities.

And Section 8.04, the "supremacy clause," provides:

> A. This Charter and the ordinances adopted hereunder shall in cases of conflict supersede all municipal charters and ordinances, *except as herein provided,* and where authorized by the Constitution, shall in cases of conflict supersede all special and general laws of the state. [Emphasis added.]

## POWERS OF THE MUNICIPALITIES

Lest there be doubt about the powers of the municipalities that may not be superseded, these powers are briefly set forth in the charter. The charter also contains provisions limiting the exercise of certain county powers as they relate to the municipalities.

### Limitations upon the County

Some of the charter provisions that impose limitations on county action have already been mentioned: those relating to municipal fire and police functions, the sale of alcoholic beverages in municipalities, the licensing of rental vehicles in incorporated areas, and the municipal prerogative to exceed the county's minimum standards in zoning, service, and regulation. Similar limitations relate to the building trades in terms of uniform county building codes and county certification of building contractors and others engaged in the building trades. While the municipalities must recognize county certification and may not impose additional requirements, persons affiliated with the building trades may obtain a municipal occupational license only after payment to the municipality of the customary fee. Likewise, the municipalities "may issue building permits and conduct the necessary inspections in accordance with the uniform codes and charge fees therefor." Still another limitation, Section 5.04, which sets forth the authority of the Board of County Commissioners to make municipal boundary changes, prohibits the board from making such changes without first "obtaining the approval of the municipal governing bodies concerned." And if annexation or separation of an area, of which more than 250 residents are electors, is contemplated, a majority of electors voting must approve the action.

### Guarantees to the Cities

In addition to the guarantee against boundary changes without their consent, other sections of the charter provide:

5.01.    The municipalities . . . shall remain in existence so long as their electors desire. No municipality . . . shall be abolished without approval of a majority of its electors voting in an election called for that purpose. The right of self-determination in local affairs is reserved and preserved to the municipalities except as otherwise provided in this Charter.

5.02.    Each municipality shall have the authority to exercise all powers relating to its local affairs not inconsistent with this Charter. . . .

5.03.A   . . . any municipality . . . may adopt, amend, or revoke a charter for its own government or abolish its existence [by a procedure described].

5.06.    Every municipality . . . shall have the power to enter into contracts with other governmental units within or outside the boundaries of the municipality or the county for the joint performance or performance by one unit in behalf of the other of any municipal function.

5.07.    Revenues realized from franchise and utility taxes imposed by municipalities shall belong to municipalities.

The powers granted municipalities, aside from the guarantees against abolition of a city, a change of its boundaries, or the impairment of its revenues from utilities or franchises, might well be construed as subservient to the powers granted to Metro. For example, a municipality has an inviolable right to alter its charter but not so that it provisions conflict with those of the home rule charter. Likewise, the right of self-determination and the exercise of powers in local affairs must not be inconsistent with the powers granted the County Commission.

## SUMMARY

In summary, the home rule charter bestowed upon Metro extensive area-wide powers, made it the exclusive local government for the unincorporated areas, and created a federal-type governmental system for Dade County in which the governance of the 26 municipalities is shared by the county and the municipalities. Unfortunately, the word "federal" has taken on a pejorative meaning among some groups in Dade County. Consolidationists, such as the associate editor of the *Miami Herald,* John Pennekamp, are vehemently opposed to its use in describing Metro because they believe there are virtually no limits to Metro's powers over the municipalities and because they are convinced that the word "federal" strengthens the position of the opponents of Metro. Pro-city forces, on the other hand, use "federal" to describe a rather narrow, static, and exact division of powers between Metro and the municipalities that is favorable to the maintenance of the status quo.

Metro, which is neither all-powerful nor narrow, static, and exact, nevertheless has those charactertistics, at least as applied to county-city relations, that are generally described by scholars as fairly typical of a federal system of government.[9] Unlike a unitary or consolidationist government, Metro is prohibited from abolishing any municipality without the consent of the voters of that municipality. Metro may make no changes in the distribution of powers between the central and local governments in Dade County, except by a charter amendment that must be approved by a majority of county electors voting on it. A charter amendment may be proposed by a resolution adopted by the Board of County Commissioners or by a petition of electors numbering 5 per cent of those who voted in the county in the last gubernatorial general election (Section 8.07).

Only in the unincorporated areas, which had about 38 per cent of the population of Greater Miami in 1960, is the county both the local and the central government. Under the provisions of the charter, Metro has the power to control area-wide functions and the municipalities have authority over local matters. There is, however, the "confederation" feature of the charter whereby minimum standards for purely local functions are laid down by the county, though enforced by the cities.[10]

Proponents of city autonomy argue that there is in the charter an exact, legal division of powers between Metro and the municipalities. However, while some of Metro's powers are explicit, others are sufficiently general to provide for considerable expansion of the metropolitan government at the expense of the municipalities. By the same token, there seem to be enough uncertainties in the charter to enable the cities to assert various claims to municipal autonomy.

Napoleon once said that "constitutions should be short and obscure." To a great extent, Metro's charter meets this prescription. Precisely what constitutes a power which is area-wide as against one which is purely local in scope is a matter of both law and fact to be determined by the courts. However, as in every federal system, questions of jurisdiction will be resolved not merely by court interpretation but by the realities of political life and the financial capabilities of the respective governmental units.

# 6

# Charter Board Decisions

THE MAJOR DIFFERENCES that developed within the second Charter Board over the provisions of the charter concerned the number of commissioners for the new metropolitan government and the method of their election—issues that to some extent were interdependent—and job security and civil service protection for municipal and county employees.

## NUMBER AND ELECTION OF COMMISSIONERS

The question of the size of the commission was influenced by such considerations as the geographical basis for representation and the form of executive control. For example, the belief persisted among some Charter Board members that the council-manager form of government could tolerate a greater number of commissioners than other forms could.

Some board members considered representation from districts superior in principle to county-wide representation, and thought that district elections would be less costly to the candidates and more useful to the electorate. Voters would be more interested in candidates who dealt with issues of immediate concern to them. Opponents of district elections contended that the arguments of the district proponents were mere subterfuge; that the truth was that some of the Charter Board members who had been on friendly terms with the "old" County Commission wanted to neutralize the power of the new five-man commission, which had taken office as a result of a clean sweep in the 1956 election. These same observers insisted that the plans of proponents of district elections to expand the Board of County Commissioners, elect a majority of its members on a district basis, and seat the new members at an early date were motivated by the desire for a drastic change in the composition of the "new" County Commission.

A number of Charter Board members advocated district elections because they feared the *Miami Herald* would dominate county-wide elections. This attitude can be explained by a combination of characteristics peculiar to Miami—a "no-party" system, the dearth of strong political leaders, the absence of a relatively strong racial or religious minority committed to the status quo, the lack of a strong labor movement, the somewhat complacent attitude of business groups, and a highly mobile population. The political vacuum created by these factors has to a significant degree been filled by the *Herald.* Over the years, the tendency to look to this newspaper for leadership has become almost a community habit. The prevailing opinion in the Miami area is that the *Miami Herald* is the most important single factor in crystallizing public opinion in Greater Miami.[1]

The *Miami Herald* in its editorials, and Associate Editor John D. Pennekamp in his own column, consistently condemned the district or ward system as retrogressive.[2] There were those on the Charter Board who maintained that the entire charter would be jeopardized if they incurred the wrath of Mr. Pennekamp on this particular issue. William C. Baggs, the editor of the *Miami News,* an evening paper and the only other county-wide newspaper, lent credence to these rumors in a striking editorial entitled "A Thing of Importance." It read as follows:

An Apache brave or a visiting editor from Rangoon might have gazed upon the scene and thought he was seeing the members of the Charter Board rendezvousing with their conscience in a pure contemplation of how best to create a more perfect government for the almost 800,000 people who live in Dade County. Not exactly. One member leaned over and whispered into the ear of another: "If we do this, John Pennekamp might get mad and kill the whole works."

Indeed as the members were leaving the room a man approached Mr. Charles Crandon, sponsor of the controversial issue, and said: "Why don't you forget this? There are too many big interests against you." [3]

The fact that the *Miami Herald* is a powerful force in the political life of the community can hardly be denied. Nevertheless, when the performance of the *Herald* in earlier consolidation movements is considered, it seems unlikely that the newspaper would have worked to destroy the entire charter in order to correct a single "flaw." [4]

The solution of the "county versus ward" method of representation was a compromise along the lines proposed in the original draft of the charter by Public Administration Service. The charter in its final form provided for 5 commissioners, 1 from each of 5 districts but elected at large; 5 district commissioners, each elected by the voters of his district only; and a commissioner elected by each city with a population of 60,000 or more. This arrangement, no doubt, was meant to win the support of the cities and suburbs by assuring them that a majority of the commissioners would be elected by and answerable to the voters of specific geographic areas. At the time the charter was drafted, only the City of Miami met the population requirements for a representative of its own on the commission. As a result of the 1960 census returns, the cities of Hialeah and Miami Beach both qualified. On August 23, 1960, Hialeah elected its representative to the Metro Commission, and later, on November 22, 1960, Miami Beach chose its Metro representative.

Despite the fact that the number of commissioners and the method of their election depended in large part upon the form of government chosen, there was little controversy within the second Charter Board over this matter. No serious consideration was given to a strong mayor type of government by either of the Charter Boards.[5] However, there were heated discussions during the first Charter Board sessions over whether the council-manager or commission form of government should be used. The commission type was advocated and defended by I. D. MacVicar, a member of the first Charter Board and, at the time, a county commissioner.[6] Ultimately, the first Charter Board favored the council-manager system of government by a vote of 13 to 2.[7] By the time this issue reached the second Charter Board, it had been fairly well resolved.

## PROTECTION OF MUNICIPAL AND COUNTY EMPLOYEES

Another major problem confronting the Charter Board involved job security and civil service protection for municipal and county employees who feared the loss of their jobs. The vigorous politicking of these employee groups had played an important role in the defeat of earlier consolidation movements. Municipal employees were particularly concerned over the status of their jobs in the event that city functions were absorbed by the county. A compromise was reached among the Charter Board members that afforded certain guarantees to municipal employees, but the compromise proved to be unacceptable to the employee factions. Under the provisions proposed by the Charter Board, when the county absorbed a municipal function, the employees retained by Metro would not lose either their accrued civil service rights or their pension benefits. The county would seek to retain as many of the municipal employees as possible and would place the others on an employment priority list, ranking them by seniority.

Both the municipal and county employees wanted a personnel system geared to protect their interests. The then existing civil service law, the Larger Counties Civil Service Law of 1955, provided for a quasi-judicial Personnel Advisory Board for Dade County with final authority to pass upon all punitive actions taken against county employees.[8] The county employees, who named two representatives to the important 5-man Personnel Board, demanded that provisions for a similar board with similar authority be incorporated in the home rule charter. However, the Charter Board refused to make these concessions, and the personnel section of the home rule charter was written in general terms giving the county commission leeway to pass a personnel ordinance vesting strong powers in the county manager.[9]

## OTHER PROBLEMS

Another issue facing the Charter Board was whether regulations governing retail liquor establishments in Greater Miami should be included in the charter. It was decided that it would be better to leave the matter to the County Commission.

While the average Dade citizen was relatively indifferent to the problems that taxed the Charter Board, he was conscious in his everyday activities of some annoyances with governmental services.[10] In most instances his problems were not major ones, but they created "talking points" among the advocates of metropolitan government. The principle of *central control* of traffic, throughways, sewage, water, and planning was accepted by the board members, as by most citizens, as a nonpolitical concept that reflected the views of impartial experts. Charter Board members, community leaders, and the public were all receptive to the recommendations of "experts." This is particularly well illustrated by the favorable reaction of the community to the PAS recommendations on nonpartisan elections and the council-manager form of government. On the whole, these propositions were viewed by both proponents and opponents of the home rule charter as principles of good government, far removed from political controversy.

Despite Charter Board compromises and efforts to woo dissident elements, some groups remained steadfast in their opposition to the charter. These included city and county officeholders, employees of the cities, and some beneficiaries of municipal business transactions. There was probably little that could be done to draw the fangs of most of these groups, although some of the business beneficiaries were apparently satisfied that the cities would not be jeopardized. The purpose and direction of Charter Board presentations was to reassure the residents of the cities that Metro was, in fact, a federal system of government with a fairly distinct division of powers between the municipalities and the county. As an evidence of good faith, the board included a provision in the charter that prohibited the abolition of any city without approval of a majority of its voters.

# 7

# For and Against the Charter

| | |
|---|---|
| 1957, April 29 | A Special Committee of the Dade League of Municipalities voted to recommend to the full league membership that it oppose the home rule charter. A group led by George S. Okell, Sr., the only Charter Board member to oppose the charter, formed a Citizens Committee Opposing Metropolitan Charter. |
| 1957, April 30 | S. D. Phillips, Jr., Charter Board chairman, accused the Special Committee of the Dade League of Municipalities of misrepresenting the Charter Board's position with regard to the demands of the league. |
| 1957, May 9 | State Senator Joe Eaton and State Representatives John B. Orr, Jr., and George L. Hollahan, Jr., publicly announced their support of the home rule charter, while Representative W. C. Herrell adopted a neutral stand. |
| | The 3M Board voted 14 to 1 to endorse the charter and to work for its ratification by the voters. |
| 1957, May 10 | A temporary injunction prevented Hialeah from spending $2,000 of its funds to fight the proposed charter. |
| 1957, May 21 | The home rule charter, as drafted by the second Charter Board, was approved by the Dade County electorate. |

The provisions of the charter designed to guarantee the continuance of cities and their autonomy in local matters did not win over city officials and their supporters. Generally, anticharter activities consisted of campaigning by individual groups within a given city rather than any extensive campaigning on a county-wide basis.

## OPPOSITION FORCES

About two months before the election to vote on the adoption of the home rule charter, it became apparent that a Special Committee created by the Dade County League of Municipalities to study the charter was thoroughly dissatisfied with the document, contrary to previous reports in the newspapers. The league voiced its sentiments in the following press release:

The Committee was of the opinion that the grant of powers to the new County Government was so general as to permit the complete extinction of all the municipalities in Dade County without their consent. If this construction may properly be placed on the Charter, then its object is contrary to the expressed representations made by the proponents of the Charter.

The Committee therefore felt that a joint meeting of the Charter Board and the members of the Committee should be held at the earliest possible time to resolve these differences if possible. It appointed a subcommittee, consisting of E. A. Evans, City Manager of Miami, Harold Spaet, Councilman of Miami Beach and myself [Mayor Paul U. Tevis of South Miami] to meet with the Chairman of the Charter Board in order to request that such a joint meeting be held forthwith.[1]

After a meeting with the Charter Board during which each side charged the other with repudiating agreements, the Special Committee recommended that the league vote against the charter.[2] The committee's main objection to the charter was that it did not incorporate the changes suggested by the league for the protection of the autonomy of the municipalities.

In this period other opposition also was building up. Municipal and county employee groups met and passed resolutions vehemently condemning the charter. The Dade Central Labor Union joined in the protest. The mayor of Homestead spoke out against his city's inadequate representation on the proposed County Commission and he expressed fears that Homestead's agricultural problems would be neglected.[3] With the exception of the Miami-Dade Chamber of Commerce, most municipal chambers, as well as municipal officials, joined in opposition to the charter.

The sentiments of Miami Beach were probably best represented by the editorials in the *Miami Beach Sun*.[4] It castigated the charter as a creation of Coral Gables college professors, discarded politicians, and Miami newspapers. The fears that plagued Miami Beach were many. First, the city felt far more secure with a state delegation aware of Miami Beach affluence and voting power than with a County Commission which reflected the views of areas hostile to Miami Beach. Second, the city was much concerned over the potential power of the County Commission to alter district boundaries within the county so as to reduce Miami Beach representation on the commission. Until the Florida Constitution was amended in 1942, Miami Beach was split into several districts, each dominated by the heavily populated areas of the City of Miami.[5] Third, the city was greatly concerned over the prospect of the municipalities losing control over tax assessments within their jurisdictions—a matter of vital concern to Miami Beach hotel owners. Finally, the city dreaded the day when its ordinances would be subordinate to those of the county.

Most Miami Beach organizations shared this anticharter view. The board of governors of the Miami Beach Chamber of Commerce voted unanimously to oppose the charter. A poll of the members of the Civic League of Miami Beach (approximately 250 members, mostly business and professional men concerned with civic betterment) produced only one vote in favor of the charter. Strong anticharter sentiments were expressed by the Miami Beach Apartment Owners Association. The only procharter groups in Miami Beach were the League of Women Voters (about 75 members) and the Taxpayers Association (about 500 members, mostly homeowners). However, the support by the Taxpayers Association may be attributed to the influence of a few strong leaders.

Other cities also indicated their opposition to the charter. A proposal in Hialeah to spend $2,000 in public funds to defeat the adoption of the charter was frustrated by a court injunction.[6] However, $325 was appropriated by the City Council of Miami Shores to oppose the charter.[7]

In addition to the opposition already described, a Citizens Committee Opposing Metropolitan Charter was formed.[8] The Committee warned that adoption of the charter would lead to an increase in taxes, the virtual elimination of the homestead exemption through increased assessments,[9] the creation of a "pork barrel" civil service, and the initiation of innumerable law suits.

Abe Aronovitz, a former mayor of the City of Miami and a highly regarded civic leader, released an eight-page statement in which he maintained that there were literally a hundred major reasons why the charter should be defeated.[10] In addition to reiterating the charges of the Citizens Committee, he cited the conflict between the competing municipal and county lawmaking bodies, the failure to limit the number of prosecutors and judges, the unlimited discretion of the County Commission to waive competitive bids, and the lack of safeguards on the issuance of bonds.

## FORCES IN SUPPORT

For the county as a whole, charter protagonists included such influential forces as the Miami-Dade Chamber of Commerce, the Dade County Research Foundation, the League of Women Voters, the *Miami Herald*, the *Miami News*, the Dade delegation to the Florida Legislature, the 3M Board,[11] and the Charter Board.[12] Unlike the suburban chambers of commerce, the Leagues of Women Voters of Miami, Miami Beach, Coral Gables, and Hialeah all gave their support to the charter. General league policy was formulated by an *ad hoc* committee composed of the presidents and representatives of each of the local leagues.[13] The Dade delegation to the Florida Legislature, with the exception of Representative W. C. Herrell,[14] publicly announced its endorsement of the home rule charter.[15] The Charter Board also campaigned for the adoption of the charter.[16] (Total funds spent by the board for all of its activities from June 27, 1955, through June 25, 1957, were $129,888.19.[17])

The procharter groups employed a variety of campaign tactics.[18] In particular, they used teams of prominent persons to address civic clubs and business groups. Various organizations were called upon to urge their members to support the charter. In addition a number of groups were approached to distribute informational pamphlets. For example, the Dade County Board of Public Instruction distributed 6,300 copies of the text and an analysis of the charter to ninth-grade civics and twelfth-grade American history and American government classes.

A number of individuals took special actions in support of the charter. Dr. H. Franklin Williams, Charter Board member and vice-president of the University of Miami, distributed a memorandum to University personnel in which he noted that Dade County could not enjoy the benefits of home rule as permitted by the home rule amendment unless the charter were adopted. A vice-president of Burdines, a major department store in the Greater Miami area, informed his employees of the advantages offered by the charter and encouraged them to go to the polls. Mitchell Wolfson, Charter Board member and owner of television station WTVJ and Wometco Theatres, in an open letter to his entire working force declared that in his opinion the home rule charter made a good start toward establishment of metropolitan government in Dade County and he urged his employees to cast their votes for the charter if they agreed with his views.

Other methods employed for the support of the charter were the use of outdoor advertising; an extensive telephone campaign; and the distribution of brochures, postcards, and bumper strips.[19]

The proposed metropolitan government was advanced by its proponents as a federal form of government in which the county would exercise complete authority over such area-wide functions as tax assessing and collecting, water supply, sewerage, waste disposal, transportation services, traffic planning, and over-all planning. The county would set minimum standards for the 26 municipalities for such functions as zoning, police and fire protection and refuse collection. If a city failed to comply with the minimum requirements, the county, after reasonable notice by the Board of County Commissioners, could assume jurisdiction over the function involved.

## THE VOTE

The charter was approved in a special election on May 21, 1957, by the narrow margin of 1,784 votes—44,404 for the charter and 42,-

620 against (Appendix D). Only some 26 per cent of Dade's registered voters went to the polls.

As expected, not one precinct in Hialeah or Miami Beach favored the home rule charter. In fact, there was almost a 3 to 2 majority against it in both cities.[20] In the Homestead–Florida City area there was somewhat more than a 3 to 1 ratio opposing the charter. Smaller cities, such as Miami Shores, El Portal, Miami Springs, and Biscayne Park, also voted "no." In addition, the unincorporated areas cast slightly more than 50 per cent of their vote against the charter.[21]

Victory for the charter was assured, however, by the 57 per cent "yes" vote in the City of Miami and the approximately 66 per cent "yes" vote in Coral Gables. The overwhelming support of Coral Gables came as something of a surprise, indicating that the "City Beautiful" was not really so proud of its autonomy as the proverbial peacock it was said to resemble. The Coral Gables vote may have reflected its higher-than-normal educational and socio-economic standards.[22] While a University of Miami poll showed that there is a high correlation between these factors and pro-Metro sentiment,[23] educational and socio-economic standards similar to those in Coral Gables failed to overcome the provincialism of Miami Shores. Suffice it to say that there were obviously other considerations influencing the voting behavior of the citizens of both Miami Shores and Coral Gables, considerations that are analyzed later in this study.[24]

## IN RETROSPECT

The opposition to the charter by the Dade League of Municipalities lacked the fervor and intensity, not to mention the personnel and funds, that were present a year later in a campaign to adopt the autonomy amendment (see Chapter 12).[25] The relatively mild opposition by the league in 1957 may be explained by the fact that the localists had recognized that some type of governmental integration was inevitable and that a federal form of government was preferable to outright consolidation. It is doubtful, however, that any formula for the division of powers between the county and the cities that affected the status quo could have won the full approval of the localists. While the core of opposition to the charter came from city officeholders and employees, the close vote in the election was the result of strong opposition of voters in major cities such as Miami

Beach, Hialeah, and Homestead, and in smaller communities such as Miami Shores. It appears that the opposition vote represented a vigorous protest against a change in the status quo.[26]

The affirmative vote, although probably cast by persons with varying views on metropolitan government, represented both acceptance of a more unified county-wide system of services and approval of a policy of upgrading services for substandard municipalities through minimum standard requirements.[27]

# 8

# Reflections
# on the Creation of Metro

To EXPLAIN THE success of the campaign for metropolitan government in Greater Miami, it is necessary to examine the relationship
of the central city to the remainder of Dade County, the socio-
economic environment of Greater Miami, the people and forces who
worked for the charter, and the methods that were used.

## THE MIAMI MILIEU

The difference between the central city and the suburbs in Greater
Miami is probably not as great as in other metropolitan areas in the
nation. Dade County, because of its youth, its many homeowners, its
relatively few apartment dwellers, and its unusual physical and geographical setting, is in many respects one big suburbia. Suburbanites
of Dade County are not an "overspill" from the core city seeking
greener pastures, but are primarily émigrés from many different
sections of the United States. These newcomers have not had sufficient time to develop deep roots or, often, even firm friendships, and
thus have few emotional ties to the Miami area. (It would seem that
the longer the residency the greater the emotional attachment to a
community).[1]

Nevertheless, these characteristics do not vitiate the reality of
the struggle between the core city and its satellites. City of Miami
officials, as well as spokesmen for the city's organized business

groups, have consistently maintained that central city residents have to bear the financial burden of county-wide facilities. These sentiments were dramatically asserted at a 1957 Congressional subcommittee hearing in Dade County. Robert M. Morgan, civic leader, certified public accountant, and a member of the executive board of the Miami-Dade Chamber of Commerce, blasted the various "parasite communities," which, he said, owed their very existence to the central City of Miami. Replying to a denunciation of Metro by the mayor of Miami Beach, Mr. Morgan declared that Miami Beach was about the least self-sufficient city in the nation. "We Miamians furnish them with water, we burn their garbage, we house their servants, we furnish them with roads leading to Miami Beach . . . we even carry it to the ultimate extreme, we bury their dead." [2]

Some observers contend that the charter, from its inception to its adoption, was a conspiracy of the "downtown Miami merchants." Undoubtedly, this group played one of the more important roles in the genesis of the consolidation movement, but its activities can hardly be classified as a conspiracy. Nor can the general dissatisfaction of a large number of the residents of the City of Miami be traced to the influence of the merchants. The political difficulties that plagued the city for many years might well have disillusioned even the most stouthearted. Despite—or because of—a council-manager form of government, with many nonprofessional managers over the years, the City of Miami was in constant political turmoil. Charges of corruption filled the air, and the police force was under perpetual attack for its failure to enforce the laws against gambling and other forms of vice. It was to counteract this state of affairs that the Greater Miami Crime Commission, a citizens' group, was formed in 1948.[3] At about the same time the Dade County Research Foundation was created to serve as a "watchdog" over governmental activities and to give assistance to the governments of the area whenever possible.[4]

At the very time that critics of the government of the City of Miami were strongly condemning the city council, these same critics had only the highest praise for the County Commission. The satisfaction with the County Commission can be attributed to its unanimity of outlook, its peace and harmony, and its fairly impressive handling, at least in the public mind, of the county parks, hospital, and Port Authority. The County Commissioners, who had had long experience in their elected offices, were acting as both administrators and policy makers under a commission form of government. The existence of this dichotomy of a "good" county government and an "evil" city government, together with the desire of the city's businessmen to have the county assume the financial burdens of metropolitan functions, helps to explain the transfer to the county of the City of Miami Port Authority and Jackson Memorial Hospital. The transfer of the hospital shifted the costs of support from the city to the county. The designation of the highly respected Board of County Commissioners as the governing board of the Port Authority was seen, by the supporters of the move, as a distinct advantage to the Port Authority in its negotiations with banks. The better credit standing of the county plus the high repute in which the County Commission was held may help to explain why the airlines and the businesses dealing with the airlines preferred county to city control of the airport. Moreover, since the spokesmen for most organized business groups in the central city see Greater Miami as a single unified area, it is to be expected that the central city businessmen would favor a governmental entity that had, in fact and in law, the power to deal with the problem of airports, harbors, and seaports.

From 1945 to 1953 all plans for geographical consolidation could be traced, in part, to the efforts of the powerful business elements within the City of Miami. The 1945 plan was abortive for a number of reasons. The members of the City of Miami Commission, at the time, were of high caliber, and there appeared to be no urgency to save the city. Moreover, the strong bond that was later forged between the Dade delegates to the state legislature and the City of Miami businessmen had not as yet materialized. Even the *Miami Herald* had not at this time realized its position of power.

In the 1948 and 1953 elections,[5] a solid alliance was established between the Dade legislators and the proconsolidation elements in Dade County. Among the latter were the *Miami Herald*, the Dade County Research Foundation, the Miami Chamber of Commerce, the Junior Chamber of Commerce, and many members of the League of Women Voters. The near victory of the 1953 move to consolidate the City of Miami with the county led to the introduction, by the localists,[6] of a modified scheme of consolidation aimed at saving the cities from destruction. Even this proposal, however, was only a counteraction to the pressures from the consolidationists.[7]

The socio-political setting of Greater Miami also was conducive to the development of a metropolitan government because of a combination of characteristics peculiar to the area: the tremendous growth of population, the pervasive tourist atmosphere, the rapid population turnover, the existence of a no-party political system, the absence of relatively strong racial or religious minorities committed to the status quo, and the lack of a strong labor movement.

One student of politics has observed that for many years to come it will be difficult, if not impossible, to integrate local governments in areas where there is a two-party system.[8] Miami with its "every man for himself" type of politics has, in effect, a no-party system and, consequently, was spared the kind of struggle that might have occurred if the fate of political parties had hinged on the outcome of the move to create a new metropolitan government. By contrast, certain other metropolitan areas with more formalized party structures, such as Cuyahoga County in the Cleveland area, have reflected sharp divisions between the parties as well as within the parties on the issue of metropolitanization.[9] One can expect a similar response in other areas where political parties stand to gain or lose power as a result of disrupting the political status quo. While stressing the logic of efficiency, economy, and unification, the advocates of integrated metropolitan government elsewhere in the nation, have generally failed to give sufficient consideration to the concrete factors of power relationships.

The opposition to recent movements to establish metropolitan governments in the United States stemmed not only from political parties but also from various pressure groups that considered themselves threatened. Minority groups which have found a *modus vivendi* in an existing government are particularly loath to change the political structure. Thus one finds that there were Negro leaders in both Cleveland and St. Louis who strongly opposed changing the existing governmental framework because of the fear that they would lose their personal influence in a larger, more rationalized government.

In Miami, Negroes constitute only 6.8 per cent of the registered voters.[10] Of those voting in the predominantly Negro precincts, an estimated 60 per cent have generally opposed the creation of a metropolitan government.[11] Although there may have been rare instances when the Negro vote on metropolitan or consolidation issues has been crucial to the outcome of certain municipal elections, this has not been the case in Dade's county elections.

In the St. Louis area, however, approximately 25 per cent of the registered voters are Negroes, and it has been estimated that as many as 80 per cent of the Negroes vote as a Democratic bloc.[12] One member of the Board of Education and six aldermen are Negroes. (Of the six Negro aldermen, four serve on the local board of the National Association for the Advancement of Colored People.) Prominent Negroes fill other important positions in the city government and are influential in the labor union movement. Obviously, if Negroes as a group oppose metropolitan government in St. Louis, it has little chance of being adopted.

The Jewish population of Miami Beach is another minority group that may have been reluctant in the past to disturb a political power setting in which it enjoyed a relatively important position. And yet, despite the overwhelming opposition to Metro from Miami Beach, Jewish leaders from that city as well as from other municipalities played important roles on the Metropolitan Charter Boards. In addition, the Jewish population in the southwest section of the City of Miami has been pro-Metro and in no way reflects the insularity of the Jewish residents of Miami Beach. Finally, it must be noted that the anti-Metro attitude of Miami Beach might better be explained by its peculiar economic interests than by its ethnic considerations.

The powerful labor unions which are found in most metropolitan areas constitute yet another political force vitally concerned with any threat to its power status. Greater Miami, however, has a relatively small number of industrial workers,[13] and although there are some 50,000 union members in the area,[14] unions have played a relatively unimportant role in Dade County politics. By contrast again, in St. Louis there are 35,000 workers in the teamsters' union alone.[15] Also, the Teamsters Local 688 is a vitally significant force in St. Louis. Labor for the most part opposed the metropolitan-oriented District Plan in St. Louis.

In a number of industrial areas throughout the nation, the businessman, or at least an important segment of the business community, has been acutely conscious of the need for the establishment of county-wide metropolitan government. Although prometropolitan business organizations in such cities as Boston, Cleveland, and Dayton generally were ineffectual and ill designed for political action, large sums of money were raised by business groups in conjunction with Ford Foundation and other organizational grants, to advance the metropolitan cause. In Miami, on the other hand, the business leaders allowed the Dade County Research Foundation, a business-sponsored "good government" group, to expire for want of funds.

It may be that the "countervailing power theory" of big business begetting big unions also works in reverse. In the case of Miami, the lack of countervailing organizations, in the form of cohesive labor or minority groups, meant that the business community had no real competitors in the political arena. Moreover, since the cause of "good government" groups coincided with the desires of the more powerful Miami business organizations, the latter were quite content to allow the newspapers, professional groups, university professors, and the League of Women Voters to assume the positions of catalytic leadership in civic affairs.

To these variables revolving about the amorphous power setting of Miami one must add two other factors: the lack of a real crisis situation in Miami except, perhaps, in the minds of the more knowledgeable, and the deep political apathy of most Miami citizens. From what we know of other studies, these conditions are probably typical of most metropolitan areas. The extent of the existence of citizen apathy in Miami is made clear by the following observations:

Any testing of levels of thought and feeling in the political substructure inevitably yields new evidence of abject apathy and gross ignorance in the citizen mass. This is particularly true in dealing with the subject of local government. To find, as we did in Survey #10, that only 15% of our registered citizens could think of anything good that the county commission had done in the preceding year, or that 24% could name something blameworthy that they had done (9% named a parks concession scandal) is routine.

However, somehow one expects a thing as big as Metro to make an impression. When only 32% say they have heard or read about a new county charter and had a sliver of a correct idea about it, while 13% have a quite wrong idea about it, that sinking sensation returns. It was not only in the telephone poll that 64½% said they did not know of any big change in the county government in the last couple of years. The same question had produced the identical 64½% shrugging response when asked in Survey #10.[16]

The authors of the above quotation concluded that those persons possessing little local political interest did not embrace a strong Metro position and, if low enough in interest, held a distinctly "neutral" position. There was also a definite correlation between high local political interest and a pro-Metro position. At first glance one might get the impression that apathy contributed to Metro's success by keeping the "neutral" and anti-Metro voter away from the polls. However, a statistical breakdown of voter turnout in the various precincts in Greater Miami refutes this. Surprisingly, it shows that there was no marked difference in voter turnout in the high socio-economic precincts, with a high degree of local political interest, and the lower socio-economic precincts with a low degree of local political interest.[17]


## PEOPLE, FORCES, AND METHODS

Although the Miami environment and the political process as explained above may have created a setting conducive to the acceptance of metropolitan government, they scarcely account for the positive actions which were necessary to plan, promote, and push Metro to successful adoption. The political environment, in short, provided a favorable matrix; it did *not* provide the "catalytic action-spark." In the following pages the roles of the main actors involved in the formation of Metro will be examined and analyzed. The taxonomy of activists includes the newspapers, the business organizations, the civic groups, the Charter Board, and the professionals.

As already noted, the political vacuum in Miami was filled to a considerable extent by the *Miami Herald*, the influence of which in crystallizing public opinion has been recognized by friends and foes alike.[18] The formulation of the *Herald* editorial policy is attributed by most civic leaders to Associate Editor John D. Pennekamp. Aspirants for political office eagerly seek the *Herald's* endorsement, which is extremely important in this no-party area. Some of

Miami's most important businessmen, elected officials, and administrative officers meet and consult with Mr. Pennekamp on important community problems. A few of the associate editor's close contacts are characterized by their enemies as "errand boys," with Mr. Pennekamp portrayed as a puppeteer pulling the strings.

The characterization of Mr. Pennekamp and the *Miami Herald* might well be compared to that of publisher Paul Block, Jr., and the *Toledo Blade* in the following:

Although . . . Paul Block, Jr. . . . would win no popularity contest in Toledo, *The Blade* is by all odds the most potent political force in Toledo. It certainly does not run the city in arbitrary, single-handed fashion. No newspaper could. But it wields immense influence. It has made, broken and chastened many a politician. It has pushed through or blocked many a public policy. . . .[19]

Mr. Pennekamp has successfully used the power of the *Herald* to crusade for many civic reforms. He has an almost artistic touch in the manner in which he gradually builds a case for or against an issue. His sense of righteousness makes him a devoted ally—and an extremely dangerous foe. The *Herald*, under the editorial guidance of Mr. Pennekamp, has fulfilled an important leadership role in the Miami area, and the legend of Pennekamp has become part of Miami's folklore.[20]

The emphasis upon the *Herald* is not intended to belittle the role of Miami's evening newspaper, the *Miami News*. During the campaign for the home rule amendment, the editorial staffs of both the *News* and the *Herald* toured the state and persuaded fellow editors to support the amendment. Both papers also strongly supported the home rule charter.

Candidates and others seeking public favor appeal to the *News* as well as to the *Herald*. The *News*, although less influential than the *Herald*, has supported candidates who have carried an election without the *Herald's* endorsement. However, while most persons who read the evening *News* also read the *Herald*, the reverse is not true.[21]

A majority of the downtown City of Miami business elements constitute another faction that has consistently supported consolidation movements. The efforts of this group to win public support for

Metro were centered around the activities of the Miami Chamber of Commerce. In 1955 the chamber changed its name to the Miami-Dade Chamber of Commerce and invited each of the chambers in the suburbs to appoint an associate director to the Miami-Dade board of directors.[22] The move was considered presumptuous and few chambers cooperated. It is significant that most of the local chambers of commerce, with the exception of the Miami-Dade chamber, have opposed geographical consolidation.

The Miami-Dade chamber, despite schisms within its membership, has played a significant role in all consolidation movements. The organization's support of the 1948 and 1953 drives lacked the fervor that was evident in later years, however. Despite the fact that chamber members were well represented on the 3M Board and the first and second Charter Boards (Appendix F), the movement for metropolitan government was never closely identified in the public mind with the Miami-Dade Chamber of Commerce.[23] The organization was considered by the public to be just another "civic" group supporting metropolitan government. This was probably fortunate, for if the Metro movement had been thought to be a chamber "conspiracy" aimed at shifting taxes from the City of Miami to the county, it would undoubtedly have failed. This is not to suggest that the chamber was in reality the moving force behind Metro and that it managed successfully to disguise the fact. At most, the chamber was part of a loosely aligned group that, along with the *Miami Herald* and the Dade legislative delegation, was responsible, before appointment of the 3M Board, for initiating geographical consolidation movements—none of which succeeded. As already indicated, the initial step toward metropolitan government was a countermovement by the enemies of consolidation, who were concerned primarily with the preservation of the cities. The consolidationists joined the "localists" in support of a federal type of metropolitan government and, according to some observers, may have succeeded in leaving their consolidationist imprint on the charter.

The Dade County Research Foundation was created in 1947 primarily by business groups in the City of Miami to help bring about more economical and efficient government. The director and full-time staff of the organization was responsible for keeping its members informed of the foundation's findings and recommendations. The foundation enjoyed the respect of the community and the support of the newspapers. It reported on matters of integrity and efficiency in the operations of the City of Miami government and later of the Dade County government. John F. Willmott, first executive director of the foundation, met with opposition when he attempted to criticize the omnipotent County Commission, and in March, 1956, he thought it best to resign.[24] It was somewhat later that the *Herald* and the *News* also began to take the County Commissioners to task.

The foundation *Newsletter* was used to inform not only the members of the organization but also the newspapers, the Miami-Dade Chamber of Commerce, and the League of Women Voters. Under the direction of Harry T. Toulmin, Mr. Willmott's successor, the *Newsletter* also was a source of information for members of the 3M Board and the first and second Charter Boards. During the campaigns for the home rule amendment and the home rule charter, thousands of copies of the publication were distributed by the Miami-Dade Chamber of Commerce and the Dade League of Women Voters. Indeed, the main function of the Dade County Research Foundation was to provide facts for those drawing up the charter and for the organizations trying to influence public opinion.

Although the League of Women Voters, prior to 1957, took no official position on consolidation movements, its members individually gave strong support to such movements. The league, at the time of the charter referendum, however, officially supported the home rule charter.[25] League members were strong allies and formidable opponents. They centered their efforts on distributing pamphlets, ringing doorbells, making phone calls, holding parades, and carrying on other old-fashioned but effective means of "politicking." This group, which is most successful if it is provided with political leadership by a "nonpartisan, good government" organization, maintained such a symbiotic relationship with the Dade County Research Foundation.

The activities on behalf of consolidation by good government groups, as well as by newspapers and business groups would have come to naught without the introduction of appropriate bills by the Dade delegation in the Florida Legislature (Appendix C). Management of both the 1948 and 1953 consolidation bills was assumed by Dade Senator R. Bunn Gautier, who, because of his experience, his strong personality, and his political leadership might well be called the father of consolidation.[26]

Considering the role of Senator Gautier in the consolidation movement, a number of questions come to mind: Was the Senator a tool of the Miami Chamber of Commerce? Was he dictated to by the *Miami Herald*? Or was it purely fortuitous that the Senator's aims were compatible with those of the chamber and the *Herald*? The answers to all of these questions must be in the negative. It would seem that Senator Gautier at times had to rally the members of the chamber to support consolidation, rather than the reverse. Although a concord did exist between him and the *Herald*, it was hardly what one would describe as a case of follow the leader.[27] On the whole, the relationship between Senator Gautier and the consolidationist organizations evolved from interaction and a mutual concern; Senator Gautier's leadership was not merely an individual manifestation but rather a reflection of the group process at work.[28]

A brief examination of some of the preliminaries to the drafting of the 1953 consolidation bill may reveal some interesting sidelights on the interaction of groups and the individual. Senator Gautier was assisted in drawing up the bill by a prominent attorney, who represented the *Miami Herald* in important litigation and who also was retained by Florida Power and Light. This latter corporation, which preferred to deal with municipalities individually, had consistently opposed consolidation; and from all evidence such was the case in 1953. The attorney for Florida Power and Light, despite his close relationship with the company, agreed to take the assignment. Senator Gautier, on the other hand, was legal counsel for Dade's major transit company, a utility favorably disposed toward, if not eager for, consolidation. Unlike the power company, the transit interests welcomed the prospect of dealing with a single governmental unit legally and financially able to purchase and consolidate the different bus systems. It should be noted, however, that the Senator was an ardent consolidationist before his association with the transit company.

In summary, Senator Gautier seemed to have the characteristics of what James MacGregor Burns calls a "pressure politician": [29] that is, he subconsciously and unconsciously tends to reflect the views of the dominant interests of the community. He may even be ahead of them, but at all times he is a member of the fraternity. He is somewhat of an alter ego of these groups. This observation, according to the writer, is not meant to be disparaging since most successful politicians are "pressure politicians."

Although Senator Gautier was the prime initiator of the early consolidation movements, he was not involved in launching the 3M Board. As mentioned before, the impetus to create the 3M Board came from the "localists" who were intent upon preserving the autonomy of the cities.

The history of the 3M Board and the first and second Charter Boards illustrates Robert Michels' concept of oligarchical leadership as a component of all organized group activity.[30] In the 3M Board the leadership was assumed by an advisory committee composed of Donald R. Larson, chairman of the Government Department of the University of Miami; William L. Pallot, attorney; and Joseph J. Orr, plumbing contractor. While Mr. Pallot and Mr. Orr were "federalists" with a city orientation, Dr. Larson might be described as a "federalist" with consolidationist leanings. To win support for Metro, however, Dr. Larson was quite willing to adopt a conciliatory position and let the future take care of consolidation. These three men worked hand in hand with the PAS consultants in planning strategy, directing public relations, and administering the 3M Board.

The same three men were the nucleus of a 5-man Executive Committee of the first Charter Board. Here, too, they consulted with the experts, directed administration, and took charge of public relations. They gave generously of time, effort, and energy. Professor Larson, experienced in the ways of government, emerged as a dominant figure of both the Advisory Committee of the 3M Board and the Executive Committee of the Charter Board.

The second Charter Board, although it did not include Dr. Larson, also had a number of influential men such as Mitchell Wolfson, owner of a chain of motion picture theaters and a television station; J. D. Ryan, town administrator of Miami Springs; George S. Okell, Sr., attorney and former legislator; and Kurt Peiser, business executive. While Mr. Okell adopted the view of the Dade League of Municipalities and refused to support the charter, Mr. Wolfson and Mr. Ryan endorsed the federal formula. Although the board had no official executive committee, Mrs. Katherine Hudson, executive secretary, often consulted with S. D. Phillips, Jr., chairman of the second Charter Board, and with Mr. Wolfson, Mr. Pallot, and Mr. Orr. Mrs. Hudson and a number of the board members also discussed their problems with Harry T. Toulmin, executive director of the Dade County Research Foundation.

As work on the charter neared completion, the board called in John D. Corcoran, PAS consultant, to assist in evaluating the "Tentative Draft of the Proposed Charter," dated February 28, 1957. In addition to Mr. Corcoran's recommendations, the board, in the final revision of the charter, relied too upon the advice of Charter Board Attorney Daniel Paul. Thus it appears that the professionals played an important role in the final stages of charter development as well as in the early and intermediate stages.

To explain the importance of professionals in molding the charter and in gaining public support for its adoption, it is necessary to examine what might be called the "expert syndrome." Before interpreting this term, however, there should be some clarification of the different types of experts. Mr. Corcoran, in an interesting article,[31] makes a rather invidious comparison between the costs and results of the PAS studies on the one hand and the "probing research" of the foundation-endowed scholars on the other. Obviously, there is need for both types of research, but it would also seem fairly evident that the PAS study was far more productive of results than the work of the scholars. The "syndrome" developed, therefore, around the "practical" expert rather than the "theoretical" expert. The practical expert's laboratory is middle-class suburbia, which has its Book-of-the-Month, its Record-of-the-Month, even its Frozen-Food-of-the-Month, and may at any moment produce its Expert-of-the-Month. The typical suburbanite, with a better than average education and fairly high socio-economic status, has escaped from the unclean realm of politics to the antiseptic atmosphere of the expert. The appeal for good government, nonpartisanship, economy, and efficiency has found a favorable response in what might be characterized as "League of Women Voters" communities. Irrational loyalties to the old and established ways of doing things have not as yet taken root in suburbia.

In Miami the image of the PAS staff as nonpartisan experts provided the symbol of good government. Public Administration Service is not only a research group but a prestige organization as well. As expert consultants analyzing the Miami area, PAS staff members were able, through their recommendations, to keep a number of issues from becoming controversial. The authority of ideas emanating from PAS influenced both the newspapers and the Charter Boards, and PAS representatives worked closely with the Advisory Committee of the 3M Board and the Executive Committee of the first Charter Board. The PAS endorsement of the charter, a sort of *Good Housekeeping* "Seal of Approval," was repeatedly emphasized by the second Charter Board in its campaign for adoption of the home rule charter.

Still another important factor in the promotion of Metro was the symbol of a nonpartisanship with which the public most closely identified the Charter Board. The members of the second Charter Board, appointed by the governor at the behest of the Dade delegation, were not representative of the Greater Miami community either geographically or economically. There were 7 members from Coral Gables, 4 from the City of Miami, 3 from Miami Beach, and 1 each from Miami Springs, Miami Shores, and the unincorporated area. The members, other than those from Coral Gables and the City of Miami, did not reflect the sentiments of the voters of their communities.

A significant number of Charter Board members were men of great wealth in agriculture, business, or finance; at least 6 of the 17 members were in this category. Among the members of the board were 6 experienced officeholders, 3 attorneys, 2 educators, 1 labor leader, and 1 housewife who was a civic leader (Appendix F). On the basis of economic status alone, the board hardly appears to be representative of the people of Dade County. The board, however, was not intended to represent narrow geographic and economic interests. Nor were the board members conscious of strong identification with any specific area or group. For example, two board members—one a labor leader and the other a prominent agriculturist—were able to disregard the sharp anti-Metro feeling of their respective groups. Similarly, those members residing in Miami Beach, as well as a very intense partisan of local government from Coral Gables, joined wholeheartedly in the support of the home rule charter.

It was not the second Charter Board but rather the 3M Board, with its representatives from the Dade League of Municipalities, that first achieved a consensus on the basic principle of federalism. Without this initial impetus, the plan for metropolitan government might have been stillborn. Strategically, "federalism" in Miami appears to have been an accommodation to both groups of antagonists: a shelter for localists against the "terror" of total consolidation, and a half-way house toward integration for the centralists. Indeed, the principle of a federal type of government that permeated the thinking of the 3M Board preconditioned the members of both Charter Boards.

The function of "representativeness" has been defined as the ability to win community consent or to gain the assent of the major power elements.[32] In Greater Miami the Charter Board was confronted with the problem of winning community consent. The board members were looked upon as public-spirited citizens sacrificing freely their time and energy. They had the respect of the community and thus they were able, despite a hard core of opposition from city officials, municipal employees, and beneficiaries of city business, to contribute to the charter referendum victory. The emphasis upon the "virtue" of the board members, made by the public relations firm assisting the board, was an extremely important selling point in the campaign for the charter.

Excerpts from a bulletin sent to the board by its public relations counsel are quoted below:

On the basis of information gained in vote research a campaign of PRELIMINARY education can be tailored with two goals:

First: to increase and solidify existing support.

Second: to hammer away with the *truth* about the Charter in simplified SLOGAN form; and the trustworthiness of its authors . . . so consistently that as the election nears the opposition will be discredited as irresponsible spreaders of confusion.

In aiming at these two goals, the PRELIMINARY campaign would:

(a) Play up the background of members of the Charter Board as the ablest and most trustworthy men and women in the community. The public must develop the utmost confidence in the Board members, because the Board will CONDUCT the final campaign for the Charter. The public must have full confidence in them.

This confidence would then outweigh and discredit self-seeking motives of most opposition from present officeholders and their spokesmen.

(b) Educate the public on Charter matters as early as possible and continuously. Members of the Charter Board should speak before clubs and at other meetings while they are still writing the Charter, and also on radio and TV. It is true that they may not yet be able to present conclusions of the Board, but they can discuss the problems of the Charter, and set forth intelligently the various alternatives being considered. They can invite their audience to present suggestions and points of view to the Board.

The Board may decide this should not be done. The decision rests with the Board, and I would abide by that decision. But it is a calculated risk on the basis of information I have been at great pains to gather on other campaigns of similar nature throughout the nation.[33]

## SUMMARY

Miami was able to create a metropolitan government with the very type of support that failed in other parts of the nation because of the ecological conditions earlier considered—particularly the absence of powerfully established political parties, labor organizations, and ethnic groups—and because Miamians have long been accustomed to depend on such non-party sources as the newspapers for political leadership. These factors, together with the astuteness of Dade's legislative delegation to the state legislature, the practical orientation of the 3M Board, the high caliber and independence of the Charter Board members, and the prestige of the Public Administration Service experts, were all responsible for the birth of Miami's metropolitan government.

9

# Implementing the Charter

| | |
|---|---|
| 1957, January 1 | A 5-man County Commission, which later became the first Metro Commission, began its 4-year term of office. |
| 1957, January 16 | Marion E. Sibley was retained by the County Commission as attorney for the county. |
| 1957, July 9 | Mr. Sibley released a list of changes to be made by the county government under the home rule charter. |
| 1957, July 21 | The home rule charter officially took effect. |
| 1957, July 22 | The County Commission inaugurated Metro government with a study of the ordinances proposed by Mr. Sibley. |

With the charter victory the County Commission was confronted with the problem of enacting appropriate legislation for the new metropolitan government. The incumbent commissioners (Appendix B) were neophytes without previous legislative experience; most of them were beneficiaries of the 1956 "kick-out-the-rascals" movement,[1] when metropolitan government was not yet an issue. These commissioners, elected at large, had taken office five months before the adoption of the home rule charter. The position they took in the charter referendum campaign could hardly classify them as Metro partisans; although two of them publicly announced their support of the charter,[2] the other three remained "neutral," on the theory that they should not try to influence the voters in making up their minds.[3] Critics not kindly disposed toward them charged that two of the three so-called "neutral" commissioners were really hostile. At a windup session of the Charter Board, several members expressed concern over what they said were "disguised efforts" by the County Commission to scuttle the newly adopted charter. They cited as an example an announcement by the commission of the necessity of a 2-mill tax hike which the commission attributed to the additional costs that would be incurred as a result of the adoption of metropolitan government.[4]

The commissioners' dissatisfaction with the metropolitan charter could be ascribed to their apprehension over losing administrative control and powers of appointment under the new council-manager government. They were also deeply concerned over the threat to their political power by the addition of at least six new commissioners in the September, 1958, elections. In fact, they attempted to interpret the Port Authority Act so as to limit the number of Port Authority members [5] to the five incumbents, but were thwarted by the county attorney's opinion.[6] The commissioners were to continue to exercise administrative functions only until a county manager was appointed.

One of the first acts of the commission upon taking office [7] was to secure a new law firm to represent the county. Three of the commissioners believed that the old firm, which had been retained from 1931 to 1956, was too steeped in the philosophy of the previous administration. Commissioner Charles F. Hall nominated his own legal adviser, Marion E. Sibley, for the position, and his nomination was supported by two of his colleagues. Despite the almost violent opposition of the other two, Mr. Hall's nominee was retained as the attorney for the county.

## DRAFTING THE ORDINANCES

In May, 1957, the commission authorized Marion Sibley to draft ordinances to spell out the basic relationships between Metro and the cities and to set out the details of county administration. Mr. Sibley was to be assisted by two committees, one of laymen and one of lawyers. Although both committees were appointed by the commission, a majority of the nine attorneys on the Metropolitan Charter

Legal Committee were the personal choice of Mr. Sibley; [8] only three were the choice of the commission. It was this committee that drew up a tentative program to launch the new government, a program that ostensibly reflected the views of the County Commission as they developed from consultations between Mr. Sibley and the commissioners.

The members of the committee decided the general approach to their tasks. Each administrative department and its functions were assigned to a member who was to draft appropriate ordinances after investigation and consultation with interested parties.

Typical of the procedure was that followed by Lucien C. Proby in drawing up the draft traffic and penal ordinances. In preparation for the traffic ordinance Mr. Proby began by assembling a number of guides for study—the model traffic ordinance of the National Committee on Uniform Traffic Laws and Ordinances, the uniform traffic ordinances passed by the Florida Legislature in 1957,[9] and the traffic ordinances of the City and County of Los Angeles. He also conferred with local traffic experts, including George H. Kunde, then director of the City of Miami Traffic Engineering Department, and J. I. Jackson, then director of the Dade Citizens Safety Council. In drawing up the draft penal code, Mr. Proby used the criminal codes of Los Angeles, San Francisco, and Denver, as well as those of the cities of Miami, Coral Gables, and Miami Beach. He necessarily correlated the code he proposed with the provisions of the Florida statutes,[10] conferring with State Attorney Richard E. Gerstein and members of his staff. On numerous occasions he met individually or in a group with Marion Sibley, Daniel Paul, and Thomas C. Britton of the Metro Legal Committee. His collaborator on both codes was Edwin E. Strickland, another attorney on the committee.

Drafts of the ordinances were submitted to Mr. Sibley and in most cases to three members of the Metro Legal Committee who acted for the entire group. A lay advisory committee of ten, formally designated the Metropolitan Government Organization Committee, was ignored save in the consideration of a few noncontroversial ordinances.[11] Although reflecting in varying degrees the views of the attorneys, of Harry T. Toulmin of the Dade County Research Foundation,[12] of interested parties, and of the advisory committee in a few instances, the final drafts were Mr. Sibley's responsibility.

## CHANGES IN CITY-COUNTY RELATIONSHIPS

The draft ordinances submitted to the County Commission to implement the charter called for radical changes in the relationships between the cities and the county.[13] In zoning, for example, the Board of County Commissioners was to set minimum standards for both the incorporated and the unincorporated areas. Whereas the cities had previously had complete jurisdiction over municipal zoning, their only power under the proposed ordinance was to adopt zoning standards higher than those set by the county. All requests for zoning changes and variances were to be made to one of four county district boards, with provision for appeal to a county zoning appeals board. The cities could ignore a decision of the appeals board only if it resulted in lowering municipal zoning standards.[14]

The zoning ordinance also provided for the creation of a county Zoning and Building Department and gave the county jurisdiction over the enforcement of building codes in both the unincorporated and the incorporated areas. The Zoning and Building Department was to have the authority to issue all building and other permits required by the codes, collect fees, and make inspections; before a building anywhere in the county could be occupied, a certificate of occupancy had to be obtained from the Department.[15] Some critics thought that the proposed ordinance just about removed the need for any city zoning and building departments.

Another draft ordinance gave the county exclusive power over the issuance of certificates of competency to contractors, subcontractors, masters, journeymen, and maintenance personnel in the building, engineering, plumbing, electrical, and mechanical trades.[16] Up to this time craftsmen had to take examinations and obtain licenses in each of the municipalities in which they were employed.

Under the proposed public works ordinance, the county was to regulate public water and sewerage systems and approve all plans for construction of public works by the cities. All such construction was to meet the minimum standards established by the County Commission.[17]

The proposed ordinances that were to cause the greatest controversy were those dealing with traffic regulations. The traffic code, as submitted to the commission, would have given the county control over traffic enforcement in both incorporated and unincorporated areas and would have permitted the county to supervise accident reporting and investigation. Traffic cases, no matter where they originated, were to be tried only in a Metropolitan Court. Cities involved in a traffic case would receive revenues from fines, less Metro court costs. Obviously, municipal courts would have to survive on other kinds of violations. The designation and location of traffic control signs, signals, and devices in the county and the cities were to be the prerogative of the county traffic engineer. All devices required in the cities were to be installed and maintained by the cities.[18]

Automobile inspection was a lucrative business for the cities. Sweetwater, a low-income area, with a population of only 327 persons maintained automobile inspection without any testing equipment and enriched its coffers by some $25,000 a year.[19] The fact that Sweetwater inspection stickers were honored by other cities where auto inspection was required accounted for its financial success. The proposed traffic ordinance would give the county exclusive authority to make inspections.[20]

There is a question whether Mr. Sibley, in drafting the ordinances, was carrying out the intentions of the County Commission or following his own predilections. Mr. Sibley had a record of being essentially nonpolitical, but he was also a person who attacked any task vigorously. The commissioners were novices who had never been too enthusiastic about Metro. Some people took a dim view of the commissioners' intentions toward Metro, suggesting that the commissioners were prepared to enforce the terms of the charter with a vengeance because of disgruntlement over loss of their administrative powers. Others, probably closer to the truth, thought that the commissioners, as neophytes, naturally leaned increasingly on Mr. Sibley and his legal expertise. Drafting the ordinances was a time-consuming technical matter, and the commission had been persuaded by Mr. Sibley that it was mandatory to have all the ordinances to implement the new government on the books by July 21, the date Metro was to be officially launched.

At least two students of government who attended one of the early sessions of the Metro Legal Committee questioned the necessity for the July 21 deadline.²¹ They suggested that it might be better to postpone ordinance drafting until a county manager had been appointed and taken office, so that he might employ his own ideas in the implementation of the new government. Mr. Sibley, however, remained unconvinced, and he was encouraged to stand by his convictions by the editorial staffs of both newspapers. In the final analysis, Mr. Sibley may justifiably be called the architect of the metropolitan ordinances.

# 10

# The Cities Declare War on Metro

| | |
|---|---|
| 1957, July 1 | Marion Sibley publicly released tentative proposals for broad changes in the county government. |
| 1957, July 19 | A rift between Metro and the cities over the proposed ordinances was reported. |
| 1957, August 9 | At an acrimonious meeting between the Dade League of Municipalities and the County Commission, the commission refused to make known its position on the ordinances. |
| 1957, August 12 | The Dade League of Municipalities circulated a petition calling for a home rule charter amendment that would insure local autonomy. |
| 1957, September 11 | The County Commission deferred action on a request by the Dade League for an election to amend the home rule charter. |
| 1957, September 15 | City of Miami Manager E. Arthur Evans claimed that the County Commissioners had ruined city finances. |
| 1957, October 11 | The Dade County Research Foundation warned that the proposed autonomy amendment would jeopardize Metro's future. |
| 1957, October 16 | The Dade League of Municipalities filed with the County Commission petitions containing 38,002 signatures to force an election on the autonomy amendment. |
| | County and city officials discussed possibilities of a compromise on the autonomy amendment. |

Few people were surprised when the tentative proposals for broad changes in county government, released to the newspapers by Marion Sibley at the beginning of July, 1957, provoked bitter criticisms from City of Miami commissioners. The gist of their arguments was that the proposals went beyond the intent of the Charter Board members. They were joined in this contention by the former chairman of the second Charter Board, S. D. Phillips, Jr., who said that the board had never envisioned that the metropolitan government would have so much power. The mayor of the City of Miami charged Marion Sibley with writing into the draft legislation, without consultation with city officials, his own interpretation of the charter. Jack R. Rice, Jr., and George S. Okell, Sr., acting city attorney and special attorney for the City of Miami, respectively, accused county officials of breaking a promise to allow them to participate in the drafting sessions of the ordinance committees.[1] Mr. Sibley had met with Mr. Okell on a few occasions but only to agree that they disagreed. There was no attempt made to compromise and, therefore, no feeling that additional meetings would be fruitful.

Taking up the cudgels for Metro were Daniel P. S. Paul, the attorney for the second Charter Board, and William L. Pallot, a member of the first and second Charter Boards. Both men had served on the Metropolitan Legal Committee, which drafted the disputed ordinances. Mr. Paul made light of the struggle as something that was more or less inevitable, drawing an analogy between the difficulties over the implementation of the home rule charter and those encountered in the implementation of the United States Constitution. Mr. Pallot conceded that Metro might be getting off to a faster start than had originally been contemplated, but insisted that the ordinances were not in conflict with the charter.[2]

The Dade County Commission attempted to calm the troubled waters by emphasizing again and again that the ordinances had merely been proposed, not adopted. The cities, however, were not reassured. The Miami Beach City Council, in a resolution to the County Commission, condemned the proposed ordinances as "an invasion and usurpation of traditionally purely local matters."[3] The Coral Gables Council adopted a resolution denouncing the ordinances as an infringement on the autonomy of the cities. The contemplated legislation was described by W. Keith Phillips, mayor of Coral Gables and a former Charter Board member, as a breach of faith with the voters.[4] E. A. Evans, city manager of the City of Miami and former president of the Dade League of Municipalities, charged that the proposed ordinances violated the promises made by the proponents of the charter during the referendum campaign.[5] According to Mr. Evans, advocates had depicted the charter as providing a metropolitan government with control over county-wide problems only, reserving to the municipalities control over all other services so long as these conformed to the minimum standards set by the county. The city manager condemned members of the ordinance drafting committee as men with little experience in government.

At the height of these attacks, a five-man advisory committee of the 3M Board urged that Metro be given a fair chance. The 3M Board had been instrumental in getting the home rule amendment ratified and in laying the foundation for the home rule charter. Ironically, at this very time, the Charter Board, which officially had been responsible for writing and promoting the charter, was planning a meeting to object to the proposed Metro laws.[6] The actions of both these bodies prompted a *Miami Herald* political analyst to observe that the boards had completed their work, and that it might be appropriate if they closed shop and went home.[7]

The Committee on Metropolitan Government of the Miami-Dade Chamber of Commerce, although defending Metro, reserved judgment on the ordinances. It lashed out at the enemies of Metro who were allegedly using the dissatisfaction with the proposed legislation to assail the principle of metropolitan government.[8] At the same time, the committee reserved judgment on the ordinances until the Charter Board minutes could be examined.[9] S. D. Phillips, Jr., and W. Keith Phillips, both members of the Charter Board, were appointed as advisers to assist the committee.

Toward the end of July, the Dade County League of Municipalities set up a committee to "coordinate and cooperate" with the County Commission in the preparation of the ordinances.[10] The board of directors of the league also appointed a stand-by legal committee, composed of the city attorneys from the cities of Miami, Coral Gables, and Miami Springs.[11] The league was ready for action.

At a meeting between the Executive Committee of the Dade League of Municipalities and the County Commission on August 9,

1957,[12] the spokesmen for the league insisted that the commission make known its position on the ordinances before the final reading. They also urged the commissioners to defer passage of the ordinances until the newly appointed county manager, O. W. Campbell, had ample opportunity to study them and make recommendations. The league spokesmen called upon the County Commissioners to adhere to the intent of the charter by not interfering with the autonomy of the cities so long as minimum standards were met.

The commissioners refused to take a stand on the ordinances in this period, saying that they would make their views known after public hearings. The only concession the league gained was an agreement by Mr. Sibley to confer with league representatives. However, since Mr. Sibley had already met with league spokesmen on several occasions, there was little to be expected from additional conferences.

Each side maintained that the charges of the other were vague and indefinite. The commission criticized the municipalities for failing to substantiate their claims that the commission had violated the intent of the charter. City of Miami Manager Evans, in turn, demanded that the commission make clear its differentiation between area-wide and exclusively local functions. Mr. Sibley and the commission had consistently maintained that they had no intention of interfering with strictly local matters, so the nub of the problem was the difference between what is "local" and what is "area-wide." The issue that was bypassed in the charter campaign could no longer be postponed.

At a league meeting on August 12, with representatives of 21 cities present, the County Commission was accused of delegating to Mr. Sibley its policy-making functions in the writing of the ordinances. Members were bitter in their complaints, contending that the proposed legislation, which they interpreted as granting the county the power to take over municipal services and revenues, had ruined the financial status of every city in the county. They gave unanimous—and dramatic—approval to sponsoring an initiative petition to provide for a referendum on a proposed amendment (Article 10) to the home rule charter.[13] The autonomy amendment, as it came to be called, read as follows:

A. Anything to the contrary herein notwithstanding, neither the political autonomy nor the right of self-government or self-determination of any of the municipalities in Dade shall be infringed upon, disturbed, or interfered with, and they shall maintain their continuous right to exercise all powers whether granted by their several charters, or by Special Act, or by General Law. This, however, shall not and does not apply to [charter provisions] Section 4.04 dealing with Assessment and Collection of Taxes, nor with subparagraph (18) of Paragraph A of Section 1.01 which permits the Dade County Commissioners to set reasonable minimum standards for all governmental units in the county for the performance of any service or function.

B. All existing ordinances inconsistent herewith shall no longer remain in force and effect.

The league's action was labeled as irresponsible by the proponents of Metro. S. D. Phillips, Jr., the former chairman of the Charter Board, upbraided the league for taking so drastic a step before Metro had an opportunity to get under way.[14] He also took the commission to task for failing to reveal its position on the ordinances.

With the situation seemingly getting out of hand, the Dade County Research Foundation urged that the commission consult with the county manager before undertaking any sweeping changes.[15] Harry T. Toulmin, the foundation's executive director, cautioned that any other approach might jeopardize the very existence of Metro. The League of Women Voters also urged a "go slow" policy.[16]

The Dade League of Municipalities requested the County Commission to initiate the autonomy amendment election so as to relieve the cities of the task of getting the 10,000 or more signatures needed for initiation by petition, but the request was denied.[17] Thereupon, the league, assisted by citizen groups in Miami Beach and Miami Shores, started the campaign for signatures. Municipal employees in a number of the cities were encouraged to circulate petitions. In the City of Miami a policy bulletin signed by the chief of police advised personnel that amendment petition forms were available to one and all, and that completed petitions could be returned to his office. The City Council of Hialeah authorized its employees to support the amendment. Dean R. Claussen, president of the Dade League of Municipalities, reported that the number of petition signatures from

Coral Gables and Miami Beach were encouraging.[18] The league, by special assessment against its member cities, raised a substantial "war kitty." [19]

On October 16 the Dade League of Municipalities filed with the County Commission a three-foot-high pile of petitions containing 38,002 names. Ironically, at the very time they were forcing an election on the autonomy amendment, league leaders were speaking of abandoning support of the amendment in favor of a compromise.[20]

# 11

# Compromise Proves Chimerical

1957, July 22    O. W. Campbell, former city manager of San Diego, California, accepted the position of Dade County manager.

1957, July 26    Mr. Campbell came to Miami to accept the position formally.

1957, September 16    Mr. Campbell arrived in Miami to assume his duties as Metro's chief administrator.

1957, October 24    A committee of 20 City of Miami business and professional men, calling itself the Committee to Stop Double Taxation, proposed a plan to the County Commission that would abolish the government of the City of Miami. The commission adopted a resolution calling for a referendum on the issue.

1957, November 6    The county manager, the city manager of the City of Miami, the president of the Dade League of Municipalities, and others met to consider an alternative to the autonomy amendment.

1957, November 12    Circuit Court Judge William A. Herin refused to enjoin the referendum on the question of abolishing the government of the City of Miami.

1957, November 13    The County Commission, upon a formal request by Hugh P. Emerson, chairman of the Committee to Stop Double Taxation, withdrew the resolution calling for the abolition referendum.

1957, December 2      County Attorney Darrey A. Davis reported that he
                      was drafting a compromise autonomy amendment.
1957, December 12     The Miami-Dade Chamber of Commerce met with
                      all the parties involved in the compromise autonomy
                      amendment controversy in a last-minute attempt to
                      reach agreement.
1957, December 13     The County Commission rejected the compromise
                      autonomy amendment to the home rule charter.
1957, December 19     The League of Women Voters announced support
                      of Metro by opposing the autonomy amendment.
1958, January 21      The Dade County Research Foundation went on
                      record as opposed to the autonomy amendment.
1958, January 25      John D. Corcoran of Public Administration Service
                      and Victor Jones of the University of California
                      Department of Political Science, "local government"
                      consultants, recommended defeat of the autonomy
                      amendment.
1958, February 5      Circuit Court Judge George E. Holt postponed the
                      referendum election on the local autonomy issue un-
                      til the Florida Supreme Court could rule on the
                      constitutionality of the autonomy amendment.
1958, February 27     City of Miami Attorney William L. Pallot organized
                      a 14-member committee of civic and government
                      leaders to make another attempt to work out a com-
                      promise amendment.
1958, July 23         The Florida Supreme Court ordered that the au-
                      tonomy amendment referendum be held.
1958, July 31         The County Commission set September 30 for the
                      autonomy amendment referendum election.

O. W. Campbell, hired by the County Commission in July, 1957,
as Metro's first county manager, was in San Diego during most of
August and consequently missed the fireworks over the proposed ordinances to implement the charter. In a telephone interview with
Miami reporters in the latter part of August, he minimized the
furor over the ordinances.[1] Mr. Campbell was of the opinion that
the cities, so long as they conformed to the standards set by the
county, would continue to perform most of their usual functions.
He explained, "I don't see how it can be anything else. The county
doesn't have the organization, manpower, or equipment to take on

everything at once."[2] He optimistically predicted that the cities and the county would iron out their differences. E. Arthur Evans, City of Miami manager, assured Mr. Campbell that the city managers of Dade municipalities were anticipating meeting with him as soon as possible.[3]

Mr. Campbell, on one of his earlier visits to Miami directly after his appointment, had been fully briefed on the new ordinances by Marion Sibley. Although at that time Mr. Campbell felt that they were too detailed and administratively too confining, he nevertheless approved of them in principle.[4] Later he took issue with a demand by S. D. Phillips, Jr., chairman of the Charter Board, that Mr. Sibley be fired because of his responsibility for the proposed ordinances.[5] According to Mr. Campbell, Mr. Sibley and he were in accord on the Metro ordinances when they reviewed them together.

The county manager was not on the job, unfortunately, until after the groundwork for the ordinances had been laid by the Metro Legal Committee. As a newcomer who had a great deal to learn about the area and its politics, he was hardly in a position immediately to take issue with the proposed ordinances, as to either substance or timing. Furthermore, he relied a great deal on Mr. Sibley, who at that time was unquestionably the spokesman for the County Commission. One might conclude that Mr. Campbell was more heir to the ordinances than midwife.

After the Dade League of Municipalities presented its petitions for the autonomy amendment referendum, Mr. Campbell, in his role of mediator, said he was confident that men of good will from both camps could together draft a compromise amendment.[6] According to George S. Okell, Sr., the league's attorney, the league shared Mr. Campbell's optimism and agreed with almost all of Mr. Campbell's ideas for implementing Metro.[7]

## THE ABOLITION RESOLUTION INTRODUCED

At the time of the uproar over the autonomy amendment, Mr. Sibley, in a public speech, adroitly planted the seed that grew into a movement to "abolish" the City of Miami.[8] The strategy of Mr. Sibley and Mr. Paul, leaders of the Metro Legal Committee, was to counterattack and divert the enemy from its main objective—getting the autonomy amendment adopted. A 20-man Committee to Stop Double Taxation, composed of City of Miami business and professional men,[9] had a resolution introduced in the County Commission that in effect would have abolished the government of the City of Miami and consolidated all its functions with those of the county.[10] The chairman of the committee, Hugh P. Emerson, prevailed upon the County Commission to put the issue on the ballot in the regular City of Miami primary election of November 19, 1957.[11] A few days later, the Miami-Dade Chamber of Commerce urged City of Miami voters to support the resolution to abolish the city government.[12] City officials, on the other hand, damned the action of the commission in putting the issue on the ballot as an usurpation of the city's power, and immediately started legal proceedings to challenge the validity of the referendum.[13]

County Manager Campbell was brought into the act by both sides. Mr. Emerson declared he had been assured by the county manager that should the voters approve the abolition of the city government, the county would be able to take over City of Miami services.[14] In a three-page letter to the county manager, which was released first to the press,[15] City of Miami Commissioner James W. High raised the question of the county's ability to take over city functions, and Mr. Campbell assured him that "the county could take over all of the services but not all at once." [16] Pressed by Mr. High for an answer to a number of questions involving the extent to which the county was prepared to reimburse the city for its property and equipment, Mr. Campbell said tersely, "In reply to your several questions, each carefully surrounded by assumptions with which I am not at all familiar, I cannot believe that your request for an early answer is serious. However, if you do need an immediate answer [to the question of whether the county is prepared to pay $33,800,000 to the city for all its property and equipment], it is No." [17]

## THE ABOLITION RESOLUTION WITHDRAWN

The City of Miami's attempt to get a temporary injunction to halt the referendum on the abolition of the city was unsuccessful.[18] The Circuit Court held that suffrage is a political right, not a civil right subject to the injunctive process. But in spite of the abolitionists' legal victory, there was growing opposition to both the tactics and the speed they had employed in getting the abolition measure on the ballot. In fact, the newspapers would not support the abolition faction.

The increased opposition also led the Miami-Dade Chamber of Commerce to change its position. The move to abolish the government of the City of Miami was reconsidered in November at a joint meeting of representatives from the Chamber of Commerce, the Committee to Stop Double Taxation, and the Miami Citizens and Taxpayers League, a pro-city organization.[19] They all agreed that both the autonomy amendment and the proposal to consolidate the functions of the city with those of the county should be modified or withdrawn and that the differences over the ordinances should be mediated. They adopted a joint resolution which read:

WHEREAS, this community is faced with a crisis affecting the future of metropolitan government, and

WHEREAS, it is vital to the people of Dade County that metropolitan government be preserved, and

WHEREAS, the present crisis has been precipitated by reason of controversial ordinances which resulted in a proposed amendment to the Charter which in effect would render metropolitan government ineffective, and an election designed to in effect eliminate the City of Miami, and

WHEREAS, the civic leaders who have actively participated in the issues involved have agreed that their main responsibility is the preservation and early implementation of metropolitan government, they

HEREBY RESOLVE to forthwith seek the following objectives:

1. The modification or withdrawal of both the proposed Charter amendment and the election transferring City of Miami services to the county.
2. The mediation of differences with regard to the contents of proposed and/or enacted ordinances of metropolitan government.[20]

A request by Mr. Emerson to withdraw the resolution calling for the vote on abolition was subsequently honored by the County Commission.[21]

## THE COMPROMISE PROPOSAL

Between the time the abolition referendum resolution was adopted and rescinded, Mr. Campbell; Robert T. Spicer, Miami-Dade Chamber of Commerce president; Mr. Claussen, Dade League of Municipalities president; City of Miami Manager Evans; Willard H. Webb, town manager of Bal Harbour; and E. B. Leatherman, circuit court clerk, met for the purpose of achieving a solution to the autonomy problem.[22] Mr. Claussen agreed to consider an alternative to the autonomy amendment as long as it guaranteed protection from extremists intent on abolishing all municipalities. Mr. Campbell favored a substitute autonomy amendment that would eliminate ambiguities. The basic issue, as he saw it, was the "wording for a substitute amendment that was both clear and acceptable to the County Commission and the League." [23] As usual, Mr. Campbell attempted to allay the fears of the cities, and the cities in turn declared their good intentions.

County Attorney Darrey A. Davis [24] and Dade League Attorney George Okell, Sr., collaborated on the drafting of a compromise amendment that they hoped would be approved. Their proposal provided for the control by Metro (1) over all functions within unincorporated areas, (2) over municipal functions if a municipality failed to maintain at least minimum standards or voluntarily relinquished its powers, and (3) over specified area-wide services. The area-wide services specified were tax assessment and collection, mass transportation, harbors, ports, health, sewage and water facilities, arterial roads and bridges, advertising and development, central records and communications for fire and police protection, and formulation and enforcement of a master traffic and parking plan on arterial roads, bridges, and turnpikes. The county could not, however, control water and sewerage plants or transportation systems owned by a municipality at the time the amendment was adopted.

The compromise amendment also included a section on uniform building and related codes enforceable as minimum standards by the county. The municipalities were to be allowed to issue permits, conduct inspections in accordance with the uniform codes, and collect fees. The county was to conduct examinations for building-trades men and issue certificates of competency binding on the cities, but the cities had the right to issue municipal licenses at the customary rate.

The proposal concluded: "All existing ordinances inconsistent herewith shall no longer remain in force and effect."

## NEGOTIATIONS ON THE COMPROMISE FAIL

At a meeting of those responsible for negotiating the compromise amendment, Daniel Paul expressed doubt that the proposal would be acceptable to both the County Commission and the cities.[25] He implied that the compromise would restrict the prerogatives of the County Commission in carrying out metropolitan functions. Mr. Okell took him to task for assuming that the compromise amendment would hamstring Metro, claiming that Mr. Paul had not read the amendment.[26]

Mr. Okell believed that Mr. Campbell, who was away from the city, would approve the proposal and lend it the necessary prestige and support. Such was not the case. In fact, the manager later said he thought it would take a miracle to bring about agreement on the compromise amendment. Despite his pessimism, Mr. Campbell believed that the county and the cities were not far apart on fundamentals.[27] The major area of contention, the county manager thought, was not disagreement on basic county and city powers but on the division of responsibility for powers they both shared. For example, some aspects of law enforcement belong to the county and some to the cities. The problem was that of drawing a satisfactory line of demarcation.

A heroic effort to settle the differences over the compromise amendment occurred on December 12, 1957. Representatives of the Miami-Dade Chamber of Commerce, the Dade League of Municipalities, the Committee to Stop Double Taxation, and the Miami Citizens and Taxpayers League met with Mr. Campbell, County Attorney Davis, Mr. Leatherman, and others to discuss the problem. By 9 P.M., when the meeting ended, most of the participants apparently approved of the final version of the amendment. During the meeting Mr. Campbell stressed his approval of a substitute amendment if it in no way would restrict Metro's authority to handle problems not yet anticipated.[28]

Fearful of its future consequences to Metro, Mr. Campbell, at a County Commission meeting the following day, refused to endorse the substitute autonomy amendment [29] and the proposal was rejected by the commission.[30] The commissioners expressed concern about (1) the effect of the substitute amendment on the basic theory of metropolitan government, (2) the confusion that might result if both the original autonomy amendment and the substitute amendment were on the same ballot, and (3) the fact that organizations supporting the substitute proposal had not had an opportunity to submit it to their members.

Reactions to the commission's rejection of the compromise ranged from bitter denunciation to reluctant acquiescence. Dean Claussen of the Dade League of Municipalities declared that "we have extended ourselves and bent over backwards by working with the businessmen and Mr. Campbell to try to find a solution satisfactory to everyone." [31] Mitchell Wolfson, a spokesman for the substitute amendment and a former member of the Charter Board, contended that the new proposal interpreted the home rule charter as it was intended by the authors of the charter.[32] County Attorney Davis maintained that although the substitute amendment was preferable to the original autonomy amendment, it, too, would undermine many of the Metro ordinances that had been passed.[33] Daniel Paul's opinion that no proposal would have been acceptable to both the county and the municipalities was probably right.[34]

Proponents of Metro were not unhappy that the substitute proposal had been rejected, apparently reasoning that it would have been far more difficult to have defeated the substitute amendment than the original. They had to go through the motions of negotiating a compromise amendment, but they felt the future was on their side and they had no intention of granting any concessions. Since the deadline for placing other substitute proposals on the February 11 ballot was past,[35] the original autonomy amendment remained to be considered at the polls.

## FORCES FOR AND AGAINST THE AUTONOMY AMENDMENT

Once the substitute proposal had been turned down, community forces began to align themselves for or against the autonomy amendment. At the outset of the campaign, Robert M. Morgan, a leading Metro advocate and prominent member of the Miami-Dade Chamber of Commerce, warned that the chamber would use every resource at its command to defeat the amendment. He was supported by Abe Aronovitz,[36] a political leader and a former mayor of the City of Miami, and by Hugh P. Emerson and J. Neville McArthur, both leaders in the Chamber of Commerce.

A "Save Metro" committee was formed by the Chamber of Commerce;[37] the League of Women Voters started a campaign against the amendment; and a poll of members of the Dade County Research Foundation, in which 47 per cent responded, showed a 90 to 11 alignment against the amendment.[38] John Corcoran and Victor Jones, nationally known municipal consultants, publicly advocated defeat of the amendment after the Dade League of Municipalities made it appear that both these men favored the autonomy amendment.[39] The newspapers, as expected, were vehemently opposed to the amendment.

Advocating the amendments were the Dade League of Municipalities, municipal employee organizations, most city officials and employees, beneficiaries of municipal business, small city newspapers, and most of the suburban chambers of commerce.

## THE COURT INTERVENES

The campaign waxed hot and heavy until a few days before the issue was to be settled. Then, on February 5, 1958, Circuit Court Judge George E. Holt upheld the constitutionality of the autonomy amendment, but ordered the vote on the amendment postponed until his decision could be reviewed by the Florida Supreme Court.[40] Judge Holt[41] opined that the court wanted to spare the voters the expense and inconvenience of an election that would be meaningless if the Supreme Court declared the amendment "a vain and illegal thing."

The ruling could hardly be called a victory for the Dade League of Municipalities and the other proponents of the autonomy amendment, since most observers believe that public sentiment at that time was with the proamendment forces. While gloom reigned in the halls of the Dade League, the opponents of the amendment were jubilant. Of the opponents, only Mr. Campbell expressed regret that the issue could not have been clarified once and for all.[42]

## FINAL COMPROMISE ATTEMPT FAILS

Some five months after the vote was postponed, another attempt was made to work out a compromise. A 14-member committee of civic and government leaders on both sides of the Metro issue was organized by the then City of Miami attorney, William Pallot.[43] A subcommittee composed of Thomas H. Anderson, attorney for the Dade League of Municipalities, and R. Bunn Gautier, proconsolidationist, reached agreement.[44] The plan they worked out, a cumbersome one, provided for a supra-administrative board that would have the power to decide whether a function was local or area-wide. The proposal never got off the ground and it probably would not have met with widespread favor in any event. On July 23, the Florida Supreme Court upheld the holding of a referendum election on the original autonomy amendment, and the County Commission called the election for September 30, 1958.[45] Dade's electorate would have to render a decision on the original autonomy amendment after all.

## 12

# The Autonomy Amendment Defeated

1957, December 19    County Attorney Davis advised the County Com-
                     mission that it could not legally use tax funds on a
                     "Save Metro" fight.
1958, August 2       Coral Gables Commissioner Winston W. Wynne
                     began organizing a pro-Metro Committee.
1958, August 9       Forty-six candidates qualified for the six County
                     Commission seats.
1958, September 5    Circuit Court Judge Marshall C. Wiseheart dis-
                     missed a suit challenging the legality of the Dade
                     League's financing of a campaign for the autonomy
                     amendment.
1958, September 9    No candidate for any of the six County Commis-
                     sion seats received a majority vote, necessitating a
                     runoff election on September 30.
1958, September 19   Mayor Robert King High of the City of Miami pro-
                     tested to City Manager Evans the printing of
                     posters by the city supporting the autonomy amend-
                     ment.
1958, September 23   The County Commission promised to end personal
                     property taxes in 1959.
1958, September 25   Time magazine predicted the autonomy amendment
                     would be adopted.
                     O. W. Campbell released a 48-page annual report
                     on the accomplishments of Metro.

1958, September 30   The autonomy amendment was defeated at the
                     polls; six new members were elected to the County
                     Commission.
                     The County Commission passed on first reading
                     an ordinance legalizing gambling casinos and slot
                     machines in Dade County.
1958, October 7      The County Commission voted 4 to 0 to kill the
                     ordinance on legalized gambling.


County Attorney Davis, appearing before the Florida Supreme
Court in early June, 1958, to appeal Judge Holt's decision upholding
the constitutionality of the proposed autonomy amendment, declared
it was impossible to conceive of any law passed by the county that
would not be in conflict with the laws of at least one of Dade's
municipalities.[1] The county attorney described the proposed amendment as a double-edged sword designed to prevent any central
metropolitan government and intended to make each municipality
supreme. Attorney Okell, representing the Dade League of Municipalities, maintained that the autonomy amendment to the home rule
charter was designed to carry out the spirit, intent, and purpose of
the home rule amendment by guaranteeing the 26 municipalities the
right of self-determination.[2] He argued that the primary purpose of
the autonomy amendment was to prevent the county from enacting
ordinances that would in effect repeal municipal charters.

In the last week of July, 1958, the Florida Supreme Court handed
down its decision upholding the referendum election on the autonomy amendment.[3] The court ruled that the referendum should
not be restrained "if an examination of the proposed Amendment
reveals that, if adopted, it would be legally operative in part, even
though it might ultimately become necessary to determine that particular aspects violate the constitution." [4] The court held that only if
the proposed amendment were unconstitutional in its entirety should
the referendum be enjoined, and expressed doubt about the constitutionality of only one aspect of the amendment.[5] Judge Campbell Thornal, speaking for the court, declared that within the provisions of the organic law, the people of the affected area could
adopt the broadest type of home rule, partial home rule, or no home
rule at all.[6]

## TAKING SIDES IN THE CAMPAIGN

The referendum election was set by the County Commission for September 30, the same day as the runoff election for the six additional County Commissioners.[7] Once again the pro- and anti-Metro groups marshaled their forces.

### The Cities—Pro-Autonomy

The Dade County League of Municipalities had a fund of some $32,000 for its campaign.[8] Far more difficult to compute but no less tangible were the pro-autonomy efforts of the cities, particularly the City of Miami. There is little doubt that City of Miami employees were led to believe that defeat of the amendment would jeopardize their jobs. City of Miami vehicles, including garbage trucks, displayed "Vote Yes" and "Save Your City" signs manufactured by the city's sign shop. City of Miami auto inspection personnel gave their clients pep talks and provided bumper strips urging support of the amendment. On election day, voters could obtain transportation to the polls by calling any of a number of the city phones.

City of Miami Manager Evans, a former army general, planned campaign strategy for the city and for the Dade League of Municipalities. Only the mayor, who was a maverick on the city commission, objected to the city's activities; the four other commissioners supported Mr. Evans' pro-autonomy activities. City Commissioner B. E. Hearn observed that $50,000 of city money had been used to launch Metro and there was no reason why an equal amount should not be used to limit its powers.[9]

Other cities also took part in the campaign. The city-owned *Miami Beach Record*, in a 4-page issue, examined what it called the dangers of metropolitan government,[10] and mailed the paper at public expense to the city's 18,000 registered voters. Anti-Metro leaflets were enclosed with all water bills in Miami Beach. Coral Gables city commissioners, by a 4 to 1 vote, approved the mailing at public expense of a "Vote Yes" letter to their constituents.[11]

The campaign efforts of the cities and the Dade League of Municipalities apparently met with marked success in the first few weeks after the date for the referendum election was announced. Indeed, there was a growing belief at the time among the proponents of Metro that they faced defeat at the polls. A *Time* magazine article, published the week before the referendum, reflected the fears of the pro-Metro forces.[12]

### The Anti-Autonomy Forces

Winston W. Wynne, the only Coral Gables city commissioner who was pro-Metro, became the chairman of the Citizens "Vote No" Committee, which raised $15,400 to defeat the amendment.[13] The committee sought to offer "leadership to offset and counteract the well organized efforts of municipal officeholders to destroy metropolitan government."[14] Some $14,435 was spent for advertising by the public relations firm hired by the committee. Aligning themselves with the "Vote No" Committee were the Miami-Dade Chamber of Commerce, the Miami Junior Chamber of Commerce, the League of Women Voters, and a number of Dade's most prominent citizens.

The board of directors of the Miami-Dade Chamber of Commerce was taken to task by disgruntled members who charged that the decision by the board to oppose the amendment was arbitrary.[15] Those who complained were the pro-city faction that came to the fore in every consolidation movement. The directors countered that there had been ample opportunity for the dissenters to express their opinions before the decision to oppose the amendment was made, and despite the protests, the chamber was active in the pro-Metro campaign.

The Leagues of Women Voters in Dade County, supporters of the home rule charter, joined the campaign against the autonomy amendment, although the Miami Beach League was not active. The leagues staged a "marching backward parade" to point up their contention that a vote for the autonomy amendment would be a backward step for Dade.[16] League members also drove behind City of Miami sanitation trucks and displayed signs refuting the city's claim of free garbage collection.[17] The ladies received a whiff of city election politics.

Television station WPST, just before the autonomy election, announced its opposition to the amendment. Station WTVJ, which supported the autonomy amendment before Judge Holt postponed the referendum, remained neutral in the final campaign. In the final weeks before the election, Ralph Renick, WTVJ news commentator, gave the most objective analysis of the amendment of any of the mass media.[18] E. Arthur Evans, City of Miami manager and leader of the pro-atuonomy forces, had accused the Miami papers and most radio and TV stations of giving only the anti-autonomy side.[19]

Other than for the effective anti-autonomy campaign of the newspapers, radio, and television, the efforts of the organized anti-autonomy groups were meager compared with those of the pro-autonomy cities and the Dade League of Municipalities.

### The County Government—Ostensible Neutrality

Unlike the cities, the county government was officially neutral in the campaign. There were no funds allocated by the county commission for any campaign purposes. The county attorney had ruled that the commissioners lacked the legal authority to incur such expenditures.[20]

Early in the campaign, County Manager Campbell publicly warned that if the amendment passed, Dade County would be thrown into political anarchy. The authority to solve area-wide problems would no doubt be nullified, he believed, and "it would take us back beyond the point where we were when we started." [21] Later, however, Mr. Campbell was reluctant to become publicly involved in political activities, directly or indirectly. During a panel discussion on county affairs he refused to talk about the amendment on the grounds that his job was nonpolitical.[22] In reply to a specific question, however, he said that contrary to rumor he would not quit his job if the autonomy amendment were adopted. On another occasion, a television station publicized an election eve debate between Mr. Campbell and Mr. Evans on the merits of the amendment. At the last moment, the station announced Mr. Campbell would not appear because he thought it improper. People close to Mr. Campbell indicated that he had turned down the invitation to debate when it had first been extended. The same day the debate was canceled, the newspapers published a story that the county manager had attacked the cities for their anti-Metro expenditures, which, he charged, approximated $1 million.[23]

Mr. Campbell told county employees that under the county civil service law they could work either for or against the autonomy amendment without being penalized.[24] They were prohibited from actively supporting any of the candidates seeking County Commission posts, however.

The County Commissioners remained in the background during most of the campaign, although one of them, John B. McLeod, is known to have contributed $1,000 to the "Vote No" Committee.[25] But the day before the referendum, to refute rumors that the commissioners favored the autonomy forces, Commissioner Edwin Lee Mason announced in behalf of the commissioners that they were wholeheartedly in favor of Metro.[26]

Between July 23, the day the Supreme Court ordered the autonomy amendment put on the ballot, and September 30, the day of the referendum election, the county announced a number of policies that had political impact and could be construed to be pro-Metro. Most important was the county's announcement of neutrality, which contrasted sharply with the often crude tactics of the municipalities. The newspapers artfully utilized the cities' campaign activities to reinforce their attack on the autonomy amendment as the "politicians' amendment." The absence of any overt campaign by the county and the mild campaign by the "Vote No" Committee may have been the most effective weapons of anti-autonomy forces.

The county took certain positive actions, however, that may also have influenced the public in favor of Metro. A tax reduction, although announced before the end of May, was repeatedly mentioned during the campaign, as was the fact that 2,000 county employees would receive pay increases after October 1.

Also announced were (1) plans for improving police protection and garbage services in the unincorporated areas of the county; (2) creation of a planning department; (3) the county's intention to abolish the personal property tax; (4) a program for uniform bus and water systems; (5) plans for a park at the edge of the Everglades; (6) a preliminary application to the federal government for aid to blighted areas; and (7) plans for two auxiliary courthouses, one at each end of the county. A few days before the referendum the county released a 48-page annual report on the accomplishments of Metro.[27]

It seems likely that the County Commission and the manager would have taken the steps they did regardless of the referendum. The fact that these activities, in most instances, were not merely schemes calculated to defeat the amendment in no way lessened their political impact.[28]

Not all the actions of the county government won friends for Metro, however. By the time of the referendum, the commissioners' personal prestige was at a new low. They were under constant attack by the newspapers, which charged they had plush furnishings in their offices, showed favoritism in awarding park and airport concessions, held secret meetings, lacked dignity, failed to grasp the concept of Metro, and had tried to push through important legislation just before the election of six new commissioners. On the day of the referendum the commission voted 3 to 2 on the first reading of an ordinance to legalize gambling casinos and slot machines in Dade County.[29]

## USE OF PUBLIC FUNDS CHALLENGED

The use of public funds to campaign for the amendment, rather than the amendment itself, was the *cause célèbre* during the closing weeks of the campaign.

A suit challenging the authority of the Dade County League of Municipalities to finance the autonomy campaign with city tax money was filed by the only County Commission candidate from the Miami Beach area who opposed the autonomy amendment.[30] He contended that the cities did not have the legal right to contribute to the campaign. The suit was dismissed, however, on the ground that the complainant was not a member of the Dade League and had no legal standing to institute proceedings.[31]

The newspapers hammered away at the iniquity of public servants using public funds to influence the voters.[32] The implication was that the activities of the cities, intended to sway the electorate, were an infringement on the free elective process. Both area-wide newspapers, the *Miami Herald* and the *Miami News*, published front-page stories and pictures of city vehicles with signs and bumper strips urging Miamians to "Vote Yes" (for autonomy).[33] In an editorial on September 21 the *Herald* charged politicians with spending taxpayers' money to defeat the will of the people, which, the newspaper said, had been expressed previously on three occasions [34] —the home rule amendment vote in November, 1956; the charter vote in May, 1957; and the first primary vote for County Commission in September, 1958, in which 9 out of the 12 candidates who qualified for the runoff opposed the autonomy amendment.

## WINDING UP THE CAMPAIGN

As the day for the vote came closer, both sides continued to argue, and many speculated on the outcome. The *Miami News* disputed the idea that the vote in the first primary on County Commission candidates was a barometer of the fate of the amendment.[35] Of the candidates who entered the primary race, 34 opposed the autonomy amendment, 9 favored it, and 3 were indecisive. Thus there were almost four times as many candidates against the amendment as there were for it. Of the 9 in favor of the amendment, 4 were from Miami Beach, and 1 each from North Miami, Opa-locka, Miami, the South Miami area, and the Miami Springs area. In view of the fact that candidates who supported the amendment (aside from those running in the Miami Beach district where it was almost compulsory to be pro-autonomy) would lose the endorsement of the two major Miami newspapers, the large proportion of anti-amendment candidates is hardly surprising. Over the years, most politicians in the Miami area have claimed it was virtually impossible to win an election without the support of one or the other of the papers.

Bitter debates between the pros and the antis over the meaning of the amendment created a great deal of confusion as to what a "Yes" vote meant and what a "No" vote meant. "No" meant "yes" you were for Metro, and "Yes" meant you wanted to negate Metro's "usurpation" of the cities' autonomy. Slogans ranged from "Vote Yes, and Save Your City and Metro" to "Vote No, and Save Metro."

There were also confusing arguments made over such issues as (1) the intent of the framers of the charter, (2) the preservation of the cities and (3) the limitations that the autonomy amendment would impose on Metro. To some it appeared that the amendment would strip Metro of most—perhaps nearly all—of its area-wide powers. Only tax assessing and collecting would be county-wide functions under the autonomy amendment, although the county could impose minimum standards for all other functions.

Both sides exaggerated and distorted—more than enough to confuse the average voter. One wit claimed that "never have so many known so little about so much." [36]

## THE AUTONOMY VOTE

The autonomy amendment was defeated in the September 30 referendum by 24,527 votes, a much greater margin of victory for Metro than in the home rule charter referendum in 1957, when Metro won by only 1,784 votes. However, 37,289 more votes were cast in the autonomy amendment referendum than in the charter referendum.

Although 124,313 persons voted on the autonomy amendment issue, this was still 20,984 fewer votes than were cast in a hotly contested state legislative race in which the segregation issue was involved,[37] and 2,162 fewer than the total vote in the County Commission district races.[38]

On the other hand, some 9,900 more persons voted in the autonomy referendum than on a measure to change the name of Dade County to Miami County, a measure that also was defeated.[39]

### Against Autonomy

In spite of all the work of city officials and employees, 53 out of 56 precincts in the City of Miami voted against the autonomy amendment. The three exceptions were predominantly Negro precincts. The Coral Gables vote was also against the amendment, just slightly less than its two-to-one pro-Metro vote for the charter in 1957. Residents of South Miami, Opa-locka, North Miami Beach, and North Miami also cast large votes against the amendment.[40]

Unincorporated areas of the county held somewhat anomalous positions in the autonomy amendment fight. The amendment, unlike the charter, dealt only with the cities and had no direct effect upon the unincorporated areas. The vote of the unincorporated areas was 66 per cent against the autonomy amendment. In the home rule charter referendum, the vote in these areas was slightly more than 50 per cent against Metro, which may be explained in part by the fear of many of its residents that a change in government would mean higher taxes. Metro had been in operation for more than a year when the autonomy amendment election was held and their fears had not been realized.

Several other factors help to explain the vote against the autonomy amendment in the unincorporated areas. Residents of the unincorporated areas can be divided into two categories—the "new type" residents and the "old type."

The new type are frequently young married couples with children, living in new, compactly built subdivisions. They expect regular garbage and trash collection, supervised playgrounds for their children, libraries, and other services. There are some within this group who are even willing to pay additional taxes to have Metro make these services available.

The old-type residents, whose counterparts elsewhere in the nation might be considered newcomers, are scattered throughout the county in various kinds of housing. Many consider themselves rugged individualists. They are not particularly fond of their city neighbors, who contend that taxes paid by city dwellers support the unincorporated areas. The old-type residents make few requests for services and are content so long as their taxes are not increased. Metro's announced reduction of the millage rate could make only a favorable impression on this group.

Both new-type and old-type residents were no doubt influenced by the newspapers, which vigorously opposed the amendment. Both groups apparently thought that since Metro was a reality and they were stuck with it, the cities should share the same fate.

### For Autonomy

The Golden Beach, Surfside, North Bay Village, Bal Harbour, and Bay Harbor Islands areas voted 58.7 per cent for the autonomy amendment, a change from 56.9 per cent vote for Metro in the charter referendum.[41] The switch probably did not reflect a change in basic attitudes as much as a recognition that the charter was not what they had initially expected.

West Miami, which favored Metro by a small percentage in 1957, supported the autonomy amendment in 1958, possibly because of strong anti-Metro leadership in the community.

In the final analysis, Dade County, apart from the unincorporated areas, was divided in 1958 along much the same lines as in 1957. The loyalty to their city governments of the voters of Miami Beach, Miami Springs, Hialeah, Miami Shores, Homestead, and some of the extremely small communities belies the contention that public officials, public employees, and business beneficiaries of the cities were the sum and substance of the anti-Metro forces. They may have been the leaders, but voters in a number of cities constituted a loyal following.

## AFTERTHOUGHTS

How can the pro-autonomy position of these communities be explained? In the autonomy election the higher income groups within any given precinct opposed the amendment to a greater extent than did the lower income groups. However, when the county's precincts were divided into four categories, based upon assessed residence values, it was found that all four divisions voted against the autonomy amendment (Appendix D). It would appear that the factor most decisive in determining whether a positive or negative vote was cast for the autonomy amendment was the particular areal jurisdiction within which the voter resided. There were both low- and high-income municipalities which supported the amendment.

A large pro-amendment vote was cast in Miami Beach, a high-income city, whose economy is largely based on tourism. Businessmen, public officials, and municipal employees, as well as other residents who benefit from the substantial taxes derived from hotels and other businesses, view the interests of Miami Beach as different from those of other parts of Dade County. The city's large Jewish population may help to reinforce this separatist feeling. The biggest anti-Metro vote in Miami Beach was in the southernmost section, an area where the lower socio-economic groups reside.

A fairly high socio-economic level is found among the residents of Miami Shores. The city's fear of encroachment from its less prosperous neighbors may account in part for its anti-Metro vote. Vigorous anti-Metro leadership was also a contributing factor.

On the other hand, Coral Gables, with similar demographic patterns and with aggressive anti-Metro leadership, aligned itself unequivocally with Metro. Needless to say, there are other factors that account for this difference in outlook between the two cities. Coral Gables is larger, more heterogeneous, more cosmopolitan, and less fearful of being engulfed by its neighbors. The only part of Coral Gables that voted for the autonomy amendment was a lower socio-economic section, which incidentally is also one of the oldest areas of the municipality. How much of the feeling of this group may be attributed to material factors and how much to tradition and loyalty is difficult to assess.

In the lower socio-economic categories are found such pro-autonomy amendment cities as Homestead and Hialeah. Homestead reflects the insularity of a city set off both economically and geographically from the remainder of Dade County. Hialeah, characterized by its mayor as a "working class community," [42] has grown from 19,676 residents to 66,972 in a period of 10 years (Appendix A). The city's economic uniformity is paralleled by its political uniformity. It has had the same mayor for the past 17 years. The residents of Hialeah enjoy what they have and are fearful of political change.

The total population of the anti-Metro cities consists of approximately one-fifth of the population of Dade County,[43] yet the faithful of these communities together with the city-centered officials of both the pro- and anti-Metro areas, will help to determine the future development of metropolitan government in Greater Miami.

13

# Fate of the Ordinances

| | |
|---|---|
| 1957, August 16 | The County Commission enacted a public works ordinance. |
| 1957, September 16 | The County Commission enacted a metropolitan traffic code. |
| 1957, September 25 | The County Commission enacted an ordinance establishing a metropolitan court. |
| 1957, October 29 | The County Commission adopted the South Florida Building Code as Metro (Dade County, Florida) Ordinance 57-22. |
| 1957, November 12 | The County Commission enacted an ordinance whereby the county would issue a single certificate qualifying building tradesmen to work anywhere in Dade County. |
| 1957, December 17 | The County Commission enacted a zoning and building ordinance. |
| 1958, June 27 | Circuit Court Judge Pat Cannon ruled that the municipalities must enforce the Metro traffic code. |
| 1958, September 30 | The County Commission repealed the section of the zoning ordinance that gave the county control over municipal zoning. |
| 1958, December 17 | The Florida Supreme Court upheld the Metro traffic code and the Metro court. |
| 1959, March 4 | The City of Miami Commission approved the use of Metro auto inspection stickers for distribution by city car-inspection stations. |
| 1961, March 6 | A story in the *Miami Herald* stated that Miami Beach and Coral Gables building codes were to be brought into conformity with Metro's building code. |

1962, January 13      Miami Beach began to enforce the Metro traffic
                      code.
1962, March 6         The County Commission enacted an ordinance
                      enabling the Metro Examining Boards to grant
                      limited certificates of competency in the building
                      trades to persons who had passed an appropriate
                      examination by qualified municipal boards during
                      the period from December 1, 1957 through Decem-
                      ber 1, 1961.

Since it was the strong opposition to Metro's controversial ordinances that led to the autonomy amendment struggle, it is important
to know what these ordinances provided and what eventually happened to them. The 1962 status of each of these ordinances is mentioned only briefly in this chapter. A more detailed account of the
struggle, particularly between Metro and the cities of Miami and
Miami Beach, over the final disposition of the more controversial
ordinances will be found in chapter 15.

## ORDINANCE CONTROVERSIES

Many provisions of the Metro ordinances did not foster any dissension; some, however, were particularly controversial.

### Zoning and Building

Zoning and building provisions under Metro were treated in four
categories: (1) the South Florida Building Code as adopted by
Metro which required uniform building regulations for both incorporated and unincorporated areas; [1] (2) a zoning code which set
zoning standards for the unincorporated areas (Part I),[2] for the
municipalities (Part II),[3] and for the Homestead Air Force Base
(Part III); [4] (3) an ordinance which enforced uniform subdivision
regulations for both incorporated and unincorporated areas; [5] and
(4) an ordinance which established a Department of Building and
Zoning to enforce the building regulations and the zoning code.[6]
    The first draft of the zoning and building ordinance would have
made the county responsible for enforcement of zoning and building

regulations in *both* incorporated and unincorporated areas, and would have given the county the right to inspect buildings and issue certificates of occupancy throughout the county. All the zoning powers of the cities, except their authority to adopt zoning standards higher than those set by the county, were eliminated. The ordinance as it was passed was modified insofar as it gave the municipalities the power to make inspections and to issue certificates of occupancy in the incorporated areas, while the county was given the power to set uniform standards for these functions.[7] The county still retained control over municipal zoning.

The ordinance was to have gone into effect on December 31, 1957;[8] it was postponed until March 31, 1958, and then again postponed until July 1.[9] During this period the cities maintained the same enforcement procedures for building and zoning that had prevailed prior to Metro. Later the July effective date was extended.[10] On September 30, 1958, the provisions in the zoning ordinance pertaining to county control over municipal zoning were repealed.[11]

Not only did Metro meet with opposition in its efforts to control municipal zoning,[12] but it also ran into difficulties over compliance with the uniform building code, which the cities themselves had been instrumental in creating. Early in May, 1958, Metro and the City of Miami disputed an alleged violation of the building code. The code allowed a property owner to build, maintain, alter, or repair a single-family residence for his own use or occupancy. The City of Miami, unlike Metro, construed the provision to apply to duplexes as well as to single homes. In an editorial on May 9, 1958, the *Miami Herald* charged that city officials were attempting "to punch a hole in the new uniform building code"[13] by violating its provisions. The newspaper interpreted the city's refusal to recognize Metro's authority as part of a plan by municipal officials to entrench themselves against the loss of their power or the abolition of their offices. Coral Gables, Miami Beach and municipalities adjacent to Miami Beach also failed to strictly adhere to the uniform provisions demanded by the building code. Instead, these rather affluent cities enforced the more strict requirements of their own city codes. However, in March, 1961, the recalcitrant cities, after negotiations with Metro, changed their building codes to conform to Metro's.

At the beginning of 1962 the county was in charge of zoning for the unincorporated areas, with each city in control of its own municipal zoning. The South Florida Building Code and the subdivision regulations remained in effect for both the incorporated and unincorporated areas. The municipalities conducted their own inspections and issued certificates of occupancy for property within the incorporated areas. A Metro building and zoning department, as created by executive order,[14] was in operation to enforce the South Florida Building Code, Parts I and III of the zoning code, and the subdivision regulations.

### Licenses and Certificates of Competency

A Metro ordinance gave the county exclusive jurisdiction over the issuance of certificates of competency to contractors, subcontractors, masters, journeymen, and maintenance personnel in the building, engineering, plumbing, electrical, mechanical, and gas installation trades.[15] The purpose of the law was to have a single license which would qualify an individual to ply his trade anywhere in the county. The cities could charge for work permits, however, as they had in the past.[16]

In open defiance of the law, Coral Gables and Miami Beach continued to give examinations in the building trades. Coral Gables stopped this practice, however, after a 1958 Florida Supreme Court decision was handed down that upheld the powers of Metro in another sphere.[17] Since that time Coral Gables has almost always granted work permits to craftsmen holding Metro licenses. However, Coral Gables did refuse to recognize a Metro plumbing license acquired under a "grandfather clause," which allowed five years' experience in the unincorporated areas, instead of an examination, to be the basis for granting the permit. The city upheld its plumbing inspector's ruling that a plumbing permit would be issued only if the licensee passed Metro's written examination.[18] The courts later ruled against Coral Gables.[19]

Although in 1959 Miami Beach still conducted its own examinations and exercised its independent judgment on the qualifications of a Metro licensee, in the spring of 1960 it gave full recognition to Metro certificates of competency. By 1962 all municipalities were conforming to Metro license requirements. As a measure of good will, the Metro Commission in March, 1962, enacted an ordinance [20] permitting the Metro Examining Board to grant restricted county certificates of competency, applicable only within a given municipality, to all persons who had successfully passed an appropriate examination by a qualified municipal board during the period of December 1, 1957, through December 1, 1961. Ironically, the period designated by the ordinance was the very period in which the cities of Miami, Miami Beach, and Coral Gables had illegally held examinations and granted certificates of competency in direct conflict with Metro's exclusive powers. It should be remembered, however, that these municipalities had standards which were at least the equivalent of Metro's.

## Traffic Code

The metropolitan traffic code established uniform traffic regulations for both unincorporated and incorporated areas as well as county control over auto inspection, traffic signal devices, and parking meters.[21] The code, adopted on September 20, 1957, was to take effect on December 1 of that year,[22] but the effective date was deferred until January 1, 1958,[23] and finally until March 1.[24] Auto inspection, as a Metro function, was postponed until July 1, 1958.[25] The testimony of Mayor Kenneth Oka of Miami Beach before a Congressional subcommittee was typical of the criticism of Metro's traffic code and of the Metro court system:

They are going to take over all the traffic. They claim under the right to regulate arterial highways that they have to expand into the cities to include all traffic offenses. They are setting up their municipal metropolitan court to virtually take the place of our municipal courts.

They are going to sit their judge in our courtroom, a courtroom which we built with our own taxpayers' money, on which we are still paying the bonded indebtedness, and they are going to try every traffic offense which occurs in the City of Miami Beach.

Miami Beach policemen, who are on the payroll of Miami Beach, will make arrests in the name of the county and issue metropolitan traffic summonses to these people who will appear before the metropolitan judges.

Now, they had a division of funds. Originally half the funds which were collected by way of fines were to be remitted to the city within which the offenses took place, and the other half was to go back to the metropolitan government; and if at the end of the fiscal year, if there was any money left, after deducting all their expenses, they were to return to Miami Beach any monies which were left.

I assume no money is ever left after a government operation; but they changed that, when the cities started to howl, to a two-thirds, one-third split. They said to the cities: "Well, we will give you two-thirds."

They were throwing us the little bone, the justification for taking over our traffic offenses, and we will keep one-third to manage our court. By the same token, just like they can keep dividing this up from half to thirds, they can come back next year and say, We will take three-quarters and give you a quarter.

Eventually, it will mean that they will take over completely the entire operation of the court system of Miami Beach.[26]

Most municipalities complained that it would be difficult to pay for a court, a city attorney, and a city judge on the income from fines for non-traffic violations. Coral Gables refused to use the Metro courts for traffic cases on the ground that to do so would reduce the city's revenue from fines by one-third and result in a $36,000 annual loss to the city.

The cities also protested the county provisions regarding traffic equipment. The traffic code permitted the county traffic engineer to designate the location and type of traffic control signs, signals, and devices for the entire county,[27] and the county paid for installation and maintenance of the equipment.[28] The code also required that the cities obtain the approval of the county traffic engineer before locating and installing parking meters.[29] This latter requirement prompted Miami Beach councilman Harold B. Spaet to express the natural reaction of Miami Beach: "We have an excellent parking system. Under the ordinances that they passed, if we want to move one parking meter we must get authority from the county government."[30]

Auto inspection is another exclusive function of the county under the traffic code, although it has been delegated by the county Public Safety Director to qualified municipalities.[31] Income from auto inspections is retained by the cities. At the beginning of 1962 the cities of Miami, Miami Shores, Coral Gables, North Miami, Miami

Springs, Opa-locka, South Miami, Homestead, North Miami Beach, West Miami, Hialeah, Sweetwater, and Surfside under county authorization were inspecting cars and granting county auto inspection stickers.[32] Only the cities of Miami, Hialeah, and Miami Beach, among those qualified, initially balked at using county stickers in place of their own. Hialeah, however, came into the fold immediately after the defeat of the autonomy amendment. The City of Miami, after a major political upheaval in March, 1959,[33] began to issue county stickers.[34] By March, 1962, Miami Beach was the only holdout against Metro auto inspection.

The traffic code, which nullified all municipal traffic ordinances, authorized municipal police to enforce county traffic ordinances within city limits, but provided that all cases growing out of such violations be tried in the Metro courts.[35] It imposed increased fines for parking violations and required appearance in court by all persons charged with moving violations. The public reaction to this requirement made it easier for the cities to continue to enforce their own municipal codes. By the end of July, 1959, however, all the municipalities except Miami Beach and El Portal were enforcing the Metro traffic code.[36] The two holdout cities, after exhausting every possible legal maneuver, began to enforce the Metro code in January, 1962, thus bringing all the municipalities into compliance.

## Public Works

The public works ordinance required the municipalities to submit plans for all public works to the County Department of Public Works; such projects would have to meet at least the minimum standards recommended by the department and set by the County Commission.[37] The cities vehemently objected to these requirements, and in July, 1958, the section of the ordinance pertaining to municipal public works construction was repealed.[38]

## THE ORDINANCES GO TO COURT

The above ordinances, especially the traffic code, moved Miami Shores to challenge the County Commission's right to curtail the exercise of a city's powers under its municipal charter. The city filed suit for a declaratory decree seeking a determination and delineation of the powers and functions of the county government and the powers and functions of the municipalities under the home rule amendment and the home rule charter.

The county, by cross complaint, sought a declaration of the rights and status of the metropolitan court and the metropolitan traffic code. In the cross complaint the county asked the court permanently to enjoin Miami Shores from exercising powers contrary to the charter and the metropolitan ordinances, if the court found that the Metro traffic code superseded local traffic ordinances.

The plaintiff, Miami Shores, in its suit questioned the validity of various sections of the home rule charter on the ground that the provisions were in conflict with the home rule amendment. The plaintiff also maintained that the charter provisions were inconsistent with each other. Miami Shores contended that the County Commission, in the exercise of its powers relating to municipalities, was limited to setting minimum standards.

Since there were widespread differences over both the home rule charter and the home rule amendment in the Miami Shores case, and since both these documents form the basis for the federal relations between Metro and the municipalities, to which frequent reference will be made in subsequent chapters, they are here considered in detail. The contested portion of the home rule amendment was subsection (1)g:

[The home rule charter] shall provide a method by which each municipal corporation shall have the power to make, amend or repeal its own charter. Upon adoption of this Home Rule Charter by the electors this method shall be exclusive and the Legislature shall have no power to amend or repeal the charter of any municipal corporation in Dade County.

The Charter provisions at issue were:

SECTION 1.01. Powers of the Board of County Commissioners.

A. The Board of County Commissioners shall be the legislative and the governing body of the county and shall have the power to carry on a central metropolitan government. This power shall include but shall not be restricted to the power to:

4. Provide central records, training, and communications for fire and police protection; provide traffic control and central crime investigation; provide fire stations, jails, and related facilities, and subject to Section 1.01 A (18) provide a uniform system for fire and police protection.

. . . . . . . . . . . . . . . . . . . . . . . .

18. Set reasonable minimum standards for all governmental units in the county for the performance of any service or function. The standards shall not be discriminatory as between similar areas. If a governmental unit fails to comply with such standards, and does not correct such failure after reasonable notice by the Board, then the Board may take over and perform, regulate, or grant franchises to operate any such service. The Board may also take over and operate, or grant franchises to operate any municipal service if:

(a) In an election called by the Board of County Commissioners within the municipality a majority of those voting vote in favor of turning the service over to the county; or

(b) The governing body of the municipality requests the county to take over the service by a two-thirds vote of its members, or by referendum.

SECTION 5.01. Continuance of Municipalities.

The municipalities in the county shall remain in existence so long as their electors desire. No municipality in the county shall be abolished without approval of a majority of its electors voting in an election called for that purpose. The right of self-determination in local affairs is reserved and preserved to the municipalities except as otherwise provided in this Charter.

SECTION 5.02. Municipal Powers.

Each municipality shall have the authority to exercise all powers relating to its local affairs not inconsistent with this Charter. Each municipality may provide for higher standards of zoning, service, and regulation than those provided by the Board of County Commissioners in order that its individual character and standards may be preserved for its citizens.

SECTION 8.04. Supremacy Clause.

A. This Charter and the ordinances adopted hereunder shall in cases of conflict supersede all municipal charters and ordinances, except as herein provided, and where authorized by the Constitution, shall in cases of conflict supersede all special and general laws of the state.

B. All other special and general laws and county ordinances and rules and regulations not inconsistent with this Charter shall continue in effect until they are superseded by ordinances adopted by the Board pursuant to this Charter and the Constitution.

The county, defendant in the original suit, conceded that municipalities have the right of self-determination in local affairs but contended that the exercise of this right is subject to the superior power of the county to enact county-wide laws. Hence if a municipal ordinance conflicts with a county-wide ordinance, the county-wide law prevails. The county cited the following provisions of the home rule amendment in support of its contention:

(1)b. . . . [The home rule charter] may grant full power and authority to the Board of County Commissioners of Dade County to pass ordinances relating to the affairs, property and government of Dade County . . . and do everything necessary to carry on a central metropolitan government in Dade County.

(1)d. . . . [The home rule charter] may provide a method by which any and all functions or powers of any municipal corporation or other governmental unit in Dade County may be transferred to the Board of County Commissioners of Dade County.

(1)f. . . . [the home rule charter] may create new courts and judges and clerks thereof with jurisdiction to try all offenses against ordinances passed by the Board of County Commissioners of Dade County and none of the other courts provided for by the Constitution or by general law shall have original jurisdiction to try such offenses. . . .

The county also pointed out that the home rule charter grants the county power to develop and enforce a master plan for control of traffic and parking and to establish a metropolitan court to try all cases of violations of ordinances adopted by the county commissioners.

Circuit Court Judge Pat Cannon accepted the arguments of Metro, and interpreted the home rule charter as giving county ordinances precedence over conflicting municipal ordinances, except where it was expressly provided to the contrary. He held that "all powers relating to local affairs were reserved in our county government except those powers expressly vested in municipalities." Judge Cannon said in part:

If it were determined that each of these twenty-six municipalities is vested with supreme power to exercise all the functions enumerated in its Charter (particularly when each municipality may amend its Charter any way it deems desirable) and that any county-wide ordinance which conflicts would be superseded by such municipal law, any semblance of the central metropolitan government in Dade County would obviously be impossible or, at least highly improbable. The rules of constitutional construction impel a more reasonable and logical conclusion—that expressed in the Charter—in cases of conflict, the Charter and the county ordinances lawfully adopted thereunder shall supersede all municipal charters and ordinances, except as to the powers expressly allocated by the Charter to the municipalities.[39]

The court held that the metropolitan traffic code was lawfully enacted under the home rule charter and therefore superseded and nullified all municipal traffic ordinances, resolutions, and codes in Dade County. Thus the Miami Shores traffic ordinances were null and void; the city was enjoined from enforcing its own code, and was required to enforce the Metro traffic code. The court ruled that all violations of the traffic code were to be tried in Metro courts, the establishment of which was also upheld.

County Manager Campbell said he hoped the ruling was only one of a series that would make Metro's position secure. "Maybe ultimately people will believe the Charter says what it means," [40] he said.

The Florida Supreme Court, six and a half months later, affirmed Judge Cannon's decision but interpreted the home rule amendment as requiring the charter to provide for municipal autonomy as to purely local functions and as authorizing the County Commission to regulate on a county-wide basis "those municipal functions and services that are susceptible to, and could be most effectively carried on under, a uniform plan of regulation applicable to the county as a whole." [41] The Supreme Court's reasoning differed from that of Judge Cannon on the circumstances under which county legislation superseded municipal legislation. Judge Cannon said that the cities' functions were those expressly granted to them in the charter and assumed that all functions not in conflict with these city powers were reserved to the county. The Supreme Court decision appears to limit county jurisdiction more narrowly and gives much more power to the courts to determine which functions are county-wide. The broad implications of this ruling are considered in Chapter 15.

## COULD CONTROVERSY HAVE BEEN AVOIDED?

Could the controversy over the ordinances have been avoided or at least greatly reduced? Some think it could; others think not.

Those who believe that a more gradual approach to metropolitan government would have avoided some of the controversy point out that when Metro was first set up it was not in a position, administratively, psychologically, or financially, to undertake a wide assortment of controversial area-wide functions. It had more than enough to do to establish a program to raise standards in the unincorporated areas and to streamline the then existing area-wide machinery. The gradualists argued that it was neither necessary nor desirable to draft and pass the ordinances so quickly.

Some of the detractors of Mr. Sibley and the Metro Legal Committee have accused them of deliberately trying to sabotage Metro by giving it too much to do too soon. City of Miami Manager Evans said, "If anyone had in mind to kill Metro they couldn't have gone about it in a better way than writing the ordinances the way it was done." [42]

Harry Toulmin, director of the Dade Research Foundation, had strongly urged that the ordinances not be drafted until after the county manager assumed his duties, [43] pointing out that Metro lacked the machinery to carry out so many functions. County Manager Campbell later acknowledged Metro's inability to administer a sweeping program when he publicly declared that "as a practical matter and speaking realistically even if the Charter were written so that the county could take over the cities and all their functions, we still couldn't do it without something to do it with." [44]

George H. Cooper, a member of both Charter Boards, thought that a more gradual approach to metropolitan government could have avoided much of the controversy. He believed that a change in government as drastic as that involved in Metro made it necessary to give the public an opportunity to adjust. Mr. Cooper deplored the "eager-beaver" approach of forcing the ordinances on the cities. He, like others, thought the attempt to pass ordinances long before they could be carried out and long before they were necessary was "a plot to kill Metro." [45] The county manager, in his annual report, conceded that the County Commission, in adopting the ordinances so quickly, may have exercised its legislative powers without regard to needs and facilities.[46]

The only convincing rationale for the rapid approach to metropolitan government was given by Daniel Paul, former Charter Board attorney, who said it was better to meet the enemy in a frontal attack and defeat him decisively than to struggle with him in a long-drawn-out battle of attrition. There are others who maintain that city officials and municipal employees would have created difficulties no matter how reasonably and gradually Metro moved. This conjecture, no matter how valid, still fails to justify the County Commission's program of immediate implementation of the charter. Such an approach could only give more ammunition to the opponents of Metro.

# 14

# Sundry Problems
# of the New Government

| | |
|---|---|
| 1958, December 16 | The County Commission passed an ordinance providing for the creation of special purpose districts. |
| 1959, January 15 | Paul C. Watt became the Metro planning director. |
| 1959, January 21 | The County Commission named 11 civic leaders to Metro's first Planning Advisory Board. |
| 1959, March 20 | Harry T. Toulmin resigned as Metro's budget director, charging that certain County Commissioners were attempting to destroy metropolitan government. |
| 1959, April 7 | The County Commission passed an ordinance providing for creation of special taxing districts. |
| 1959, April 20 | County Manager Campbell fired James Picola, whom he had hired as budget director two weeks earlier. |
| 1959, May 27 | George M. McSherry, $30,000 a year director of the Dade County Port Autherity, was fired by the County Commission, sitting as the Dade County Port Authority. |
| 1959, July 13 | The Miami-Dade Chamber of Commerce created the Government Research Council. |
| 1959, November 3 | Five home rule charter amendments, aimed at changing the size and method of electing the County Commission and at returning the positions of sheriff and tax assessor to elective status, were rejected at the polls. |

| 1960, February 9 | A Metropolitan Dade County Urban Renewal Ordinance was adopted. A Metropolitan Special Taxing District ordinance was enacted which superseded earlier ordinances on special purpose and special taxing districts. |
| 1960, April 5 | Metro agreed to construct and operate a seaport on the Dodge Island site. |
| 1960, July 1 | Metro received a half-million-dollar payment for the Florida Power and Light franchise. |
| 1960, July 5 | A Metropolitan Dade County Water and Sewer Board was created. |
| 1960, August 2 | A Metropolitan Dade County Transit Authority was established. |
| 1960, October 11 | Metro was involved in the last stages of negotiating for the purchase of four water companies. |
| 1961, January 17 | The Metro Commission ordered the Transit Authority to purchase Pawley's bus lines. |
| 1961, March 7 | Metro rejected the agreement to purchase the four water companies. |
| 1961, May 9 | The final purchase contract for the bus lines was approved by the Metro Commission. |
| 1962, January 29 | A bus strike against the Pawley Bus Company began. |
| 1962, February 6 | Metro agreed to borrow funds on a "pay-as-you-go" basis to finance the building of recreation facilities in the unincorporated areas. |
| 1962, February 9 | Metro took possession of buses at 12:01 A.M. |

## MANAGER-COMMISSION RELATIONSHIPS

The decision of the Charter Board to turn over the new government to the holdover commissioners was questioned by some observers at the time the charter was drafted. The home rule amendment, although stipulating that the Board of County Commissioners would be the governing body under the charter, in no way limited the discretion of the Charter Board to determine the fate of the old commission and the composition of the new one. The decision to continue the incumbent commissioners in office so as not to antagonize either them or their supporters—particularly John Pennekamp, associate editor of the *Miami Herald*—was acclaimed by some as astute statesmanship.[1] The incumbent commissioners were already alienated from the Charter Board, however, because the charter provisions creating a council-manager government stripped them of their administrative powers. Furthermore, since they were neophytes as legislators, it could hardly be argued that the new government would need their experience.

One of the most pressing problems confronting Metro was the establishment of a working relationship between the county manager and the County Commission. Mr. Campbell was approved as county manager by only a three to two vote of the commissioners; he never knew when Charles Hall, the pivot man on the commission, might, by a change of vote, force him out of office—a situation that made good working relationships difficult.

Despite Mr. Campbell's unenviable position, the holdover commissioners gave him and Budget Director Harry Toulmin a great deal of leeway in reorganizing the administrative branch of the government. The commissioners preferred to focus their attention on the Dade County Port Authority, for which they were also the governing body and over which the county manager had no jurisdiction. The Port Authority at the time was expanding the Miami International Airport and making plans for a new causeway from Dade County to Key Largo, an island 100 miles from Key West. There was sufficient action—reviewing studies, discussing methods of financing, negotiating contracts, resolving a controversy over the proposed causeway, and formulating other plans—to keep the commissioners interested. As the governing board of the Port Authority, the County Commission continued its "commission form" of control. The director of the Port Authority, who is hired by the county commission and is answerable to it, is in a position hardly comparable to that of county manager. The port director, like the manager, may be fired by the Board,[2] but he has none of the manager's safeguards and independence of action.[3] The fact that the commissioners could control the administration of Port Authority activities more closely than they could county activities may explain why they directed so much of their attention to the Port Authority.

Despite the preoccupation of the commissioners with the Port Authority, Mr. Campbell's position remained tenuous. The hope was that the election of six additional County Commissioners on September 30, 1958, would strengthen the manager's position.

In the months preceding the election Glen R. Peterson, newly appointed director of the Dade County Research Foundation, started a movement (which both newspapers allegedly were pledged to support) to establish a strong nonpartisan citizens' group to recruit, endorse, and elect the "right kind of candidates" to support the county manager in a program of action to make metropolitan government a reality. The executive committee of the Dade County Research Foundation, however, refused to support Mr. Peterson's move and, furthermore, voted to discontinue the foundation, which was in financial difficulties. The businessmen, who had previously contributed to the foundation, may have thought that once they had Metro the foundation was no longer necessary.

The campaign for the six commission seats was waged primarily as an attack on the five incumbent commissioners who were to continue in office for two years after the six new members took office. Besides assailing the incumbents for their extravagance in office furnishings, secretarial help, and use of official Metro cars, and for awarding questionable contracts, the candidates for the six new positions, in most cases, distinguished themselves from the incumbents by promising to support the manager or at least to give him every opportunity to demonstrate his ability.

The promise of a more stable position for Mr. Campbell did not, however, materialize after the six new commissioners took office. Some, indeed, maintained that he was worse off after the election than before. With the airport near completion and the causeway issue stalled,[4] the "old five" commissioners were no longer distracted by Port Authority business, and it was almost inevitable that the "new six" would take a great interest in the administration of Metro. The 11-man commission now turned its attention to the county administrative organization and began to object to the manager's actions on the budget, to his hiring of certain personnel, and to the lack of communication between him and themselves.

The strained relations between the manager and the commission were climaxed by some bloodletting in the administration. Harry Toulmin, budget director and, in effect, assistant manager of Metro in charge of internal affairs, resigned in March, 1959, charging that some members of the County Commission interfered with the administration of Metro at every turn and were determined to destroy it.[5] Mr. Campbell, after reluctantly accepting Mr. Toulmin's resignation, expressed great admiration for the former budget director, and concurred with the latter's view that the tactics of some of the commissioners were obstructionist.

Mr. Toulmin's resignation seemed to take the pressure off Mr. Campbell, at least temporarily.[6] However, when Mr. Campbell fired the new budget director, James Picola, in April, 1959, only two weeks after he was appointed, a furor was raised all over again. Mr. Picola charged that Metro was top-heavy with high-salaried administrators and that Mr. Campbell's own office was one of the worst offenders. Alexander Gordon, chairman of the County Commission's budget committee, ordered a thorough investigation of the charges, commenting that "Mr. Picola's statements reflect what we have been thinking all along. . . ."[7] The commission disapproved when Mr. Gordon proposed the investigation, however, and some commissioners labeled Mr. Picola's charges reckless and irresponsible.[8] After Mr. Picola was fired, relations between Mr. Campbell and the commission were, for a brief period, more cordial, although the rapprochement was based only on mutual tolerance.[9]

In May, 1959, George M. McSherry, director of the Port Authority, was fired by the County Commission on the ground that he was indecisive and lacked leadership. William C. Baggs, editor of the *Miami News*, said in his column that firing the port director might lead to similar action against County Manager Campbell.[10] Mr. Baggs applauded Mr. Campbell for creating a top-notch administrative structure, for maintaining his administrative independence of the County Commission, and for behaving like a professional. Metro, the editor of the *News* pointed out, was an innovation in government and he warned that firing Mr. Campbell would jeopardize the whole experiment.

Perhaps the key issue exacerbating manager-commission relations in mid-1959 was Metro leadership. Each side contended that responsibility for leadership rested with the other. Until there was understanding and mutual respect between Mr. Campbell and the commissioners, there would, apparently, be no effective leadership from either side, and the consequent inaction could result only in a loss of public confidence in the new government.[11]

## METRO ACTIONS

The community leaders showed increasing signs of impatience with Metro's apparent lack of accomplishments. Hugh Purvis, president of the Miami-Dade Chamber of Commerce, at a directors' meeting in December, 1958, said, "I and others feel we have had Metro long enough to see tangible results." [12] He made it clear that although the public had not lost faith in Metro, they hoped for action within months instead of years. Mr. Purvis suggested that in the immediate future Metro deal with the problem of traffic control; purchase and unify transit facilities; create a central police records bureau; reappraise county projects; establish a uniform county-wide business licensing system; expand parks and beaches; and maintain closer contact with the municipalities. In the months and years that followed, Metro did undertake to act in a variety of these fields.

### Bus Line Negotiations

Negotiations for the purchase of the Miami Transit Company, the Miami Beach Railway Company, and the South Miami Coach Lines (which combined carried approximately 84 per cent of Dade's transit passengers), reached an impasse in March, 1959, over the purchase price. Abe Aronovitz, former mayor of Miami and a leading political figure in the Greater Miami area, contended that the price demanded by Mr. Pawley, owner of the three bus lines, was exorbitant. Charges of bribery raised by a County Commissioner went to the grand jury which, on November 10, 1959, cleared all involved in the bus lines transaction "of any violation of the law or any wrong-doing whatever." [13] Negotiations were resumed but subsequently broke down and no additional action was taken until after the election of four new commissioners in May, 1960.

A Metro ordinance adopted on August 2, 1960, provided for the purchase, development, and operation of an adequate mass transportation system by the county. The transit system would be operated on a self-sustaining basis by a governmental instrumentality to be designated as the Metropolitan Dade County Transit Authority.[14]

The authority was given the power to ascertain the necessary facts concerning public transportation; to make findings and recommendations to the County Commission relative to the acquisition of a public transit system; and to operate, control, and manage under the supervision of the Board of County Commissioners any and all transit systems acquired by the county.

Some four months later, on January 17, 1961, Metro ordered the Transit Authority to purchase Pawley's bus lines for a price of $7,705,274. The vote of the commission was 7 to 4 with 2 members absent.[15] The purchase contract was approved by the commission on May 9, 1961.[16] On November 7, 1961, the commission voted to take over the bus lines before validation of the bond issue by the court.[17] However, because of legal complications and the threat of a bus strike, Metro did not take actual possession of the buses until February 9, 1962. By then the bus union had already been out on strike for 12 days against Mr. Pawley's company. Because Metro and the bus union were unable to settle differences over the right of the union to bargain and to strike "against the government," the strike continued and the Transit Authority began to hire bus drivers as civil service employees. Only a small percentage of union drivers returned to work. By March, 1962, normal bus service was beginning to resume but the bitterness of the striking bus drivers and of organized labor toward Metro continued. The bus union by an initiative petition signed by 25,000 voters called for a referendum to repeal the ordinance authorizing the bond issue for the purchase of the bus lines. The referendum, placed on the May 8 ballot by the County Commission, was defeated by a vote of 82,394 to 47,268.

## Central Water and Sewage System

The need for creating a central water and sewage system has concerned Metro since its inception. As noted earlier, there are some 57 water and sewage companies in Dade County and most of Dade's residents rely on septic tanks for sewage disposal. Since there seemed to be some question of the county's authority to regulate these utilities,[18] Metro turned its attention to acquiring the companies. Metro was also faced with the difficult task of obtaining the rather extensive holdings of the City of Miami Water and Sewer Board. The financial question of compensation to the City of Miami for the assets of its water board and the legal question of the bondholder obligation both had first to be settled.

In the closing months of 1960 Metro was involved in what were believed to be the final stages of negotiation with the General Water Works Company to purchase 4 water companies—Consumers, Estates, Oakridge, and Key Biscayne. Metro would pay for the companies with tax-exempt bonds to be retired with future revenues earned by the companies.[19] Some months later the County Commission reneged on the purchase after a "crown of thorns" speech by one of the commissioners charging that the people of Dade County were paying far in excess of the value of the companies. Other commissioners were concerned about the problem of operating the companies. Because of these doubts, the commission voted 6 to 3 to reject the agreement.[20]

After its unsuccessful effort to enter the water business, the county enacted in July, 1960, an ordinance creating a 5-man Metropolitan Dade County Water and Sewer Board. Authority was given to this board to regulate rates, establish standards of service, and issue certificates of public convenience and necessity for the operation, construction, or extension of any private water or sewer system. Municipally owned and operated utilities were required only to register with the board, to comply with minimum standards prescribed by the board, and to obtain a certificate for expansion or enlargement of existing service areas.[21]

By the beginning of 1962 the board had established a series of regulations pertaining to private water and sewage companies for (1) quality of service, (2) water main extensions, (3) uniform bookkeeping, and (4) certification. In addition, the board was slowly feeling its way on the question of fair rates (although no actual control over rates had been established) and cooperating with the Public Safety Department in an endeavor to provide adequate water flow for fire hydrants. For the first time the residents of Dade County were able to bring their complaints as to both services and rates to a local agency. Regulations, when they become more formalized, will no doubt be challenged in the courts as a usurpation of the authority of the Florida Railroad and Public Utilities Commission over all private water and sewage companies.

## Urban Renewal

In 1959 a Florida Supreme Court decision upholding a state urban renewal act, applicable only to the City of Tampa,[22] established the principle that urban renewal programs, when serving a public purpose, were not in conflict with the Florida Constitution. Dade County, under its home rule powers, has enacted an ordinance which to a large extent parallels the Tampa act. The Metropolitan Dade County Urban Renewal Ordinance, adopted on February 9, 1960,[23] provides for the rehabilitation, clearance, and redevelopment of slums and blighted areas in Dade County in accordance with urban renewal plans approved by the County Commission. The ordinance, although giving Metro jurisdiction throughout Dade County, may be applied to a given municipality only upon the adoption by the County Commission of a resolution declaring that one or more blighted areas exist in the municipality and that redevelopment is necessary in the interest of public health, safety, morals, or welfare.

The central Miami Urban Renewal Area, the initial project approved and undertaken by the county, essentially embraces the central Negro area in the downtown section of the City of Miami. The county applied for and received a federal advance of $83,722 to prepare a general neighborhood renewal plan, which was expected to be completed by January, 1963. Actual ground-breaking should follow in approximately six to eight months.

One particularly fortunate aspect of the timing of this urban renewal project is its dovetailing with the building of an expressway through the central Negro area in the city of Miami. The federal highway construction act makes no provision for the relocation of the thousands of persons displaced by the expressway, but the county as a result of its urban renewal program has been able to deal with the problem.

### Planning

Metro's Planning Department in November, 1960, reported on a preliminary land use plan for the whole of Dade County.[24] The plan is intended to advance community health and safety, the citizens' tastes and comforts, government efficiency and economy, and the economic prosperity of the entire area. The policies advocated by the planning department for achieving these objectives were: (1) containing the rapidly spreading urban sprawl, (2) creating a new focus inward to the Miami core, with particular emphasis on developing downtown city centers,[25] (3) establishing a new focus in the southern portion of the county to care for future growth, (4) encouraging the proper development of the offshore Keys, and (5) stimulating and developing the Homestead area for productive agricultural and agricultural-industrial activities.

## The Expressway Bond Issue

Dade County property holders were asked to approve a $46 million expressway bond issue in the May 3, 1960, election. The purpose of the bond issue was to complete the southern portion of the North-South Expressway (part of the federal interstate system) by 1963 and the entire expressway by 1966. The idea was to start building the expressway immediately rather than await federal funds, which would not be forthcoming for a number of years. According to Metro officials and State Road Board member William D. Singer (from Dade County) there was an implicit agreement between the federal government and the state road board acting for the county that the federal government, beginning in 1968, would repay the state, which in turn would reimburse the county. The payments would be at the rate of $10 million a year. The 1.25-mill tax which would be assumed by the property owners to pay for the bond issue would be discontinued after ten years.

The Miami-Dade Chamber of Commerce was responsible for conducting the campaign for the bond issue; the *Herald*, the *News*, television stations, and Mr. William D. Singer also vigorously endorsed the proposal. A number of rather impressive advertisements appeared in the newspapers urging the freeholders to vote for the bond issue. (Funds for the advertisements and for a large billboard were forthcoming, in a number of instances, from cement companies which might be involved in the construction of the expressway.) In addition, the chamber sent out over 40,000 pieces of literature explaining the bond issue to the freeholders.

Relatively few ads appeared in opposition to the bond issue. These were paid for by the "Citizens to Vote No on Expressway Bond." The group was headed by B. E. Hearn, City of Miami commissioner, and appeared to include property owners who felt they would be adversely affected by the building of the expressway. The bond issue was approved by 62.3 per cent of the freeholders.

Litigation by the Hearn group contesting the election, and opposition by the DuPont interests to the proximity of the expressway to DuPont Plaza (where they own property), led to delay in the building of the expressway. The ruling against Hearn by the courts and an alternative route approved by the State Road Board and the Metro Commission in February, 1962, reactivated the project.

### Administrative Reorganization

It was hardly feasible to launch an undertaking of such magnitude as metropolitan government with the obsolescent machinery of the old county government. Before Metro, there were 35 county departments, 23 of which were administered by the County Commission and 12 by other elected officials. A county budget commission, appointed by the governor, reviewed all budget requests. Metropolitan government itself could not take hold unless it, in turn, was predicated on an efficient and economical administration. There is little doubt that it was politically advantageous to include the changes for both external (Metro-city relations) and internal (legislative-executive-administrative relations within the county government) in both the home rule amendment and the home rule charter.

The council-manager system, established by the charter, was expected to take the old county administrative structure in hand and bring order out of chaos. A report by Budget Director Toulmin in February, 1959, gave every indication that a first-rate administrative organization had been established. The pre-Metro county government had been completely reorganized, reducing the number of departments from 35 to 17. Insurance, purchasing, and budget and finance procedures had been changed, and a full complement of staff services such as records management, data processing, building and property management, central motor pool control, and internal auditing had been developed.[26]

By the beginning of 1962 a good many of Metro's administrative strains and stresses had been eliminated. New departments like Planning and Law were in full operation, and old departments like Public Safety, Health, Welfare, Hospitals, Parks and Recreation, and Public Works [27] had been reorganized and streamlined.

### Recreation

A new recreation program began in 12 school recreation centers in the unincorporated areas on February 1, 1961. The school facilities were made available without cost, and Metro agreed to bear the cost of salaries, operation, and maintenance. By the beginning of 1962 there were 15 such centers maintained by Metro in the unincorporated areas. School cafeterias, auditoriums, and gymnasiums were also utilized. The Recreation Department, in cooperation with the Board of Public Instruction, provided special classes for children and adults in arts and crafts, music appreciation, creative writing, and typing.

On July 1, 1960, Metro received approximately a half-million dollars as a payment for the Florida Power and Light franchise for the unincorporated areas. (The franchise payments are expected to reach a million dollars a year by 1970.) A year later, in July, 1961, the Metro Commission approved an administrative proposal to pledge $4,500,000 of Florida Power and Light Company franchise payments to construct within the unincorporated areas 27 neighborhood recreation parks, 7 neighborhood swimming pools, a centrally located athletic stadium, and a series of smaller projects including boating facilities, a camping area, sidewalks, roads, and drainage areas. In addition, Metro contemplated the purchase of Castellow Hammock in South Dade and the creation of a $1,000,000 special improvement district revolving fund.

Although it had initially intended to finance these projects by floating a bond issue supported by franchise payments, Metro, on February 6, 1962, decided to embark on a policy euphemistically referred to as "pay as you go." The county government would borrow some $2,500,000 from the First National Bank and pay off the debt with the annual franchise payments. A resolution passed by the commission at its February 20, 1962, meeting provided that all of the franchise payments be marked exclusively for expenditures in the unincorporated areas.[28]

## Other Program Growth

An additional convenience for Dade's residents was the establishment of public safety, and building and zoning substations in the northern and southern sections of the county. Also, the Metro radio communication system was expanded and improved until Metro contended that it could provide a central police communications system for the entire county.

By the beginning of 1962 Metro was providing police communication services to its own public safety department and, on a contract basis, to the police departments of 9 municipalities. Metro also had expanded its hospital facilities, built a Museum of Science and Natural History, renovated the old Dade Court House, and completed a public safety building and a jail. In addition a criminal courts building was nearing completion.

## ATTACKS ON METRO'S GOVERNMENTAL STRUCTURE

During the summer of 1959 several attempts were made to change Metro's internal structure by amending the home rule charter. Five proposals eventually were placed on the November ballot—3 on the composition of the County Commission itself, 1 on the sheriff's office, and 1 on the tax assessor's office.

The 3 amendments which intended to alter the number of commissioners and the method of electing them were placed on the ballot by the commission itself. All 3 provided for an increase in commission salaries from $6,000 to $15,000 a year. Of the 3 amendments, one would have reduced the size of the commission to 5 members who would be elected on a county-wide basis. Another would have limited the number of commissioners to 7 who would also have been elected on a county-wide basis. The last amendment would have changed the commission to a 9-member board with the commissioners elected by districts.

Despite the commissioners' receptiveness to the proposals on the size and method of choosing the commission, they denied a request to place any proposed amendments on the ballot which would have restored the offices of sheriff, tax assessor, and tax collector to elective status.[29] County Manager Campbell charged that the latter proposals were an attempt to ruin Metro by destroying the principle of a co-ordinated, central approach to the problems of government.[30] A "Committee for Elective Government" composed of friends of the incumbent sheriff and tax assessor succeeded, through the initiative process provided by the home rule charter, in placing the sheriff and tax assessor measures on the ballot. The committee campaigned on the Jacksonian theme of popular and direct democratic election of responsible public officials.

All 5 amendments were opposed by the Government Research Council of the Miami-Dade Chamber of Commerce, the League of Women Voters, the *Miami Herald*, the *Miami News,* and Ralph Renick, leading television newscaster. In the November election, with only 25 per cent of the registered voters going to the polls, all the amendments were defeated.[31]

The 3 proposals concerned with the make-up of the county com-mission were defeated by large majorities. The proposal for the 5-man County Commission, which received the largest number of votes of the 3 amendments, was defeated by an opposition vote of 87.7 per cent. That the "commission" amendments were evidently not thought of as pro- or anti-Metro is borne out by the fact that the cities in both camps voted overwhelmingly against these amend-ments.

The proposals for an elective sheriff and an elective tax assessor [32] were also defeated but by smaller majorities: 53,349 to 42,278 on the sheriff's amendment, and 53,916 to 38,781 on the tax assessor's amendment. Voters in the lower socio-economic categories cast the highest number of votes in favor of these amendments. Conversely, the higher socio-economic groups provided the most opposition. Even the consistently anti-Metro areas of Miami Beach and Miami Shores voted against both the sheriff and tax assessor measures. The issues seem to have been conceived in terms of responsible administration versus spoils politics and not as a clash of pro- or anti-Metro in-terests.

# 15
# Metro and the Cities

1959, February 17    Circuit Court Judge Vincent C. Giblin ordered post-
                     ponement of the trial of a City of Miami traffic
                     violator until a decision could be made as to whether
                     the city or the county had jurisdiction.

1959, February 23    Circuit Court Judge Ray H. Pearson ruled that
                     Metro had full authority to take over regulation
                     of liquor sale hours, motor vehicle inspection, trades-
                     men licensing, traffic control devices, building codes,
                     sewage collection and disposal, and water supply.

1959, March 2        City of Miami Manager Evans was fired by a 3 to
                     2 vote of the city commission. Commissioner James
                     W. High resigned in protest.

1959, March 4        The City of Miami Commission approved the use
                     of Metro auto inspection stickers.

1959, May 11         Circuit Court Judge Robert H. Anderson ordered
                     the City of Miami to refund to traffic violators
                     more than $1 million in traffic fines collected after
                     the effective date of the Metropolitan traffic code.

1959, May 29         The City of Miami Commission informally endorsed
                     a referendum on the question of transferring to the
                     County Commission "all powers, authority, rights,
                     duties and obligations granted to the City by its
                     charter or other authority."

1959, July 1         The Metropolitan traffic code and the Metro court
                     system were initiated on a county-wide basis.

1959, July 21        Circuit Court Judge Pat Cannon ordered Miami
                     Beach, Miami Springs, and El Portal to close their
                     traffic courts.

1959, September 2    The City of Miami Commission tabled the City
                     of Miami-Metro merger proposal.

1959, November 4   The Florida Supreme Court upheld Circuit Court Judge Anderson's ruling that the City of Miami traffic court was without jurisdiction, but reversed the order that the fines be refunded.

1959, November 13   The Florida Supreme Court upheld Circuit Court Judge Pearson's ruling that Metro had authority to regulate liquor sale hours, motor vehicle inspections, sewage collection and disposal, water supply, traffic control devices, building codes, and licensing of tradesmen.

1960, April 1   Metro and the City of Miami entered into an agreement whereby Metro would construct and operate a new seaport on Dodge Island.

1960, June 21   The City of Miami gave the Inter-American Cultural and Trade Center (Interama) Authority the right to encumber the entire Graves Tract, thus enabling the authority to float the necessary bond issue.

1960, July 1   Metro absorbed all municipal traffic engineering departments.

1960, October 26   The Miami Beach City Commission voted to take action to secede from Dade County and form a separate county, Greater Miami Beach.

1960, November 20   Metro's Planning Department reported on a preliminary land use plan for the whole of Dade County.

1961, October 31   Metro as a *quid pro quo* agreed to give the City of Miami not less than $800,000 rental credit in a proposed city-county building.

1962, January 13   Miami Beach for the first time began to enforce the Metro traffic code.

1962, February 28   The City of Miami and Metro agreed to hold joint monthly meetings.

1962, March 9   Interama arrived at an agreement with Goodbody and Co. on the terms of a $21-million bond indenture.

## DIVISION OF POWERS

The problem of distinguishing between local and county functions is a knotty one. The division of powers between Metro and the cities could, of course, have been spelled out in the charter—but it was not.

Several possible explanations for the failure of the Charter Board to delineate more clearly the division of powers are: (1) Charter Board members were unaware that the problem would arise, (2) they wished to dodge the problem, (3) they were lulled into a false sense of security by the experts, and (4) most likely, they were determined to have a flexible system of government which could move in any one of several directions.

In probably no other metropolitan area of the nation could a home rule charter granting such broad powers to a metropolitan government be adopted. In fact, a proposed charter for the Cleveland metropolitan area encompassing a small number of area-wide activities was defeated at the polls in November, 1959, and the Cleveland proposal was not nearly as broad as the Dade County charter.[1] Many delegates, from both the Illinois and Milwaukee metropolitan study groups which visited Miami in 1958, observed that the authority of any government created for their areas would be limited to those functions that the cities freely and voluntarily relinquished.[2]

Although federalism was the only form of government for the Dade County complex that both the consolidationists and the localists would accept, an emergent federalism is bound to cause difficulties before an accommodation is reached. The Charter Board members were probably aware of the potential difficulties but had no alternative. They probably also realized that the success or failure of the Dade metropolitan government, like that of the United States federal system, would be determined more by time and experience than by constitutional absolutes.

The role of County Manager Campbell as a mediator between Metro and the cities has been considered previously, but his importance in the federalist scheme of county-city relations deserves particular attention.

Mr. Campbell got a warmer welcome from the various city officials when he came to Greater Miami than he did from his employers— the five holdover County Commissioners. Even before his arrival the *Miami News* noted that, on the basis of his public statements, his views seemed to coincide with those of the Dade League of Municipalities.[3] Yet, once on the job, Mr. Campbell repeatedly rejected league proposals on the controversial ordinances and the autonomy amendment.

Were the manager's first statements,[4] which evoked an enthusiastic response from anti-Metro forces, a reflection of Mr. Campbell's philosophy or simply balm to the opposition? His speeches and papers show that he was a consistent advocate of grass-roots democracy, but that is not to say that he was a "cities' righter." Rather he was an exponent of a federated system of government—one with strong centralized powers—which he felt was the only solution to the manifold problems of the metropolitan complex.

In a speech to the League of California Cities in 1958 Mr. Campbell gave his views on the division of powers:

Practically all functions of local government are divisible into levels of service which might be called wholesale and retail in nature. The police function, for instance, is not a single standardized activity. It consists of a series of things, some of which may be handled adequately and even more effectively on the community and neighborhood level, while others require unification and central direction. An analysis of any area of local government operations will usually disclose a similar pattern.[5]

Elsewhere he noted:

Personally . . . I do not support the idea of one major city. In our history of local government the biggest cities have been the seats of most of our corruption, and the city hall has been a lot further, in most instances, than the state capital or even Washington. And I can conceive of the future of the metropolitan government as a series of self-contained municipalities bound together by some kind of initial interest in a collective program of providing the overall regional services.[6]

It is apparent that Mr. Campbell believed in a "federal approach" to the division of powers between the municipalities and the county government. The Dade League of Municipalities embraced his general theory, but they parted company on the implementation of the federal system. (A somewhat similar situation existed in the early history of the nation, among the founding fathers.) The league apparently recognized as metropolitan responsibilities only those functions that are not confined to municipal boundaries, either physically or legally—i.e., mass transportation, sewerage, water supply, health, and hospitals. These functions also require large financial outlays, which most cities cannot afford. The league considered all other functions local, although subject to the county's minimum standards. Mr. Campbell was more flexible, as well as more nebulous, in what he considered local functions and what he considered metropolitan.[7]

William Pallot, former attorney for the City of Miami, believed, as Mr. Campbell did, that there should be no real difficulty in differentiating purely local from county-wide functions, although he and Mr. Campbell disagreed completely over such issues as zoning, traffic, and the Metro courts. However, most people agree on a broad principle in the abstract; it is in its implementation that they differ. These "practical" differences were not to be resolved by debate but by the decisions of the Florida courts and actual governmental developments.

It should be recalled that the home rule amendment authorized the charter "to grant full power and authority to the Board of County Commissioners of Dade County to pass ordinances relating to the affairs, property, and government of Dade County . . . and to do everything necessary to carry on a central metropolitan government in Dade County." The Florida Supreme Court construed the home rule amendment to require autonomy of the municipalities in purely local functions and to authorize "regulation and control on a county-wide basis of those municipal functions and services that are susceptible to, and could be most effectively carried on under, a uniform plan of regulation applicable to the county as a whole."[8] What constitutes a purely local function, the court said, "is a mixed question of law and fact to be determined judicially if, as and when the authority of the board to legislate any particular municipal function or power is controverted."[9]

The Supreme Court decision, although a significant victory for Metro, may have given some encouragement to the cities to contest Metro actions which they believed infringed upon their powers. It may also have contributed to a change in emphasis by Metro from compulsion to persuasion.

Even before the Supreme Court decision was handed down, there was a tendency on the part of the 11-man County Commission to adopt a more conciliatory attitude toward the cities. The new chairman announced that the commission would try to foster cooperation between Metro and the cities.[10] He said he believed that county-wide functions could be expedited through negotiation and consultation with representatives of the cities.

The *Miami Herald* opposed the commission's new philosophy, however. In an editorial published on December 31, 1958 the editors said:

### Back On The Course, Metro!

The 12 men in charge of Metropolitan Government here ought to do a little soul-searching this New Year's Eve. We mean the 11 Metro commissioners and their chief executive, County Manager O. W. Campbell.

Their job is to get rid of duplication and overlapping in local government, improve efficiency and stop waste. That is what the people have voted for not less than four times.

Yet what has been happening? The Dade County League of Municipalities, made up of city officeholders, has been indoctrinating the commissioners and Campbell with the theory that Metro should be just another government on top of all the others here.

So effective has been the constant ding-donging of this line that the 12 top men of Metro seem to be sinking into a featherbed of peaceful coexistence with the league. . . .

Let the Metro commissioners and County Manager Campbell start the New Year right. They can do so by getting back on the straight course pointed out to them emphatically and repeatedly by the people.[11]

## LEGAL RAMIFICATIONS

As a result of the Miami Shores decision, most municipalities adopted a policy of watchful waiting. The City of Miami, however, vigorously opposed the jurisdiction of Metro courts over municipal traffic violations. City of Miami Attorney Pallot interpreted the Miami Shores decision as upholding Metro's power to set minimum traffic standards with which the city had to comply, but insisted that the judicial enforcement of the code remained the prerogative of the city courts,[12] an attitude that the *Miami Herald* branded as open defiance of the court decision.[13]

The City of Miami's position on the traffic code resulted in a series of legal actions. Circuit Court Judge Vincent C. Giblin restrained the city from trying a traffic violation case in its own courts until a decision was handed down as to whether the city or the county had jurisdiction in the case.[14] Judge Giblin, a controversial and colorful figure, warned that any city judge who disobeyed the injunction would stand trial for contempt.[15]

Even more far reaching than Judge Giblin's decision was Circuit Court Judge Robert H. Anderson's ruling in a case decided on May 11, 1959. The judge decreed that the City of Miami refund more than $1 million to traffic violators who had been "illegally fined" after March 1, 1958, when the Metropolitan traffic code went into effect.[16] He said that under long-established principles against unjust enrichment it would be unconscionable to allow the city to retain the fines. Judge Anderson declared that the city courts had been divested of jurisdiction to try traffic violations and ordered the city traffic courts closed immediately. The following day Judge Anderson withdrew his order to refund the money, pending a Florida Supreme Court ruling on an appeal by the City of Miami. The Florida Supreme Court subsequently upheld Judge Anderson's ruling that the city's traffic court was without jurisdiction but reversed the order that the fines be refunded.[17]

Another case that was watched with great interest was instituted by Miami Beach. The suit, challenging provisions of the home rule charter and Metro ordinances pertaining to the cities, had been pending for some time before Circuit Court Judge Ray H. Pearson.[18] On February 23, 1959, the judge, who had been awaiting disposition of the Miami Shores case, held that Metro had full authority to take over regulation of hours for liquor sales, inspection of motor vehicles, collection and disposal of sewage, operation of water systems, approval of municipal traffic control devices, formulation of building codes, and issuance of certificates of competency for building contractors and tradesmen.[19]

The Florida Supreme Court, on November 13, 1959, upheld Judge Pearson's ruling that the ordinances attacked by Miami Beach dealt with functions or services that "are susceptible to, and could be most effectively carried on under, a uniform plan of regulation applicable to the county as a whole." The contention of Miami Beach that the home rule amendment authorized Metro to operate only in the unincorporated areas was held "untenable for reasons so obvious as to make discussion thereof unnecessary." [20]

Both County Manager Campbell and Metro Commission Chairman Walter Weiss were pleased with the decision in the Miami Beach case but both indicated it did not mean that Metro activities in the cities would be expanded overnight. The *Miami News* commended the two officials for their decision to move "slowly and studiously before transferring the new powers to Metro." [21] The *Miami Herald*, on the other hand, in a "Let's go, Metro" editorial said it could not understand why the county government was "pulling back on the reins" 584 days after the birth of Miami's metropolitan government. [22]


## METRO-CITY OF MIAMI RELATIONS

The greatest stumbling block to the expansion of Metro functions through February, 1959, was probably the opposition of City of Miami officials. The City of Miami, as the central city, with control over a significant part of Dade County's water supply and with large and well-established police and fire departments, was the logical core for metropolitan government—not the county. And, on the basis of past efforts at consolidating the city and county, City of Miami residents apparently were not particularly concerned with preservation of the city government as such. Furthermore, most of the powerful business interests and the newspapers were eager to abolish the city's government. In view of these facts, it was strange that City Manager Evans and the city commission were leading exponents of municipal rights.

On February 21, 1959, the *Miami Herald*, commenting on a demand by Abe Aronovitz, a former mayor of the City of Miami, that City Manager Evans be fired, concluded: "To dismiss Evans from his $25,000-a-year post would require a majority of the five-man commission. This is generally considered unlikely since the commission has been politically aligned with Evans." [23] However, the move to fire Evans was already under way at this time.

Dramatic action on March 2, 1959, by the majority of the City of Miami commissioners [24] resulted in the summary dismissal [25] of City

Manager Evans and the resignation of Commissioner James W. High, a vigorous Metro antagonist. The reasons publicly given for firing Mr. Evans were his anti-Metro role in the autonomy amendment movement and his assumption of policy-making powers. Actually, in his fight for the autonomy amendment, Mr. Evans had had the support of 4 of the 5 members of the commission; the mayor was the only one who had opposed him. Some observers said the firing of Mr. Evans was politically expedient for 2 of the commissioners who needed support from pro-Metro forces if they were to be re-elected. These same commissioners had also begun to feel that they were bearing the brunt of public indignation over some of Mr. Evans' other actions and policies—the registration of automobile hubcaps, a Christmas cocktail party at the manager's home that was paid for with city funds, police roadblocks to check drivers' licenses,[26] and failure of the manager to prod the police chief to take action against bolita and bookmaking.

The two commissioners who voted against Mr. Evan's dismissal castigated the other three. Commissioner High resigned from the commission in protest of the dismissal. He attacked the firing of Mr. Evans as "filthy politics" and declared that it was inspired by powerful special interests. Commissioner Hearn, who along with Commissioner High had supported Mr. Evans, correctly insisted that the manager had been carrying out the wishes of the commission in the autonomy amendment campaign, and he characterized the action of the majority as complete capitulation to the *Miami Herald*.[27]

Ira F. Willard, a former Coral Gables city manager who had left public service to go into the banking business, reportedly had been approached by Mayor High about the job as city manager some two weeks before Mr. Evans was dismissed. Mr. Willard indicated that he would be interested in the position. Immediately after Manager Evans' dismissal, Mr. Willard was hired.[28] The next day, Fred C. Davant, a former City of Miami judge, was appointed to fill the vacancy left by the resignation of Commissioner James High. The *Miami News*, in a sarcastically worded editorial, suggested that the commissioners should really have appointed John Pennekamp of the *Miami Herald* and saved themselves innumerable trips and phone calls to the *Herald*.[29]

With a new attitude prevailing in the City of Miami Commission, the olive branch was extended to Metro. At a joint meeting of the city and county commissioners an agreement was made to assign city traffic cases to the Metro courts, and a committee was appointed to work out the mechanics of consolidating the City of Miami courts with those of Metro. The Metro Commission set July 1, 1959, as the deadline for county-wide enforcement of the Metropolitan traffic code, and by a 7 to 2 vote approved the findings of a traffic court study made by the American Bar Association. In its report the ABA recommended that the number of Metro judges be increased from 3 to 13, a list of prospective judges be obtained from the Dade County Bar Association, a central records office be set up, and municipal courtrooms in the cities of Miami and Miami Beach be used for Metro courts.[30] By July 1, 1959, the Metropolitan traffic code was in effect in the unincorporated areas, the City of Miami, and most other municipalities. Violations of the code would be tried in the Metro courts.

The City of Miami's acquiescence to the Metro court system, following the firing of City Manager Evans, was only one of a series of peacemaking moves by the city. County Manager Campbell and City of Miami Manager Willard also discussed the sale of the privately owned Miami Transit Company to the county;[31] the city commission approved the use of Metro auto inspection stickers; and city officials considered the transfer of the city water system to Metro.[32] Mr. Willard suggested integrating such city and county services as publicity, weights and measures operations,[33] public libraries, tax assessments and tax collections,[34] and bus transportation. Mayor High proposed that a joint city-county board be named to chart the orderly transfer of municipal functions to the metropolitan government.

A more radical step was the informal endorsement by the City of Miami Commission of a proposal for a referendum in November, 1959, on the question of transferring to the Metro Commission "all powers, authority, rights, duties and obligations granted to the city by its Charter or other authority." While the majority of the city commissioners were opposed in substance to the transfer, they voted to have it submitted to the people.

Most County Commissioners also believed that the City of Miami-Metro merger was premature and concurred with County Manager

Campbell, who maintained that the transfer of city functions to Metro would be more effective if done on a piecemeal basis.[35] Other critics of the merger contended that a vote on the abolition of the city government would once more split the community and lead to increased antagonism between the cities and Metro. Metro, they believed, should consolidate its gains before attempting to take over more functions.

The *Miami Herald*, on the other hand, editorially bemoaned the Metro commissioners' coolness to the proposed merger and found it difficult to comprehend the commissioners' support of a policy of gradual unification of county and city services. The editors declared that a dramatic merger of the city with Metro, if soundly conceived and executed, would go far toward establishing confidence in Metro.[36]

The ardent consolidationists thought the time was ripe. An increase in city taxes in conjunction with Metro promises to absorb certain city functions encouraged the consolidationists to believe that City of Miami voters, who had favored Metro in earlier elections, would vote for abolition of their local government. Consolidation, they argued, would be extremely beneficial to Metro, since it would provide the nucleus of a truly metropolitan government.

In August, 1959, the Government Research Council of the Miami-Dade Chamber of Commerce, organized in July of that year, requested that the City of Miami Commission take no further action toward putting the merger proposal on the November ballot. The council, claiming the merger was premature and "might result in harmful confusion," also pointed out that if Metro took over the City of Miami's municipal functions it would divert Metro from its more pressing county-wide problems. On September 2, 1959, the city commission tabled the referendum proposal.

New friction began to develop between the City of Miami Commission and the Metro Commission in the summer of 1959 over the financing and building of a seaport, the proposed sale of city-owned property in connection with the seaport, and the construction of a skyscraper city hall.

The long-standing question over where to locate a new seaport, which had plagued Miami for many years, was handed over to Metro's Planning Department. The department, in a report issued in July, 1959, recommended that a new seaport for Miami be built on Dodge Island,[37] an island situated in the middle of Biscayne Bay between the cities of Miami and Miami Beach. With acceptance of that recommendation by both the City of Miami and the county, the controversy over location of the seaport was ended,[38] but not the controversy over whether the city or the county should finance and construct the port. In early October the city announced that it intended to sell the 1,700-acre property called the Graves Tract and use the proceeds to build the seaport—an announcement that caused a good deal of consternation, particularly in the Inter-American Cultural and Trade Center Authority and the Metro Commission.

The Interama Authority, appointed in 1951 to build and operate a trade and cultural center in Miami,[39] had no means of financing itself other than through contemplated earnings. The authority had an understanding with the city that the Graves Tract would be transferred to Interama for the trade center. The announcement, therefore, that the land was to be sold brought bitter protests from the authority, as well as from the Metro Commission and the *Miami Herald*. In fact, the Metro Commissioners were so incensed that, on the first reading, they unanimously voted for a bill to prohibit any city in Dade County from selling property without first giving the county an opportunity to buy it. Before the final reading, however, the bill was amended to require that the municipalities conform to a county-wide comprehensive plan for the development of public lands in Dade County. Meanwhile the Dade County Development Committee, an important group of business and civic leaders organized to promote capital improvements for the Greater Miami area, urged the county to finance and build the seaport.

Metro agreed in April, 1960, to accept full responsibility for constructing and operating a seaport on the Dodge Island site.[40] Funds for building the port were allocated from Metro's general fund and amounted to approximately $2 million for the 1960–61 and 1961–62 fiscal years respectively. The City of Miami on its part agreed to convey to the county title to the Dodge Island site and to permit the county to administer temporarily the existing City of Miami port. Revenues from the port would be used by Metro solely for the construction of the Dodge Island port. Thus the City of Miami went out of the port business and all City of Miami port personnel became

Metro employees. It should be noted that the City of Miami port, aside from its inability to incur large expenditures for repairs and improvements, had been self-supporting and had even operated at a profit.

The Interama Authority and the City of Miami had earlier concluded an agreement (February 15, 1960) under which the city would turn over to the authority the deed to the Graves Tract for the purpose of creating a trade and cultural center. In return, the city would receive certificates of indebtedness to the amount of $8.5 million which would be secured by a designated portion of the Graves Tract, not subject to encumbrance without prior consent of the city. Since the latter provision limited Interama's ability to float a loan, the City of Miami in June, 1961, agreed to forfeit the equivalent of its first-mortgage privileges. Now with the entire Graves Tract as collateral, the Interama Authority, on March 9, 1962, was able to consummate an agreement with Goodbody and Company on the terms of a total $21-million bond indenture. Interama prepared to advertise for bids on drainage and fill after the Florida Supreme Court validated its first bond issue.

For the fiscal year 1961–1962, the Metro Commission, sitting as the Dade County Port Authority, committed the Port Authority to underwrite Interama's budget to the amount of $327,368.27. The authorization stemmed from a resolution, adopted by the Metro commission in December, 1958, pledging a sum, not to exceed $500,000, to assist the Interama Authority in the initial administrative expenses of launching the center.[41] The $327,368.27 was the unused portion of the $500,000, the remainder having already been allocated to Interama.

Another problem, the conflict over the construction of a city hall in downtown Miami, was not settled until October 31, 1961,[42] when Metro in effect agreed to give the City of Miami a rental credit of not less than $800,000 in a proposed city-county building. The construction of the proposed building would be contingent upon the county's financial ability and legal power to undertake the project. The rental-credit stipulation was part of an agreement in which Metro exchanged a parcel of county-owned land for land owned by the city. The purpose of the latter arrangement was to provide a site for the construction of a 16-story federal building directly opposite the Court House in the heart of downtown Miami. The latter site, which was successfully promoted by City of Miami businessmen, was accepted by the United States government as a suitable location for its office building. Since the land swap entailed a loss of at least $800,000 to the City of Miami, the enactment of the Metro resolution was an attempt to compensate the city. In reality, the county was actually aiding rather than exploiting the city since establishment of a federal building within the downtown city area would benefit both the City of Miami and its businessmen.

There were a few areas like traffic engineering and publicity in which the transition to a new type of Metro–City of Miami relationship was relatively painless. On July 1, 1960, Metro began to exercise jurisdiction over all traffic control devices and vehicular traffic for Dade County. The absorption by Metro of the City of Miami Traffic Engineering Division resulted in an annual saving to the city of approximately $260,000. In 1960 Metro and the Dade County Port Authority also began to make an annual contribution of some $200,000 to the City of Miami publicity department for a joint program to promote tourism in Dade County.

At the beginning of 1962 there still existed a number of City of Miami–Metro problems which it was hoped might be amicably settled by the two commissions. Among these problems were the transfer of the city's stockade and misdemeanor court; [43] the reconstituting of the city's Water and Sewer Board as a county-wide agency; the establishing of joint central purchasing; and a number of other less urgent problems. In February, 1962, the City of Miami and Metro commissions agreed to hold monthly meetings in order to ascertain which functions might lend themselves to county-wide control or which might be jointly supported by both governments.

## THE BITTER RESISTANCE OF MIAMI BEACH

If Metro's relations with the City of Miami were difficult, its relations with Miami Beach, at least through 1960, were even more so. Aside from its concurrence with Metro's absorption of traffic engineering responsibilities, Miami Beach resisted Metro to the bitter end—in 1960 it still was following its own traffic code, trying traffic cases in its own courts, issuing its own automobile inspection stickers, and in accordance with its own standards giving limited recognition to the South Florida Building Code and Metro licenses in the building trades. As a culmination of Miami Beach resistance, the city council, on October 26, 1960, voted to attempt to secede from Dade County and to set up a separate county, Greater Miami Beach. The city commission was responding to a resolution of 22 leading citizens requesting the Florida Legislature to create "a separate county with the usual form of county government which exists in 66 counties and in the state, and not the Metropolitan form of government existing in Dade County. . . ." [44]

The resolution pointed out that Miami Beach and the neighboring cities were geographically separated from the Dade mainland and, unlike the remainder of the county, were dependent primarily upon the tourist industry. After passage of the resolution, the attorney for Miami Beach was instructed to take the necessary legal steps to bring about secession. Leaders from such adjacent municipalities as Surfside, Bal Harbour, Golden Beach, and North Bay Village indicated that they favored the proposal. [45] The Dade delegation to the state legislature opposed the secession movement and the issue was never presented to the Florida Legislature. (Even if it had been presented, the possibility of the Florida Legislature approving the creation of another county was nil.)

By the beginning of 1962 relations between Miami Beach and Metro had greatly improved. With its appeal on the Metro traffic code denied first by the Florida Supreme Court and finally by the United States Supreme Court, [46] Miami Beach in January, 1962, began to enforce the Metropolitan traffic code. Earlier the city had agreed to abide by the strict terms of the South Florida Building Code and had ceased giving examinations for certificates of competency in the building trades. Metro had previously absorbed the traffic engineering departments of all the municipalities including Miami Beach. The two County Commissioners representing the Miami Beach area in 1961 had opposed the anti-Metro McLeod amendment, [47] as had a number of Miami Beach City Commissioners. A new spirit seemed to prevail.

## METRO-MUNICIPAL AMITY

The areas of agreement and understanding between Metro and the cities of Miami, Miami Beach, and most other Dade municipalities, give promise of a greater degree of unity and harmony in the future than has existed in the past. The new spirit existing between Metro and the Dade municipalities was reflected by the creation by the Dade League of Municipalities of the new post of coordinator. The chief function of the coordinator is to provide closer liaison between the municipal governments and Metro.

It would seem, from experience to date, that a most effective means for Metro in wooing the cities is to reduce the municipalities' operating costs. Even Miami Beach, at a time when it was fighting Metro on almost every count, was willing to have its traffic engineering department taken over by Metro. By the beginning of 1962 Metro had absorbed 127 city employees from various municipalities into its traffic courts, traffic engineering division, and seaport.[48]

The desire to reduce city taxes has also brought about a meeting of minds between the representatives of the Dade League of Municipalities and the Government Research Council of the Miami-Dade Chamber of Commerce. It should be recalled that the chamber normally reflects both pro-Metro and pro-consolidationist tendencies. Both the league and the chamber believed that the tax structure in Dade County favored the unincorporated areas at the expense of the cities, and insisted that some appropriate means be found to compel the residents of the unincorporated areas to bear their proportionate share of the tax burden. The legal difficulties encountered in such a scheme will be considered in Chapter 17.

The municipalities' reactions to Dade's metropolitan government may be gauged from their responses, at hearings in late 1961 and early 1962, to a reconsideration of the home rule charter.[49] Relatively few basic changes were proposed by spokesmen of most of the municipalities. The return to the municipalities of the responsibility for traffic and traffic engineering was requested by Miami Beach, which at the time of the hearings was maintaining its own municipal traffic code. The election at large of the Metro Commission chairman was requested by the City of Miami. Both these cities also desired clarification of city and county functions, with the City of Miami underscoring the need for an amendment to the charter equivalent to the Tenth Amendment in the United States Constitution.

Most of the municipalities, including the two aforementioned, were generally sympathetic to the concept of metropolitan government. Representatives from such hard-core anti-Metro cities as Hialeah and Homestead attributed past difficulties to misunderstandings and faulty implementation of the charter rather than to any basic structural defects of the charter. Surprisingly, Coral Gables officials, whose voters had been among Metro's staunchest supporters, unleashed a stinging attack on the basic principles of the home rule charter. (The dichotomy of views between city officials and voters was not a new experience for Coral Gables.)

The results of the 1961 referendum election, which will be discussed in the following chapter, seemed to reinforce the more amicable relations between Metro and the municipalities. Furthermore, the city officials have confidence in the ability of Irving C. McNayr, new county manager,[50] to apply common-sense solutions to Metro-city problems. The spirit of amity, if it continues, will presage better days for both Metro and the municipalities.

# 16

# The McLeod Amendment
# and Its Aftermath

On October 17, 1961, a grave threat to Dade County's home rule charter was repelled, when the voters of metropolitan Miami rejected the McLeod amendment by a bare majority (52 per cent against— 48 per cent for).

The McLeod amendment, containing 37 proposed changes, was in effect a new charter which would have stripped Metro of its control over such area-wide functions as sewage, water supply, transportation, traffic, and central planning. In addition, the amendment would have abolished the council-manager form of government and substituted in its stead the commission form in which the commissioners act as both legislators and full-time executive administrators. The County Commission would have been reduced to 5 members elected at large. The commission at the time of the proposed amendment was composed of 13 members; 5 elected at large, 5 by individual county districts, and 3 by individual cities with a population of 60,000 or more.[1] Under the McLeod amendment, salaries for the commissioners were to be increased from the existing $6,000 a year to $15,000.

Another major change in the McLeod amendment was the provision for an elective sheriff in place of an appointed sheriff responsible to the county manager. The amendment also provided for the popular election of the tax assessor. The elective assessor would hold office until January 1, 1964, at which time his position would be eliminated and his authority assumed by a 5-man board of tax assessors appointed by the County Commission. Each of the 5 new tax assessors would hold office for four years and represent one of the 5 county commission districts.

The McLeod amendment also would have substituted a county court for the Metro court. The jurisdiction of the county court would have been limited to the unincorporated areas, although a municipality could contract to have the county court try municipal traffic violations.

Finally, the McLeod amendment, although maintaining amending procedures identical with those in the existing home rule charter, provided that the new charter could be abolished only by a majority vote of *all the electors registered to vote in the county*. Amendments to bring about particular changes could still be added in the traditional manner, but an amendment of the scope of the McLeod amendment, for example, might well be construed as abolishment and consequently be interpreted as requiring the consent of a majority of the registered voters in Dade County. Actually the 202,267 voters who voted both for and against the McLeod amendment totaled only 50 per cent of all the registered voters.

After the defeat of the McLeod amendment, even the adherents of the amendment admitted that their proposals had contained a number of basic flaws. How then does one account for the closeness of the election? The actual contents of the amendment seem to have been relatively unimportant. In a poll taken by the University of Miami Government Department,[2] completed ten days before the election, 48 per cent of some 500 interviewees had no idea at all as to the substance of the McLeod amendment. Of those who revealed any knowledge, only 37 per cent were aware of the change in the size of the commission; 15 per cent of the abolition of the county manager; and 12 per cent of the increase in the power of the cities. Some 11 per cent mentioned a possible tax reduction which apparently would stem from the changes brought about by the McLeod amendment. Since so little was known about the contents of the amendment, one must conclude that there were other factors that motivated Dade County electors to vote for or against it.

## REASSESSMENT: THE KEY ISSUE

Reassessment was one of the issues played to the hilt by the McLeod forces and, although only tangentially related to the content of the amendment, it was probably the most important factor contributing to the heavy vote for the proposed changes. The home rule charter provided for reassessment of all real and tangible property within both incorporated and unincorporated areas no later than January 1, 1961. In order to fulfill its obligation by this date, Metro undertook a crash program which expended approximately $1.5 million. The projected reassessments were based on 100 per cent of the market value of all real property, as ostensibly required by a state law.[3] The total net real estate valuation as a result of reassessment increased from approximately $2 billion to $4 billion. The 100 per cent assessment was in striking contrast to the approximate 50 per cent assessment (i.e., 50 per cent of market value of property) to which the taxpayers of Dade County had previously been accustomed.

When the new reassessment rolls were opened to the public in February, 1961, newspaper reports indicated a dearth of complaints. Taxpayers were informed that the effect of the 100 per cent reassessment on their tax bill was still unknown, but that the increase in assessments would, in general, be compensated by a corresponding 100 per cent decrease in millage. As applied to most homeowners, however, this reassurance was deceptive. Since under the Florida Constitution a $5,000 homestead exemption is granted to each home-owner residing in his own home, the owner of a home assessed at $10,000 and taxed at 40 mills per dollar would normally pay $40 × 5 or $200. However, if the assessment were increased to $20,000 and the rate reduced to 20 mills, the homeowner would end up paying $20 × 15 or $300, an increase of $100. In addition, some three-fourths of the 40,000 homes heretofore assessed under $5,000 (and consequently exempt from all county real property taxes) would now be placed on the tax rolls for the first time.

Irving C. McNayr, who assumed the office of county manager on May 1, 1961, urged the County Commissioners, on May 16, to postpone reassessment for two years. McNayr maintained that the reassessments might be inaccurate in view of the speed with which they were carried out and he further warned that the 100 per cent increase in assessment values would be too much of a shock to the homeowners. The commission by an 8 to 5 vote refused to go along with McNayr's recommendation but raised no objection to an "administrative action" by McNayr reducing the new assessment by 20 per cent. The manager justified his action on the grounds of a recent downward trend in economic conditions in Greater Miami which had brought about a corresponding reduction in property values. The commission also agreed by a vote of 9 to 4 to provide $15,000 for the tax assessor's office to mail the new assessments.[4]

During the final weeks of May, postcards were mailed to the owners of each of the 318,000 parcels of land in Dade County. Upon receipt by the taxpayers of the reassessment notices which included McNayr's 20 per cent reduction, there was a violent reaction. Hundreds of persons swamped the assessor's office, and thousands of calls tied up the switchboard. According to a statement later made by the county manager, there were over 200,000 complaints.[5] On June 8, 1961, because of the public pressure, the commission voted 7 to 5 to call a special election on August 15, 1961, to give Dade voters the opportunity to cast a "Yes" or "No" vote on the question: Shall the home rule charter of government for Dade County be amended, revised, and modified by repealing Sections 9.03 (A) and 9.03 (B) relating to reassessment of all real and tangible personal property in Dade County?[6] The commission resolution also directed the county tax assessor, subject to the outcome of the election, to prepare the 1961 tax assessment rolls upon substantially the same basis as the 1960 rolls.

On July 12, 1961, a taxpayer instituted mandamus proceedings to compel the county manager and Chief Deputy Tax Assessor Thomas A. O'Connor to file a tax roll based upon the 1961 reassessment program, which the petitioners contended was a "full cash value" appraisal, or, alternatively, to submit to the County Commissioners a tax roll predicated upon the reassessment of all real and personal property in Dade County at full cash value. Petitioners alleged that the 1960 tax roll was grossly unfair since an assessment based on anything less than full value would, because of the homestead exemption provision of the Florida Constitution, necessarily result in an inequality in favor of the homestead owner.

The Dade County Circuit Court dismissed the petition for a writ of mandamus.[7] Circuit Judge Philip Goldman based his decision on the "undisputed evidence" that valuations in the reassessments were "the judgments of various and sundry untrained and unqualified personnel."[8] The judge also accepted the county's contention that it would be physically impossible to create a new tax roll based upon full cash value by the deadline of October 2, 1961. In observing that the state law requires assessments to be made at full cash value, Judge Goldman noted that the concept of full cash value does not lend itself to certainty and that consequently considerable discretion was granted to the official making the assessments. He added, "In fact, absent arbitrary and capricious action on the part of the county assessor of taxes, his discretion or judgment will not be disturbed."[9]

On appeal, the Florida Supreme Court affirmed the ruling of the Circuit Court and emphasized that the purpose of mandamus is to enforce a right which is already established, not to establish a legal right. Justice Campbell Thornal declared for the court: "When reduced to its simplest terms, the conclusion reached by the trial judge was that the petitioners had not demonstrated that they had a legal right to compel the preparation and submission of a particular tax roll which the record revealed was itself invalid. The trial judge merely held that the respondent taxing officials were not subject to any legal duty to prepare and submit a particular tax roll which was illegal."[10]

The next test for reassessment was to be at the polls on August 15. The *Miami Herald* editorially took the position that the voters should defeat the proposition to repeal the reassessment sections of the home rule charter.[11] The *Herald* declared that the commission's holding of a reassessment referendum was analogous to Congress holding a national referendum for each new federal tax law. The editorial further observed that the tax aggregate would not be raised as a result of reassessment but would simply be redistributed so as to make the total burden more equitable. The *Miami News*, although favoring the principle of reassessment, urged Dade electors to vote for the repeal of the reassessment provisions because the newspaper believed that postponement of the new reassessment program would give Metro at least a fighting chance to defeat the McLeod amendment on October 17.[12] The *News* feared that a sharp rise in taxes would cause the voters to turn against Metro.

County Manager McNayr placed large advertisements in the *Miami Herald*, the *Miami News*, and the *Miami Beach Sun* urging the voters to defeat reassessment by voting for its repeal. The advertisements signed by County Manager McNayr recommended a "Yes" vote for the following reasons:

1. Reassessment was only half completed.
2. There was not enough time to do the job properly.
3. Qualified appraisers did not make individual assessments.
4. The program lacked public understanding and acceptance.

The rationale for spending $1,884 of county funds for these advertisements was the need to counteract the false impression, allegedly created by the *Metro Bulletin* of August 4, 1961, that the county was urging Dade electors to vote against the repeal of reassessment. The *Metro Bulletin*, an official publication of Dade County, is distributed to civic groups and interested citizens.

On August 15, 1961, the electors of Dade County voted by a 10 to 1 ratio (115,026 to 11,927) to repeal the Metro charter provisions requiring reassessment. Not one of the county's 210 precincts voted to retain the reassessment provisions.

Neither the repeal of the reassessment provisions of the charter nor the decision of the courts on reassessment quieted the fears of many who gloomily foresaw further reassessment at 100 per cent of market value. Both proponents and opponents of the McLeod amendment interpreted the state law requirement that all property be assessed at "full cash value" to mean that property must be assessed at 100 per cent of market value. The fact is that this law has been on the books since 1941 and an overwhelming number of Florida counties continue to base their assessments on 50 per cent or less of market value.

The McLeod forces used giant billboards and newspaper ads warning the public that reassessment would be coming back unless a "Yes" vote was cast for the McLeod amendment. These ads quoted the county manager and County Attorney Darrey A. Davis as testifying under oath that full reassessment would be brought back as soon as possible.[13] Reference was also made to a statement by the Florida

Supreme Court that the Metro tax assessor was preparing a tax roll based on full cash value.

In a poll taken by the Government Department of the University of Miami, the majority of respondents in every category—those opposed to the McLeod amendment, category 1; those in favor of the amendment, category 2; and those who were uncertain of their position, category 3—indicated that they were against the reassessment program. The percentage of respondents in each of the above categories who opposed reassessment was as follows: category 1, 58 per cent; category 2, 83 per cent; category 3, 58 per cent; and the overall average for all three categories, 69.4 per cent. As might be expected, those favoring the McLeod amendment expressed the greatest opposition to reassessment.

## THE PRO-McLEOD FORCES

The pro-McLeod forces were led by John McLeod and the People's Committee to Amend Metro. John McLeod, *l'enfant terrible* of metropolitan Miami, is a former County Commissioner who specializes in the sensational and is an expert at manipulating meetings and debates in such a manner that confusion and chaos reign. This "dapper Dan," by his very indifference to normal conduct and to the rules of the game, is able to drive his opponents mad. Typifying Mr. McLeod's air of abandon was his response to a question asking him to quote his authority for a particular statement he had made. "I am my own authority," McLeod declared arrogantly but whimsically. In another instance, he dramatically called attention to the fact that the people had spoken on reassessment and therefore the issue was foreclosed from further discussion. When his interrogator pointed out that the people had also spoken against an elected sheriff in the 1959 election, McLeod nonchalantly insisted that the people would change their minds.[14] Inconsistency, *non sequiturs*, and extravagant and fantastic statements mixed with a dash of humor and whimsy made McLeod something of a giant killer.

The pro-Metro forces took out after McLeod's scalp. They accused him of calling veterans "drunk stumblebums," of pleading for gambling casinos, of displaying a disrespect for churches, of squandering county money, of opposing a $46-million expressway bond issue which had been overwhelmingly approved by the freeholders, and of participating in county matters involving a conflict of interest. The indomitable Mr. McLeod charged his adversaries with character assassination, and declared that the *Herald*, the *News*, and the television stations were biased, and furthermore that his detractors were begging the issue by discussing his personality rather than the amendment.

Whatever motivated McLeod to submit his amendment, it was not love for the municipalities or fear of too much centralization. As early as September, 1957, McLeod had publicly advocated the abolition of all Dade municipalities. In December, 1960, during his final weeks as a Metro Commissioner, McLeod requested the Metro Commission to call a special referendum election for either of two proposals: (1) abolition of all the cities except the city of Miami, which would become the parent city for the entire county or (2) abolition of Metro. McLeod at one time had also fathered a plan to have Dade secede from Florida and establish Dade County as a separate state.

McLeod and the other members of the original five-man commission (elected under a commission form of government in November, 1956) inherited the Metro government as a result of the adoption of the home rule charter in May, 1957. These five commissioners, who under the terms of the charter held office until 1961, were unhappy with both the council-manager form of government and with the later election of six commissioners in September, 1958. On more than one occasion Mr. McLeod expressed his dissatisfaction with both Mr. O. W. "Hump" Campbell, the original county manager, and with the six additional commissioners.

After McLeod's term of office expired, he attempted to persuade the commission to place what later came to be known as the McLeod amendment on the ballot. When this request was denied, McLeod secured some 64,000 signatures for an initiative petition which he submitted to the commission on May 22, 1961. The county manager, by a technicality, foreclosed the possibility of the McLeod amendment appearing together with the reassessment amendment on the August 15 ballot. After 15,000 signatures on the petition were certified by the supervisor of registration, a referendum date, October 17, 1961, was set by the commission.

Relatively few organizations endorsed the McLeod amendment. These included the People's Committee to Amend Metro, the Polish-American Club of Miami, the Voters and Taxpayers Political League of Miami and Dade County, the Dade County Police Chiefs Association, the Bus Drivers Union, the Dade Federation of Labor, and the Senior Citizens Protective League. Foremost among those who spoke in behalf of the amendment were Johnny McLeod; Art Green, radio and TV commentator; Dan Chappel, president of the People's Committee to Amend Metro; John Gautier, former Dade County tax assessor; Joseph Marcus and William Pruitt, attorneys; Malvin Englander, vice mayor of Miami Beach; William Dickinson; and Robert Quinn, public relations man.[15] According to an official McLeod spokesman, the amendment was approved legally by such outstanding attorneys as Edward L. ("Ted") Semple, city attorney for Coral Gables; E. P. Brigham; former Circuit Court Judge Vincent C. Giblin; former attorney for Dade County Marion E. Sibley; Miami Beach city attorney Joseph A. Wanick; and special counsel for the City of Miami John W. Watson, Sr.

The People's Committee to Amend Metro and its spokesmen stressed the following arguments:

1. Metro would bring back 100 per cent reassessment.
2. Metro meant rule by bureaucratic and dictatorial management, and by an outsider at that (referring to County Manager McNayr, who came to Miami from Columbia, South Carolina).
3. Metro had created a multi-million dollar bureaucracy.
4. The McLeod amendment would restore government by the people.
5. The Metro court system was Metro's biggest boondoggle.[16]
6. The McLeod amendment would give the public "neighborhood" tax assessors conversant with local tax problems.

During the campaign persons affiliated with the McLeod group, made a number of veiled references to "1313" and John D. Corcoran of Public Administration Service.[17] Pamphlets and mimeographed letters were circulated, by groups not always identified, insinuating that "1313" was a Communist conspiracy. In addition, some bumper

strips appeared proclaiming that "Metro and Castro Both Gotta Go."
At least two suburban newspapers expressed a similar type of editorial view.[18] However, the extremist propaganda had no significant
impact on the public mind. The University of Miami poll found that
of some 500 persons interviewed, only a handful made even remote
references to this type of view.

It might be worth noting the reactions of the county manager, the
Miami-Dade Chamber of Commerce, and the area-wide newspapers
to the extremist charges of dictatorship and Communism that were
levied against Metro. Mr. McNayr condemned the attack on "1313"
as the "familiar scare tactics used by radical, anti-Semitic, anti-
integrationist, and anti-professional reactionaries." [19] The president
of the Miami-Dade Chamber of Commerce characterized the "red
smear" as ridiculous. The Miami News observed that the Communist
issue in the Metro debates was the work of afflicted persons who discovered this issue lurking beneath the surface of every debate.[20] The
Herald called attention to the "scurrilous accusations" [21] levied against
the county manager and other pro-Metro personalities. Ralph Renick,
TV newscaster, said that "to believe this tripe and cast a ballot based
on this reasoning is to perform an injustice against the privilege of
voting." [22]

## THE PRO-METRO FORCES

The pro-Metro forces, led by the Citizens Committee for Good Government, operating out of the Miami-Dade Chamber of Commerce,
attacked McLeod personally, and in addition charged the People's
Committee to Amend Metro with spending exorbitant funds for
billboards and newspaper, radio, and television advertisements.
The implication was strong that the money for these expenditures
came from illegal gambling interests. Speakers against the McLeod
amendment openly charged that the amendment was to be used as a
springboard for a power grab by the gamblers.

Other issues hammered at by the pro-Metro forces were:
  1. Dade County needed a stable government to attract industry.
  2. Chaos would result if the McLeod amendment were adopted
     since the McLeod amendment made no provision for a transi-
     tion period.

3. The check and balance system would be destroyed if the legislators and administrators were one and the same.

4. The McLeod charter was written by unidentified persons, who held no public hearings. In contrast, the original charter board was composed of prestigious persons who provided an opportunity to the public to participate in the writing of the home rule charter.

5. A five-man commission would need only a three-man quorum, which could result in just two men controlling the destiny of Dade County.

6. A separate tax assessor appointed for each of the five commission districts could lead only to confusion and favoritism.

7. Capital improvements, pending at the time of the election, would be jeopardized.

8. Reassessment was removed as an issue in the McLeod amendment campaign by the results of the reassessment referendum held on August 15, 1961.

There were many more civic, business, and political organizations opposing the McLeod amendment than favoring it.[23] A number of prestigious persons debated against the amendment, including County Manager McNayr; William T. Kruglak of the Miami-Dade Chamber of Commerce; Metro Commissioners Alexander S. Gordon, Harold B. Spaet, and Ben C. McGahey; Mrs. H. Franklin Williams of the League of Women Voters; R. Bunn Gautier, former state senator; Daniel P. S. Paul, former Charter Board attorney; William Singer, former State Road Board member; and Dr. H. Franklin Williams, vice-president of the University of Miami. Both Mr. Singer and Dr. Williams had served on the Charter Board.

The anti-amendment forces also included a number of other persons prominent in public life. Three of the four members of the Dade delegation to the Florida State Legislature publicly announced their opposition. State Senator William ("Cliff") Herrell maintained that the adoption of the amendment would retard the county by 20 years. Of the three Dade representatives in the Florida House, one warned that Dade would forfeit its home rule privileges; another, that the amendment was not the proper way to right Metro wrongs. The third adopted a neutral position. Circuit Court Clerk E. B. ("Buck") Leatherman, who had held office for 34 years and generally maintained an image of nonpartisanship, openly condemned the McLeod amendment. Former County Commissioner Charles Crandon, an elder statesman in Dade County, insisted that the adoption of the amendment would destroy not only Metro but the entire county. In addition to these impressive endorsements, there was also the very strong and active opposition to the McLeod amendment by the *Miami Herald*, the *Miami News*, and Ralph Renick, newscaster of TV station WTVJ.

County Manager McNayr played a most important role in the defeat of the McLeod amendment. According to the findings of the University of Miami poll, the county manager was the second best known source for activity against the McLeod amendment; only the *Miami Herald* was better known.[24]

## THE IMPACT OF THE MASS MEDIA ON THE CAMPAIGN

The complexity of a typical primary election contest in Dade County helps to explain the dependency of the electorate upon the mass media. In the May 3, 1960, election there was a miscellany of some 32 elective offices for which 160 candidates were competing. In view of the long ballot and the general political vacuum in Dade County, it can readily be understood why the Dade voter has had to turn to some "authority" for guidance. Both public opinion polls and the election results bear out the importance of newspaper endorsements. In the Greater Miami area the *Miami Herald* has become the dominant authority to which the local voter turns for leadership.

The great influence of the *Herald* has filled a basic need in the Greater Miami area, and the *Herald* has used its power to help bring about many civic reforms. Certainly, the *Herald*, in alliance with the *News*, played a most important role in creating the new metropolitan government in Dade County. Furthermore, the *Herald* and the *News* have supported the new metropolitan government against all attacks to reduce its powers.

Despite its basic support of Metro, the *Herald* and its associate editor, John D. Pennekamp, have been among its most bitter critics. On repeated occasions the *Herald*, in editorials and in Mr. Pennekamp's columns, has lashed out at Metro for its failure to eliminate what were constantly referred to as the duplicating and overlapping functions of Metro and the municipalities. Particular attention was called to the existence of the many police, fire, and other municipal departments in Dade County. That the *Herald* has assumed this position is no surprise to those who are acquainted with the philosophy of its editorial staff. The *Herald*, since the passage of the home rule charter, has been strongly opposed to the interpretation of the division of powers between Metro and the municipalities as a federal type of government, and instead has favored an outright consolidationist position. The *Herald*, in fact, posits the issue as one of good government (i.e., the elimination of duplication and overlapping of services with the resultant economy and efficiency) versus downright sin.

The impact of the mass media during the McLeod amendment campaign may be ascertained from the findings of the University of Miami poll. Respondents were asked: "Whose advice or help has been most valuable to you in coming to a decision about your vote on this Amendment, sometimes called the McLeod Amendment?" The replies to this question, divided on the basis of whether the respondents were for, against, or uncertain about the amendment, were as follows as pertains to the mass media:

| Category | Against | For | Uncertain | Total | Per cent |
|---|---|---|---|---|---|
| Herald | 75 | 39 | 27 | 141 | 25 |
| News | 36 | 23 | 13 | 72 | 13 |
| All Television | 56 | 42 | 34 | 132 | 24 |
| WTVJ | (32) | (17) | (16) | (65) | (12) |
| WCKT | (12) | (10) | (8) | (30) | (5.4) |
| WPST | (9) | (12) | (6) | (27) | (4.9) |
| General | (3) | (3) | (4) | (10) | (1.8) |
| All Radio | 15 | 18 | 12 | 45 | 8 |
| Courtney | (8) | (10) | (4) | (22) | (4) |
| Other | (7) | (8) | (8) | (23) | (4) |
| All Suburban | | | | | |
| newspapers | 6 | 3 | 5 | 14 | 2.3 |
| Miami Beach Sun | (3) | (2) | (2) | (7) | (1.7) |
| Other | (3) | (1) | (3) | (7) | (.6) |

The mass media together accounted for 72.3 per cent of all the sources listed as aiding respondents in determining their views on the amendment. Other sources listed were friends, neighbors, and work

178 PART FIVE: PROGRESS OF METRO

companions, 13 per cent; families, 5.4 per cent; government officials, 3.4 per cent; and miscellaneous, 5.9 per cent.

The *Herald* and the *News* together constituted more than one-third (38 per cent) of the total responses. If WTVJ, the next most popular source, is combined with the area-wide newspapers, the percentage is raised to 50. WTVJ's leading position is due in large part to the two-minute editorial comment of Ralph Renick on his 6:30 P.M. newscast. The responses to the University poll showed that the public was well aware of the position taken on the McLeod amendment by the *Herald*, *News*, and television station WTVJ on the McLeod amendment. Few references were made in the polls to TV stations WCKT and WPST, since neither station took an official position on the election.[25]

The amendment received little support from the mass media with the exception of the suburban newspapers and commentators Alan Courtney of radio station WQAM and Art Green of TV station WPST. Mr. Courtney was mentioned as a source of influence 22 times, which constituted 4 per cent of the total responses and 50 per cent of all references made to radio. A smaller number of references were made to Green. Those who named either Courtney or Green were aware of their pro-McLeod sentiments.

Mr. Courtney conducts an audience participation program via telephone from 10:00 P.M. to 1:00 A.M. Monday through Saturday, on which local affairs are frequently discussed. Courtney makes his microphones available to all candidates during an election campaign and to speakers for both sides of any contested election issue. Mr. Courtney is decidedly anti-Metro in his views. Art Green, the other commentator, had a five-minute editorial program both in the early evening and after 11 P.M. on TV station WPST. In addition, Mr. Green was an active participant in behalf of the McLeod amendment and appeared before many groups.

There is little evidence that the dozen or so suburban papers had much effect on the outcome of the election. Only 2.3 per cent of the 72.3 per cent of the persons alluding to the helpfulness of the mass media made any reference to the suburban press. The community papers for the most part are small papers with a smattering of local news and editorial comment, and do not compete with the area-wide papers in either circulation or opinion molding.

ELECTION RESULTS

To what extent does the McLeod election compare with former elections challenging Metro? The initial home rule charter was approved in a special election held on May 21, 1957, by the narrow margin of 1,784 votes (51 per cent to 49 per cent) with a turnout of only 26 per cent of the registered voters. The opposition to the charter was particularly strong in the Homestead–Florida City area (3 to 1), in Hialeah and Miami Beach (2 to 1) and in a number of smaller cities such as Miami Shores, El Portal, Miami Springs, and Biscayne Park.[26] The unincorporated areas cast somewhat over 50 per cent of their votes against the charter. On the side favoring the charter were the City of Miami (56.4 per cent), Coral Gables (2 to 1), and a number of smaller municipalities such as Bal Harbour, Bay Harbor Island, North Bay Village, Golden Beach, Surfside, South Miami, West Miami, North Miami Beach, and Opa-locka.

The first significant challenge to Metro, the autonomy amendment, was defeated by a 3 to 2 margin with a 34.2 per cent turnout of the registered voters. Fifty-three of the 56 precincts in the City of Miami opposed the amendment. The overall city majority was 6 per cent higher than the county average. Voters in South Miami, North Miami Beach, North Miami, and Coral Gables also cast large votes against the autonomy amendment. The unincorporated areas switched from their narrow margin of opposition to Metro in the charter election to a heavy margin (2 to 1) in favor. Miami Beach, Miami Springs, Hialeah, Miami Shores, and Homestead constituted the bulk of the support for the anti-Metro forces. In the final analysis Dade County, except for the unincorporated areas, was divided in the 1958 autonomy elections along pretty much the same lines that it had been in the 1957 charter election.

Metro was to face still additional challenges. On November 3, 1959, Dade County voted on five amendments to the Metro charter. Three proposals, which were placed on the ballot by the Metro commissioners, would have altered the number of commissioners, their salaries, and their method of election. The two other amendments, which were placed on the ballot through the initiative process, were intended to restore the offices of sheriff and tax assessor to elective status. Only 25 per cent of the registered voters participated in the election and all five amendments were defeated. The issue seems to have been viewed in terms of responsible administration versus spoils politics rather than as a clash of cities versus Metro. There was possibly a greater emphasis in this election on socio-economic factors than on municipal identification.

The McLeod amendment which came to the fore in October, 1961, was not just another attack on Metro by Dade municipalities. The Dade League of Municipalities took no part in the campaign and, a number of municipal representatives to the league actively fought the amendment. Certainly the reaction of the league in 1961 differed radically from the position it had assumed in the anti-Metro autonomy amendment election in 1958. At that time the league had sponsored the autonomy amendment and had raised a $32,000 campaign fund to carry the fight to the voters. The results of the autonomy election were interpreted as a definite defeat for the league and for the hard core of anti-Metro cities.

The division of voting patterns along socio-economic lines in the McLeod amendment election resembled the 1959 sheriff and tax assessor elections much more closely than it did either the 1957 charter or the 1958 autonomy election. If the 1959 sheriff and tax assessor election results are excluded, the greatest difference between the lowest and highest socio-economic groups in any Metro election contest was never more than 12.2 per cent. On the McLeod amendment the division between the highest and lowest socio-economic categories was much sharper, amounting to almost 20 per cent. (See Appendix D.)

In 1961, there were also a number of changes in municipal voting patterns. The reaction of cities like Miami Beach and Miami Shores differed substantially from their positions in the 1957 and 1958 elections. Miami Shores, which had opposed Metro in both the charter and autonomy amendment elections, cast 2 out of every 3 of its votes against the McLeod amendment. Although Miami Beach, unlike Miami Shores, did vote for the McLeod amendment, the vote was relatively close—53.8 per cent to 46.2 per cent. As indicated earlier, a number of officials from Miami Beach, as well as civic and business organizations from that city, publicly opposed the McLeod amendment.

The City of Miami, although opposing the McLeod amendment, did so by a vote of only 50.9 per cent as against the overall anti-amendment vote of 51.5 per cent for all the cities and 52 per cent for the entire county. It was the first time in a Metro election that the City of Miami vote for Metro was less than the overall county average. In 1957 the margin provided by City of Miami voters was primarily responsible for victory in the home rule charter election.

The unincorporated areas, although voting against the McLeod amendment, did so by a vote of only 53 per cent as contrasted to the 66 per cent vote cast by that area against the autonomy amendment in 1958. However, since the autonomy amendment did not directly affect the residents of these areas, a more meaningful comparison would be between the votes cast by the unincorporated areas in the charter and McLeod amendment elections. Voters in these areas were obviously more pro-Metro in 1961 than in 1957, since they cast a 53 per cent vote opposing the McLeod amendment as against a vote of somewhat less than 50 per cent in favor of the home rule charter.

In the past, the high socio-economic areas of Miami Beach and Miami Shores were exceptions to the generally low socio-economic status of most of the anti-Metro areas. This situation, however, was modified during the McLeod amendment election. In that election, there was a sharp division along almost purely economic lines between the proponents and opponents of the McLeod amendment— the affluent cities and the high income groups opposing the amendment, and the less well-to-do cities and the lower income groups favoring it. The results of the McLeod amendment (what Professor Thomas J. Wood describes as the rise of neo-populism) would seem to presage great difficulty for Metro if it should attempt to impose heavy financial burdens on the lower socio-economic groups or try to shift some of the tax load from the business groups to the home-owners in the relatively low or middle income brackets. Laborers and white-collar workers in Greater Miami do not generally enjoy the protection of strong unions but they are able to reflect their economic dissatisfaction at the polls.

## SEQUEL TO THE McLEOD AMENDMENT

A vigorous criticism of the McLeod amendment was that it had been hurriedly drawn up by a secret group without any opportunity afforded the public to participate in its considerations. To cut the ground out from under the McLeod amendment adherents, the Metro Commission, at the height of the McLeod campaign, created a six-man Charter Review Board [27] to hold public hearings regarding the need for changes in the home rule charter. This may have been an unfortunate move since the hearings and the attendant publicity tended to create the impression of a strong need to amend the charter.

In general, the board felt that although there were many complaints of the manner in which Metro was being administered, there was no great or widespread demand for revision of the charter. The board shared the opinion of many responsible persons that Metro needed a period of respite in which to concentrate on metropolitan problems instead of having to expend its energies on the battle for survival. Nevertheless, because this latter view was not acceptable to some prominent civic leaders, the board felt impelled to offer a number of charter amendment recommendations to the Metro Commission.

The Charter Review Board's decision to propose amendments, some substantive, was influenced in large measure by an eight-man group which came to be known as the Crandon Committee. The committee was headed by Charles H. Crandon, former county commissioner and venerable elder statesman in Dade County. Also included in the group were such notable figures as Mitchell Wolfson, owner of television station WTVJ, former Charter Board member and active public and civic figure; County Commissioner Robert Haverfield; and others.[28]

The Crandon Committee made its debut at the tail end of the Charter Board hearings. The committee's recommendations were first made public during a meeting with the Government Research Council of the Miami-Dade Chamber of Commerce. The proposals met with a cool reception from the Research Council. Later the Crandon Committee met with the Charter Board and the County Commission. The proposed amendments of the Crandon Committee would:

(1) Divide the county into 9 districts and provide for the election of one commissioner from each district.
(2) Require the commission's approval for the appointment of major county department heads.

(3) Allow the commission to exercise a veto over administrative orders issued by the county manager and require the approval by the commission of any administrative order creating, merging, or combining departments.

(4) Create an independent Port Authority Board which in effect would have all the powers presently exercised by the commission in its capacity as the Dade County Port Authority.

(5) Provide for a Metropolitan-Municipal Court in each municipality having a population in excess of 2,500 to try offenses under county ordinances occurring within the boundaries of such municipalities; prescribe minimum standards for all Metro-Municipal courts; and designate the number, qualifications, term of office, methods of appointment and removal of the judges for all such courts.

The Charter Review Board recommendations to the Metro Commission, as a sop to the Crandon Committee, included proposals (1) and (2), adding to the former a provision for a commission chairman elected at large. Both of these proposals and an additional Charter Review Board proposal to raise commission salaries from $6,000 to $10,000 were rejected by the commission. The County Commission, however, did approve for placement upon the May 29, 1962, ballot three Charter Board amendment proposals which would have prevented county officials from holding any other elective office; required appointed county officials to resign their positions in order to run for elective office; set a new deadline for filing as a candidate for County Commission office; and required competitive bidding for transactions involving $1,000 or more. These proposals were characterized by Charles Crandon as insignificant items, which indeed most were. (Subsequently, all three amendments were overwhelmingly approved by the voters.)

The Crandon Committee, after having the commission formally deny its request to place the Crandon amendments on the ballot, proceeded to distribute petitions in order to place the committee's five proposed amendments on the May ballot. Under the charter an initiative petition must be signed by 5 per cent (some 14,446) of the voters who cast their ballots in the last gubernatorial election. However, the committee did not succeed in having its proposals placed on the May, 1962, ballot, but on May 1, its initiative petition was certified by the County Commission and a referendum election on the five Crandon amendments was set for August 21, 1962. The Crandon Committee is composed of honorable and respectable men. A number of its members are prestigious persons who fought valiantly against the McLeod amendment. These members, although lacking the color and verve of Mr. McLeod, are potentially far more formidable opponents than were Commissioner McLeod and his supporters. The *Herald* has labeled the Crandon Committee proposals as the McLeod amendment in spats.

The Crandon Committee proposal to return the traffic courts to the municipalities would be a serious blow to Metro and the proposal to weaken the county manager's authority over appointments and administrative orders, although not of the same import, would tend to undermine the principles of council-manager government. The committee's most important argument is that the people be given an opportunity to accept or reject their proposals. But why these— there are so many other conceivable amendments. Nor does the committee give proper consideration to Metro's need for stability. Most political scientists long ago became disillusioned, and understandably so, with the reformers' great secular trinity—initiative, referendum, and recall. These devices when too easily accessible become powerful weapons with which to harass orderly democratic government.

The Crandon Committee's leadership of a populist movement, strengthened by a powerful assist from television station WTVJ, is not to be taken lightly. Such a movement could rally organized labor, the alienated, the dispossessed, and, in general, the lower socio-economic groups and provide them with respectable middle-class leadership.[29]

17

# Finance

THE METROPOLITAN DILEMMA has been equated in many areas with legal inability to create a single governmental entity coexistent with the problems of a metropolis and with financial inability to bear the costs for the solution of these problems. Dade County has the legal instrumentality to deal with area-wide problems but, unfortunately, the home rule amendment failed to grant the new metropolitan county government any additional taxing powers. This was a necessary concession in order to persuade the state legislature to enact a resolution which later, upon the approval of the state electorate, became the home rule amendment.

Florida's tax structure is even more irrational than that of most other states, chiefly because of a constitutional $5,000 homestead exemption for every residing homeowner in the state.[1] Thus the owner of a $10,000 home in Dade County, assessed at approximately only 50 per cent of market value, is exempt from all ad valorem real property taxes.

The tax situation is further complicated by a requirement of the Florida Constitution that all ad valorem taxes levied by the county, in both incorporated and unincorporated areas, be of a uniform nature. Thus, homeowners in the municipalities, in addition to bearing municipal taxes, must also pay county property taxes at a rate identical to that paid by the residents of unincorporated areas. The equal tax rate was justifiable so long as the county provided equal

# PERCENTAGES OF TOTAL MUNICIPAL REVENUE

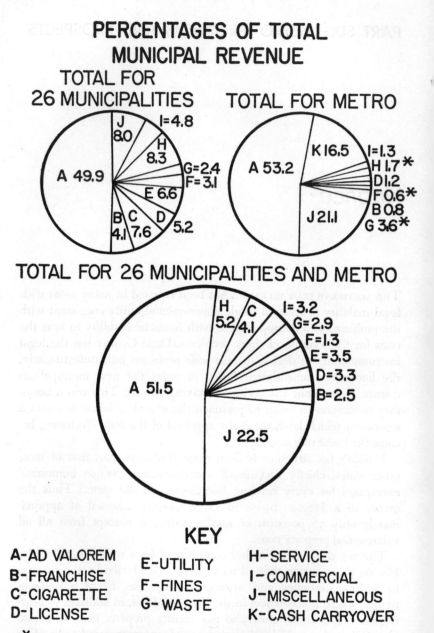

TOTAL FOR 26 MUNICIPALITIES

J 8.0
I=4.8
H 8.3
G=2.4
F=3.1
E 6.6
A 49.9
B 4.1
C 7.6
D 5.2

TOTAL FOR METRO

K 16.5
I=1.3
H 1.7 *
D 1.2
F 0.6 *
B 0.8
G 3.6 *
A 53.2
J 21.1

TOTAL FOR 26 MUNICIPALITIES AND METRO

H 5.2
C 4.1
I=3.2
G=2.9
F=1.3
E=3.5
D=3.3
B=2.5
A 51.5
J 22.5

## KEY

A-AD VALOREM
B-FRANCHISE
C-CIGARETTE
D-LICENSE

E-UTILITY
F-FINES
G-WASTE

H-SERVICE
I-COMMERCIAL
J-MISCELLANEOUS
K-CASH CARRYOVER

*REVENUE FROM UNINCORPORATED AREAS ONLY

services to all of its residents. However, the county government, in effect, has also become a municipal government for the unincorporated areas, providing municipal-type services (essentially police, fire, and road maintenance) without additional charge to the 380,-000 residents of these areas. Naturally, city taxpayers resent sharing the cost of providing these municipal-type services to the unincorporated areas, when the unincorporated areas do not share in the cost of such services within the cities.

The total local revenue collected by the governmental units of Dade County during the 1960 fiscal year amounted to some $185 million.[2] Roughly one-third was collected by each of the following: the school board, the county government, and the cities as a group. All three relied most heavily on property taxation, which accounted for $98 million or 53 per cent of the total.[3]

An examination of exclusively city revenues shows that 55 per cent of such revenues was collected by the City of Miami, which contained half of the population of the 26 municipalities. The cities of Miami, Miami Beach, Coral Gables, Hialeah, North Miami, and North Miami Beach collected more than 90 per cent of the total revenue of all municipalities. The greatest sources of city revenues were ad valorem taxes, 50 per cent; service charges, 8 per cent; cigarette tax rebates, 8 per cent; utility taxes, 7 per cent; and licenses, 5 per cent—a total of 78 per cent.

Municipalities in Dade County rely far more heavily for their support on the property tax than do sister cities elsewhere in Florida —49.9 per cent for Dade cities as against 30.46 per cent for Florida cities as a whole. The differences in sources of revenue between the cities in Greater Miami and in Florida as a whole may well be explained by the almost complete absence of publicly owned electric power systems in Dade County, and by the failure of many of Dade cities to take advantage of utility taxes and garbage removal charges. The City of Miami receives 7.57 per cent of its revenues from utility taxes (an excise paid by consumers), Coral Gables 10.44 per cent, South Miami 13.84 per cent, and six other cities an average of 10.62 per cent; but Miami Shores, Miami Beach, and 15 other municipalities receive no revenue whatsoever from this source. Twelve cities have no special garbage charges. Both utility taxes and garbage charges provide a means whereby all homeowners, regard-

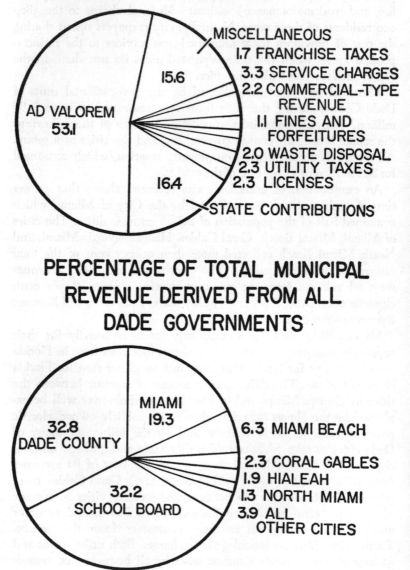

# SOURCES OF TOTAL MUNICIPAL REVENUE DERIVED BY ALL DADE GOVERNMENTS

MISCELLANEOUS

1.7 FRANCHISE TAXES

3.3 SERVICE CHARGES

2.2 COMMERCIAL-TYPE REVENUE

1.1 FINES AND FORFEITURES

2.0 WASTE DISPOSAL

2.3 UTILITY TAXES

2.3 LICENSES

15.6

AD VALOREM 53.1

16.4

STATE CONTRIBUTIONS

# PERCENTAGE OF TOTAL MUNICIPAL REVENUE DERIVED FROM ALL DADE GOVERNMENTS

MIAMI 19.3

32.8 DADE COUNTY

32.2 SCHOOL BOARD

6.3 MIAMI BEACH

2.3 CORAL GABLES

1.9 HIALEAH

1.3 NORTH MIAMI

3.9 ALL OTHER CITIES

less of their assessment, may be compelled to contribute to the support of municipal services.

The only apparent impact of metropolitan government on the revenues formerly collected by the cities has been fines and forfeitures. The total city revenue from this source has declined substantially, some $740,000 annually. The City of Miami alone accounts for the greatest part of the loss ($566,000). With the purchase of the bus lines by Metro,[4] the municipalities will sustain an additional annual loss of $216,000. A number of cities, however, have benefited financially by Metro's takeover of the traffic engineering function. In addition, Coral Gables has achieved a substantial savings as a result of the absorption by Metro of its 10 traffic policemen, a concession made by Metro in July, 1959, to win over Coral Gables to the Metro traffic code. The estimated annual savings to the municipalities from both traffic engineering and the Coral Gables arrangement is approximately $400,000. Metro and the Port Authority also contribute approximately $200,000 annually to the City of Miami toward the support of a joint publicity program.

The county is somewhat more dependent on property taxes (53 per cent) than are the cities as a whole (50 per cent). This can be explained by the existence of certain forms of municipal revenue that are wholly or partially unavailable to the county. These revenues are from cigarette tax rebates, utility taxes, and those business and occupational license fees that exceed the county rate or that affect businesses and occupations not covered by the county.[5] Most of the county's non-ad valorem sources of revenue, therefore, are much less than comparable sources for the cities.

As can be seen from the chart on page 191, the greater percentage of city expenditures (65 per cent) went for debt service (19), police (18), fire (10), waste removal (10), and street maintenance (8). On the other hand, county expenditures in the areas of debt service (4), police (10), fire (1.0), waste removal (5), and street maintenance (5), amounted to only 25 per cent. The small county figure can be explained by the fact that more than half of all county expenditures were made solely for area-wide functions such as health, hospitals, welfare, state courts, and mosquito control. Slightly more than $5 million of the total county budget of some

$55 million was expended exclusively for the support of the unincorporated areas.[6] The remainder went either for functions benefiting the entire county area or for functions benefiting the unincorporated area but paid for by fees from that area (waste removal and building permit charges).

Professor Reinhold P. Wolff has characterized the expenditures in the municipalities as property-oriented, with emphasis on services enhancing property values; those of the county as individual-oriented, with stress on services of a personal nature such as health and hospitals.[7] This division is rather interesting since property-oriented services are visible to the ordinary citizen while individual-oriented services, like hospitals, affect only those persons who are immediately concerned. Metro's largest single expenditure has been in the area of hospitals, although Metro's needs lie in both the individual and property-oriented categories.

## METHODS OF INCREASING REVENUE

The nub of the problem confronting Metro is how to raise sufficient revenues to care for expanding county-wide functions while at the same time providing improved municipal-type functions, as well as a few amenities, to the 380,000 residents in the unincorporated areas. To do this, Metro must find new sources of revenue. Some possible sources will be examined.

### Reassessment

One method provided by the charter for obtaining additional revenues and correcting "inequities" in property taxation was the requirement for mandatory reassessment of all real property by 1961. Metro's policy was to increase assessments from approximately 50 per cent of market value to 100 per cent of market value. Reassessment would add some 30,000 homeowners to the tax rolls, and increase significantly the tax return of the greater number of Dade property owners.[8] It was estimated that 100 per cent reassessment would increase the total net taxable value of real property in Dade County from about $2 billion to $4 billion. The overwhelmingly negative response by the voters on August 15, 1961,[9] to the reassessment pro-

## GOVERNMENT EXPENDITURES FOR ALL DADE GOVERNMENTS

| Function | All gov'ts Per cent | County Per cent | All Cities Per cent | Cities over 100,-000 Per cent | Cities 25,-001- 100,-000 Per cent | Cities 5,000 25,000 Per cent | Cities under 5,000 Per cent |
|---|---|---|---|---|---|---|---|
| Administration | 5.4 | 6.1 | 5.0 | 3.7 | 4.9 | 10.4 | 11.6 |
| Police | 14.4 | 9.7 | 18.0 | 18.4 | 16.4 | 18.7 | 26.7 |
| Fire | 6.0 | 1.0 | 9.8 | 12.1 | 7.4 | 8.2 | 3.1 |
| Legal | 2.5 | 4.7 ‡ | 0.8 | 0.9 | 0.6 | 1.2 | 1.2 |
| Streets | 6.6 | 4.8 | 7.9 | 6.3 | 1.6 | 7.8 | 6.3 |
| Traffic | 1.0 | 1.4 | 0.7 | 1.0 | 0.4 | 0.1 | * |
| Parks | 4.1 | 3.8 | 4.3 | 3.0 | 5.5 | 7.5 | 2.8 |
| Recreation | 2.0 | 0.4 | 3.3 | 1.7 | 5.3 | 5.0 | 1.3 |
| Library | 1.5 | — | 2.4 | 3.3 | 1.2 | 2.1 | 0.6 |
| Buildings | 1.8 | 2.3 | 1.4 | 0.1 † | 2.3 | 4.2 | 5.7 |
| Planning | 1.9 | 2.3 | 1.5 | 1.8 | 1.3 | 1.5 | 0.2 |
| Garbage | 7.8 | 4.7 | 10.1 | 8.7 | 10.5 | 15.1 | 15.9 |
| Lighting | 1.2 | — | 2.1 | 2.6 | 1.7 | 1.4 | 1.5 |
| Publicity | 1.3 | 0.2 | 2.1 | 2.0 | 2.7 | 0.5 | 0.8 |
| Debt service | 12.5 | 3.8 | 19.0 | 22.6 | 17.0 | 6.2 | 15.2 |
| Other functions | 8.9 | 5.2 | 11.6 | 11.8 | 12.2 | 10.1 | 7.1 |
| Areawide functions | 21.1 | 49.6 | —— | —— | —— | —— | —— |
| TOTAL | 100.0 | 100.0 | 100.0 | 100.0 | 100.0 | 100.0 | 100.0 |

* Less than 0.1%
† An additional 1.1% is included in departmental budgets
‡ Three-fifths of this item is for state and county courts; two-fifths for Metropolitan courts

posal has pretty well eliminated the possibility of any such radical program of reassessment in the near future. It should be noted that the term reassessment is now euphemistically referred to as equalization and that a somewhat vague plan of equalization was being proposed in the early part of 1962. However, there seems little doubt that any reassessment program, no matter by what name it is called, will have to be both realistic and gradual.

Millage Increase

A second method of obtaining additional revenue would be to increase the millage rate, but here too we run into the low tolerance point of the lower socio-economic groups. Assuming that it would be possible to bring about a substantial gain in revenue from real property taxes, service charges, user taxes, and the like, such additional amounts would be insufficient to support both area-wide services for the county and municipal-type services for the unincorporated areas.

Permissive State Legislation

Because Metro can levy only those taxes authorized by general law,[10] a third possibility would be to persuade the state legislature to provide Metro with the additional authority to levy a gasoline or sales tax or to permit Metro to retain the $2 million cigarette rebate which in 1962 was still reverting to the state treasury. Earlier in 1959 Metro had requested the state legislature to pass a permissive one-cent gasoline tax as well as a law to permit Dade County to retain the tax rebate on cigarette sales in the unincorporated areas. An estimated $5.5 million would have accrued to the county if both these measures had been passed. However, the gasoline tax proposal died in committee and the cigarette tax rebate request was withdrawn at the behest of the Metro commission.[11] There is little hope in the immediate future that Dade's fiscal problems will be solved by state legislation.[12]

Special Districts

The creation of special tax districts is another possible solution.[13] This alternative would provide a means whereby the residents of the unincorporated areas could be taxed for particular services rendered to them. Since the question of creating special tax districts is of extreme importance, it is dealt with in detail in the following pages.

The home rule charter, by authority granted by the home rule amendment, provides in section 1.01 A(11) that the county may "establish . . . special purpose districts . . . for police and fire protection, recreation activities . . . and other essential facilities and services." The money for such facilities and services "shall be provided by service charges, special assessments, or general tax levies within such districts only."

While the home rule amendment and the home rule charter explicitly permit Metro to establish special purpose districts, a Florida Supreme Court ruling [14] on the general nature of such districts raises doubt as to their utility. The court held that assessments for special benefits must be direct, proximate, and capable of being computed according to the special benefits derived by the assessed property. In the case in dispute, a special tax was to be levied annually on all real property within the special district, including homesteads, on the basis of the assessed valuation of each property. The proceeds from the tax were to be used to pave and repair streets and provide street lighting within the particular district. Maintenance and repair of the improvements were to be financed the same way. A majority of the homeowners involved had approved the tax in a referendum. However, the court held that the so-called assessment was, in fact, a device to avoid homestead exemption (which applies only to ad valorem taxes), since it could not be established that the properties would benefit in proportion to their assessed valuation. The assessment was held to be an ad valorem tax and, consequently, null and void.

It seems reasonable to infer from the court's ruling that charges levied within special districts must be computed on the basis of a standard or measure, such as the front footage of each property, to equate it with direct benefits to the property. In previous cases the Florida courts had held that a special tax could not be assessed to collect garbage, waste, and trash or to create a county health unit. [15] In addition, the courts have held that need or justification for a proposed improvement must be established.

Although aware of these difficulties, Metro in 1958 attempted to cope with the problems of special districts by the enactment of appropriate ordinances. However, because of the requirements of the bonding houses, a Metropolitan Special Taxing District Ordinance repealing the 1958 ordinances [16] was enacted in February, 1960. [17] Under the provisions of the new ordinance appropriate "local improvements" for water mains, sanitary sewers, storm sewers, streets, side-walks, and beach erosion controls might be financed by special assessments against the particular property benefited. Combined with the special assessment features for "local improvements" is the additional authorization to create special taxing districts for the purpose of acquiring and constructing water and sewerage systems, storm sewers, street and sidewalk improvements, police and fire protection, recreation facilities, street lighting, incinerators, beach erosion control, and such other facilities or services as the commission may deem essential.

Such special tax districts, as contemplated in the Metro ordinance, are predicated upon the fact that the entire district would benefit; consequently, the facilities and services provided may be financed by general taxes assessed against all the property within the district. A bond issue or the levy of a general tax in lieu of bonds would have to be approved by a majority of the property owners within the special tax district. In addition, service charges or special assessments on benefited property, or both, might also be utilized. The joining of these two revenue-producing features was intended to make it easier for Metro to utilize both actions simultaneously. Thus, for example, Metro might levy general taxes for building a sewerage system within a special taxing district and then provide for special assessments for tie-ins by the individual homesteads.

The nub of the legal problem is whether the Florida courts will permit the levy of a general tax within a special tax district for functions such as police, fire, and recreation. Special tax districts were created by the ordinance to bypass the limitations of financing improvements through special assessments only. The legal questions involve an interpretation of both the home rule amendment and the home rule charter.

Section 1(e) of the home rule amendment states that the home rule charter could provide a method for establishing special taxing districts and prescribing their jurisdiction and power.[18] Since the home rule charter is interpreted in the light of the constitutional amendment, the bond counsel felt that the courts would have no hesitation in upholding the County Commission's power to create special taxing districts for the purposes set forth in section 1.01 A(11) of the home rule charter.[19] However, section 1.01 A(11) of the charter specifies special purpose districts rather than special taxing districts—this distinction may create some legal difficulties. Although section 1.01 A(11) provides for the financing of such special purpose districts by service charges, special assessments, and general tax levies within the districts, special purpose districts have normally been associated with special assessments, not general tax levies. And although the home rule amendment gave the Charter Board the right to create special taxing districts, the latter category is nowhere mentioned in the home rule charter unless we are to imply that the power to create new municipalities under section 5.05 of the charter also includes the right to create special taxing districts. However, it would appear from a reading of section 5.05 [20] that the charter refers to municipalities similar to the existing municipalities in Dade County rather than to any type of special districts.[21]

The Florida courts may interpret the powers of the special taxing district to be the same as those of the special purpose district. The real problem is whether the courts will allow a general tax levy to be imposed on the special tax district, or will insist that such a tax district be treated like special purpose districts, which in the municipalities, at least, are financed by special assessments.

### Annexation and Incorporation

The revenue potential of the county as a whole may be increased by annexation or incorporation. Incorporation of the now unincorporated areas could make available to these areas the following new sources of non–ad valorem revenue: cigarette tax, $1,900,000; 10 per cent utility tax, $3,150,000; business licenses, $1,400,000; total, $6,450,000. This sum represents a total per capita yield for the residents of the unincorporated areas of $18.43—a figure lower than the per capita revenue of all but one of the 26 cities. However, it might still act as an incentive for either annexation or incorporation by the residents of the unincorporated areas.

*The Lakewood Plan:* An incorporation method which purportedly would allow the residents of the unincorporated areas to eat their cake and have it too is the so-called Lakewood Plan. The home rule charter requires that the creation of one or more cities from the unincorporated areas must be approved by a majority of electors voting and residing within the proposed boundaries of the new city. Thus, the residents of the unincorporated areas would have to be induced to incorporate. They also would have to be convinced that in most cases they could support a new municipality to a substantial degree from non–ad valorem taxes, i.e., cigarette, utility, occupation, and license taxes.

This is where the Lakewood Plan, or at least a modified version of it, comes into the picture. For a city to create a completely new administrative plant would normally not only be costly but also would preclude the possibility of employing supervisors, experts, and technicians of high caliber. Under the Lakewood Plan, however, the residents, through their municipal councils, could determine the nature and quality of the services they desired and Metro, utilizing its facilities and personnel, could contract to provide such services at the lower unit cost of the larger county entity. As of 1962 no section of the unincorporated area had succumbed to the charms of this plan.

*Induced Annexation:* Another possible solution, recommended by the first county manager [22] but never seriously considered by the commission, would indirectly bring about a merger of the unincorporated areas with adjacent neighboring cities. Under this scheme the county, pursuant to its power under the home rule charter, would set minimum standards for services for both unincorporated and incorporated areas. Metro would impose a general ad valorem county tax which would be sufficiently high to pay the costs of services in the unincorporated areas as well as provide a substantial surplus. This surplus would allow Metro to grant a rebate, on the basis of a prearranged formula, to each municipality meeting minimum service standards. Rather than levy taxes of their own, the cities would use the rebated county taxes to finance services and facilities. If this plan resulted in a heavy tax burden for the residents of the unincorporated areas, they might be induced to merge with neighboring municipalities.

Some of the difficulties of the county manager's plan would be: (1) the question of the legality of the rebate provisions; (2) the means by which the commission could be compelled to get tough with the unincorporated residents (who constitute 38 per cent of Dade's population), particularly if these groups organized to fight the plan; and (3) the methods by which the unincorporated areas could be persuaded to annex to adjacent municipalities.[23] It should be remembered that Section 5.04 B of the home rule charter requires the approval of the majority of electors voting and residing within the area to be annexed. The requirement does not apply to unincorporated areas of 250 electors or less. It is hardly feasible, however, to foster the annexation of the unincorporated areas by hundreds of separate actions.

There are, nevertheless, some possible advantages to the rebate plan. First, taxes would be made more nearly equal for city and county residents. Second, if the unincorporated areas were annexed to the cities, Dade County would be freed from providing municipal-type services to the unincorporated areas and instead could concentrate on the county-wide problems of planning, transportation, traffic, roads, parks, welfare, health, and hospitals. Whether Metro might eventually take on such other functions as fire and police protection would depend, not so much on its legal powers, as on the needs and development of the county.

As of early 1962 Metro was surviving on basically the same county tax structure that existed before the creation of the new metropolitan government. Yet Metro was able to meet a budget increase from $45 million in 1958 to approximately $60 million in 1961. This was accomplished through several means: a revenue program which included a 2.15 millage increase, a policy of gradual or creeping reassessment, the employment of funds borrowed prior to Metro, and increments in aggregate taxes due to the normal growth of the area.

There have been but a few scattered efforts to employ other methods of financing. For example, only one special tax district for street lights was approved. A long drawn-out effort to establish a special tax district for sewerage for the motel area failed because of the opposition of the relatively small number of homeowners residing in the area. Attempts at annexation have been confined primarily to the squaring of boundaries of a few municipalities. Enthusiasm for incorporation by residents of a southwest section waned when they discovered that they could not create a municipality which could survive purely on non–ad valorem taxes. Dade County's metropolitan government is still confronted with the dilemma of having to use its pre-Metro tax structure to provide area-wide services to the county and municipal-type services to the unincorporated areas.

# 18

# Leadership

DURING METRO'S APPROXIMATELY five years of existence, it has been plagued by the problem of inadequate leadership.

## LACK OF CIVIC LEADERSHIP

Informed observers blame Metro's slow start and bungling infancy chiefly on the dearth of cohesive community leadership in the Greater Miami area. The question has been raised whether Miami's leaders may not have been more successful as obstetricians than they have been as pediatricians.

Since the advent of the new metropolitan government, the alignment of businessmen, newspapers, League of Women Voters, professionals, and college professors which was successful in promoting the home rule charter has functioned only when Metro was directly under attack. These groups allegedly failed to assume the responsibility for providing the new government with an action program, creating public support for such a program, and influencing the County Commission to enact appropriate legislation.

Dade County, according to some observers, lacks both strong political leaders and aggressive civic organizations. Dennis O'Harrow, executive director of the American Society of Planning Officials, in a report on planning for metropolitan Dade County concluded that "in Dade County there is no clear and apparent group of leaders as there is in most cities and metropolitan areas. There is nothing to correspond with . . . any of the numerous . . . strong leadership and power groups that are found in nearly every city." [1]

Mr. Campbell also emphasized the need for support of community leaders. His outlook was summed up by a city manager in Robert Wood's *Suburbia:* "God bless all civic associations. They are the city manager's ward machines." [2]

Until the summer of 1959 no such civic action organization was created for Dade County despite the urging of the county manager and others.[3] The do-gooders, the intellectuals, and the professionals in social work and other fields, who might have sparked such a movement, displayed no initiative whatsoever in this direction.

Furthermore, the significant position of the *Miami Herald* in the pro-Metro alliance was weakened by the ultra-consolidationist position of the newspaper and its associate editor, John D. Pennekamp. However, both the area newspapers, the *Herald* and the *News,* as well as the League of Women Voters, fought the frenetic efforts of the localists to weaken Metro. Without the guidance of the Dade County Research Foundation, which had been allowed to lapse, the League of Women Voters was unable to initiate action. Last, the professors were busy with their teaching and research at the University of Miami.

The failure to establish a good-government group until the summer of 1959 may be attributed to the complacency of the pro-Metro forces, who apparently felt no need for such a group.

In May, 1959, County Manager Campbell was quoted as saying that Dade County's 22-month-old experiment in metropolitan government was sure of survival.[4] However, the manager expressed uncertainty as to his own position, because he alleged that the leaders responsible for creating Metro had allowed the experiment to shift for itself. Campbell explained that almost every community has a few pace-setting civic organizations "backed by the 'fat cat interests' which look after things" [5] and that until this was evidenced in Miami, he, himself, could not provide the necessary leadership. Mr. Campbell had previously met with community leaders who were seeking to resurrect the Dade County Research Foundation, or to create a similar organization.

The events of the day following Mr. Campbell's statement brought renewed hope of organized community support. Robert M. Morgan, former president of the Dade County Research Foundation, announced that he would ask about 100 of Dade's prominent businessmen to meet with him for the purpose of re-establishing the Research Foundation. The organization, he believed, would require a minimum of $30,000 a year, which the business leaders would have to contribute. The money would hardly be a stumbling block if the businessmen were truly convinced of the critical need for such a private research group to help bolster metropolitan government. Such financial backing did not materialize, however.

Subsequently the Miami-Dade Chamber of Commerce, recognizing the need for organized Metro support, created the Government Research Council. The stated objectives of the council were to study and analyze matters pertaining to government affairs, draw conclusions from their analysis, propose public policies, and seek acceptance of these policies by the government agencies involved and by the public. The council also served as an advisory committee to the Board of Directors of the chamber.

The Government Research Council made its public debut in the summer of 1959 by opposing the holding of a referendum to abolish the City of Miami. Immediately thereafter it challenged the attempts to amend the home rule charter which were intended to change the size and method of electing the County Commission and restore the offices of sheriff and tax assessor to elective status. Council brochures analyzing the amendments and urging a negative vote in the interest of Metro's future were distributed to the members of the chamber. Spokesmen for the council appeared on local television programs to debate the issues of the proposed amendments; and the council even utilized television for paid political announcements. In general, the council openly assumed the position of leadership in the battle against the amendments. In 1962 the Government Research Council was the only organization continuously functioning among Dade County businessmen that was concerned exclusively with the broad governmental problems of Greater Miami.[6] (The council had assumed an important leadership role in the expressway bond issue in 1960[7] and in the McLeod amendment campaign in 1961.[8])

There were those who hoped that the Research Council might provide a vehicle to promote the businessman's expectations for

Metro as well as meet the county manager's need for support. What the business and professional men expected from the development of Metro, what kind of image they had of Metro, and what their views were of metropolitan leadership are best shown by some preliminary findings obtained from a leadership questionnaire circulated toward the end of 1959.[9]

Most of Miami's leaders, like the founding fathers of Miami's metropolitan government, held a decidedly "federal image" of Metro. Many also agreed that the county government had improved considerably since pre-Metro days and they anticipated a number of basic reforms. Foremost among the anticipated reforms were an end to duplication in administration, lower taxes, improved government services, and a more responsive and responsible government. The "leaders" recommended that Metro give priority to such vital matters as traffic relief, county-wide planning, coordinated zoning, equalization of assessments, sewage disposal, county police protection, airport development, highway safety, and unification of transportation facilities. They were generally indifferent to such issues as Interama, recreation, urban renewal, and county-wide fire prevention and control.

The organizations and persons deemed by the respondents to be most influential in affecting Metro policies were as expected. Named most frequently were the Miami-Dade Chamber of Commerce (108 times); the Dade League of Municipalities (41); the Miami Herald (40); and the Miami News (22).[10] So far as influential individuals were concerned, County Manager Campbell and Associate Editor John D. Pennekamp led the list.[11]

County Manager Campbell, who headed the list, was criticized by a number of the respondents for "lack of leadership," "poor administrative ability," "poor personality traits," and "poor public relations." On the other hand, he was also commended by others for "trying to do a good job, although hampered by an opposing County Commission"; for "courage" and "integrity"; for making a good record as county manager; and for creating an effective administrative organization. The different views of Mr. Campbell may be explained in part by the interviewee's belief as to whether or not it was the responsibility of the county manager to provide strong political leadership.

## POLITICAL LEADERS: THE ROLE OF THE MANAGER

In the absence of a two-party system to dramatize Miami's needs and in the absence of any aggressive business elite to provide continuous leadership, more and more stress is being placed on the need for a strong political leader who can rally the people. Some persons would bestow such a role upon the county manager and were deeply disappointed that Mr. Campbell failed to provide the expected political leadership. It was ironic that Mr. Campbell was damned by the very persons who consistently heralded the office of county manager as a "nonpolitical" position.

Campbell himself came to question the nonpolitical role of the county manager's office. The "political" environment of Miami led him to the rather startling conclusion that "it might have been better to have the county manager elected." [12] He believed Metro would progress far more rapidly if the county manager had 100,000 solid votes behind him. According to Mr. Campbell, the major problem, if the manager were to be elected, would be to induce qualified administrators to run for an office that would be reduced in both professional prestige and security. [13]

Although Campbell was being criticized for inept leadership, there was little possibility of his being fired as long as the *Herald* supported him. A change in the newspaper's attitude toward Mr. Campbell was foreshadowed by a *Herald* feature story on October 14, 1960, which reported that Mr. Campbell was expected to resign in January, 1961. [14] According to a *Miami News* story of the same evening, however, Mr. Campbell denied the report of his resignation and maintained that the story was a deliberate concoction of the *Herald* reporter who had interviewed him. The *News* also reported that Don Petit, Metro administrative analyst, who had been present at the interview, affirmed Campbell's denial of the *Herald's* story. Mr. Petit quoted the *Herald* reporter as stating: "I have been instructed to write a story saying that you [Campbell] are going to resign." [15]

The Government Research Council of the Miami-Dade Chamber of Commerce, in midsummer 1960, prevailed upon the County Commissioners to declare a truce with Mr. Campbell until January 3, 1961. There was, however, no understanding—tacit or otherwise—

that Mr. Campbell would resign by that date. It was the chamber's intention that the future relations between the County Commission and the county manager be resolved after the seating of the new commission in January, 1961.

On October 15, 1960, the *Herald* editorially declared:

. . . Neither arm of the manager-commission system has functioned well: the Commission hasn't legislated and the manager hasn't managed.

It is no secret that the county has been marking time for weeks and even months; that no major programs are getting basic attention, and that local government is on a stand-by basis.

What we are awaiting, evidently, is the seating of new Commission members in January, Mr. Campbell has indicated that at that time he will give the Commission an opportunity to accept his resignation.

That this relationship has not improved and that a caretaker atmosphere prevails at the County Courthouse is no fault of the Metro concept. It can work: it has worked in important details of executive reorganization which are much to Mr. Campbell's credit.

But it is not going to work smoothly under the stresses and strains of clashing personalities and mutual lack of confidence.

Let's quit pretending that it does.

The sooner this situation is remedied by competent prescription the better it will be for metropolitan government in Dade County. Mr. Campbell's gesture offers that opportunity.[16]

The same day that the editorial appeared, the *Herald* carried a news story that Mr. Campbell was not expected to last as county manager until January 3. A *Herald* story the week of October 17 reported that the Metro manager had put his house up for sale. Regardless of the validity of the *Herald's* report of Mr. Campbell's resignation or of the validity of Mr. Campbell's repeated denials, it appeared by late December that the *Herald's* "kiss of death" would lead to the manager's dismissal. Campbell was fired in February, 1961, with only one member of the 13-man commission dissenting.

Mr. Campbell, as the first county manager of the new metropolitan government, was faced with a range of problems—administrative, legal, and psychological—of truly Herculean proportions. At the end of the three and one-half years in which he was manager, Metro had emerged victorious in all the attempts to amend the home rule charter, in most of its legal battles,[17] and in many of its encounters with obstructionists, both inside and outside the government. "Hump" Campbell subscribed to the classical view of council-manager government—the manager as administrator and the council as policy-maker. He believed it was his job to carry out the ordinances that others might prevail upon the commission to enact. Mr. Campbell and his staff did assume leadership, however, in constructing and reconstructing the administrative structure of Dade County. Different periods in the evolution of a government call for different types of leaders and Metro may have been fortunate in having a technician as its first manager. Mr. O. W. Campbell deserves a significant part of the credit for the early accomplishments of Metro, which provided a solid base on which Metro could build.

On April 6, 1961, the Commission named Irving C. McNayr, former city manager of Columbia, South Carolina, to succeed Mr. Campbell. The vote was 12 to 1, providing Mr. McNayr much firmer support than Mr. Campbell ever had. Since assuming the position of county manager, McNayr has conferred frequently with civic leaders, neighborhood citizens' groups, municipal officials, and the press. He misses no opportunity to appear on radio and television to explain Dade's metropolitan government and program. He has also instituted a weekly news conference with the press, radio, and television.

McNayr projects an image of a soft-spoken, articulate, reasonable, and responsible official. He exudes a sense of fairness that seems to imply there is no reason why decent and well-meaning persons, regardless of their differences, should not be able to reach a reasonable settlement. McNayr has been critical of those who would have Metro move too rapidly and he stresses evolution rather than revolution or cataclysmic change. He has constantly spoken of the need for cooperation between Metro and the municipalities, and there is no doubt that he means it. The philosophy of the manager as well as his personality seem to have reassured many municipal officials.

Most Dade voters (92 per cent) polled during the battle over the McLeod amendment expressed either a favorable or a neutral impression of McNayr, who had been county manager for close to five months at this time. The most frequently mentioned reason for the approval of Mr. McNayr was that "McNayr was a good man trying to do a good job." Of the 84 persons who expressed this sentiment,

49 opposed the McLeod amendment, 26 favored the amendment, and 9 were uncertain. Since these responses were elicited during a period of intense feeling for and against the McLeod amendment, at a time when Mr. McNayr was actively campaigning against the amendment, the public attitude toward Mr. McNayr seemed remarkable.

Shortly after the defeat of the McLeod amendment, the chairman of the County Commission condemned the county manager for speaking out on the question of the need for a city-county building which, the chairman alleged, was a policy matter to be determined by the commission. McNayr stated that he could not be expected to refrain from commenting on such matters and his stand was affirmed.

The strong position of the county manager is due to favorable public reaction, support of the newspapers and the Miami-Dade Chamber of Commerce, and the belief of city officials in his practical-mindedness. Nevertheless, the manager has antagonized certain groups by his firing of administrative personnel, by his active role in both the McLeod amendment and the reassessment referendum campaigns, and by his clash with organized labor during the bus strike. The manager must guard against alienating too large a segment of the community, lest he destroy his utility.

## POLITICAL LEADERS: THE COUNTY COMMISSIONERS

Rather than turn to the manager for political leadership, it has been suggested that a member or members of the Metro Commission provide such leadership.

Under the council-manager form of government, elected commissioners, who usually serve on a part-time basis, determine the broad policies that are carried out by a full-time professional administrator. But the manager and his staff "have a virtual monopoly of vital intelligence and technical competence" which leaves no alternative to the commission but to turn to these professionals for knowledge and guidance. Furthermore, "the creation of a climate of support, acceptance or sometimes hostility or indifference, has become (whether we like it or not) a function of the administrator." [18]

Manager leadership is further reinforced by the failure of council-

men to fulfill their roles as policy-makers. A study made at Michigan
State University on leadership in council-manager cities indicates
that councilmen who become involved in controversial issues frequently jeopardize their political careers.[19] It can be concluded, somewhat cynically, that a commissioner is far better off if he is less a
leader and more a follower. Should a commissioner become a community leader, he does so at the risk of antagonizing his fellow
commissioners. As commissioners become more experienced, they are
likely to try to insure their future by avoiding the hazards of political
leadership.

Another factor tending to support the leadership role of the county
manager in Greater Miami is V. O. Key's "law of institutional compensation." Professor Key suspects that the "law" accounts for the
rise in Florida of substitute stabilizing mechanisms to counteract the
divisiveness of Florida politics. On the state level the development
of the cabinet system is an excellent example of a stabilizing influence, and on the county level the managerial form of government
tends to serve a similar purpose. This is not to preclude the possibility of any other substitute mechanism, but in Miami's amorphous
political setting the manager seems to be in a better position to provide continuity of government than an elected leader. The election
by the voters of a county commission chairman, under a council-
manager form of government, might under some conditions have
merit. This observer believes, however, that for Miami in 1962 such
a move would be considered by the county manager as a threat to his
authority and thus tend to create discord.

The question is, then: *Can council-manager government provide
the leadership needed to meet the challenge of the sixties?*

The consensus of scholars in the field of municipal government is
that the manager in the small and medium-sized city, where the emphasis is on functions of a housekeeping nature, has been on the
whole successful. Customarily, the manager, in undertaking to perform his duties in the most efficient and economical fashion, seeks
the support of the community by working in a rather oblique manner through the business-civic type organization. However, in the
large city or metropolitan area the council-manager institution is
confronted by a far greater challenge. Leadership in such areas must
be forthright, imaginative, continuing, and "popular." The manager

in the metropolitan area must be more resourceful than his counter-
part in the small municipality. He must, in fact, assume the role
of a Don Quixote as well as that of a Sancho Panza.

To what extent can a county manager engage in "politics" even if,
like McNayr, he is a fine blend of minister, diplomat, and teacher?
In an article published early in 1961, before McNayr came to Miami,
this observer suggested that the danger in Greater Miami was drift
and anarchy—not managerial despotism. The absence of a two-party
system and strongly organized labor or ethnic groups to dramatize
Greater Miami's needs, and the lack of an aggressive business elite
to provide continuous leadership created the need for a strong political leader. The conclusion was:

In the final analysis, the manager's job in the complex affairs of
tomorrow will probably not be vastly different from that of the elected
executive. Like the mayor, he too must court favor with his council,
and, like the mayor, he can be far more effective if he has a strong following of civic groups, newspapers, and the public to support him. To be
sure, the appointive manager can always be fired; but, if he serves the
community as prime mover and star salesman of forceful governmental
action, he will build up his own clientele—a clientele which the council
will antagonize only at its peril. In [Greater] Miami it would appear
that such a leadership role must soon be accepted by the manager or
there will in time be an attempt to supplement the present system with
a popularly elected chairman or president of the council. There is reason
to believe that the strong tradition of city-manager government in Miami,
the local middle class admiration of the expert, and the non-party atmosphere of local and state government will influence the county manager, with the support of existing "good government" groups, to assume
the leadership initiative which is so vital to the success of Miami's metropolitan experiment.[20]

Mr. McNayr seems to have fulfilled this prophecy, although it
should be remembered that he has been in Greater Miami for a
relatively short period, and that he has become embroiled in some
politically dangerous battles such as the McLeod amendment campaign in the fall of 1961 and the bus strike in early 1962.

After actively campaigning against the proposed Crandon amendments in the summer of 1962, the county manager was confronted
by a group of county commissioners determined to prevent him from

speaking out in the future on any proposals appearing on the ballot to amend the home rule charter. The clash between the manager and the commissioners took place on August 24, 1962, just three days after Dade's electorate cast its vote on the Crandon amendments. (Only 16.6 per cent of the registered voters turned out at the polls.) Three of the Crandon proposals were rejected; two were approved by a narrow margin. The two amendments that passed limited the county manager's powers but did not involve either the powers of Metro or its relations with the municipalities. One of the amendments required that the nomination of major department heads by the manager be approved by the county commission, thus narrowing the manager's power over appointments. The other amendment required positive approval by the commission of all managerial orders relating to departmental reorganization; previously such orders went into effect as long as they were not formally disapproved by the commission.

County Manager Irving C. McNayr interpreted the passage of these amendments as a reflection of dissatisfaction with his work on the part of the voters. Actually, according to a University of Miami poll taken just before the special election, a strong majority of those interviewed (70 per cent) were neutral or favorable to Mr. McNayr. The poll also revealed, however, that the interviewees supported the limitations upon the manager's powers, presumably because of a belief in the democratic process of checks and balances.

After the Crandon amendment election, the county manager announced that he would request a vote of confidence from the county commission. A *Herald* front page headline of August 23 proclaimed "McNayr Assured of Metro Confidence Vote." As predicted, the commission at 9 A.M. on August 24 gave McNayr a unanimous vote of confidence. The auspicious beginning of the meeting belied the events that were to follow later that day. Immediately after the vote of confidence, County Commissioner Hughlan Long offered a resolution which required the county manager to refrain from campaigning on any issue that was to appear on the ballot. The resolution was withdrawn, however, and the commission met later in the day with the manager at an informal session to discuss the resolution and its ramifications. Mr. McNayr insisted that the commission make known its position on the Long proposal and warned that unless the commission voted it down, he would tender his resignation to be effective in 30 days. Commissioner Harold Spaet then made a motion to put the commission in formal session. The motion was passed by a vote of 6 to 5, whereupon the 5 dissenters walked out of the meeting leaving the commission without the required 7-man quorum. Mr. McNayr then announced his resignation.

Pandemonium broke loose in Greater Miami. Newspaper editorials, commentaries, letters to the editor, and even news items excoriated the 5 commissioners who had participated in the walkout. All kinds of proposals to amend the charter were offered as panaceas for Metro's latest crisis. Tremendous pressure was brought to bear upon Mr. McNayr to reconsider his resignation but he firmly insisted that his decision to resign was irrevocable.

What factors influenced Mr. McNayr to resign? The manager was still somewhat sensitive about the passage of the two Crandon amendments. He also believed apparently that he would have a great deal of difficulty working with the newly constituted commission (6 of the 13 commissioners, three of whom were newcomers, were elected in May, 1962). There is no question that Mr. McNayr could subsequently have secured the defeat of the Long proposal by a vote of at least 8 to 5. (Two of the manager's supporters were out of town at the time of the August 24 meeting.) Mr. McNayr contended that the 5 commissioners who walked out of the meeting constituted a bloc which would have continually harassed him. There is a good possibility that some of the 5 commissioners might have harassed Mr. McNayr but there is little or no evidence to support the manager's contention of a 5-man bloc. Three of the 5 commissioners were first sworn in on July 31, 1962; the other two were strong individualists.

Just as everyone despaired of dissuading the county manager from withdrawing his resignation, he suddenly announced that he would reconsider. Mr. McNayr declared that he was moved to make this announcement because of the suggestion from many sources that "he was quitting under fire and letting down thousands of citizens who had fought long and hard to develop, keep and strengthen the home rule charter."

A special commission meeting was called by Chairman Alexander S. Gordon for August 31. Amid the glare of television lights and the hubbub of a fully packed house, Mr. McNayr officially withdrew his resignation. The issue that had led to Mr. McNayr's resignation was settled by a motion that the county manager be instructed to go forward with public statements in those areas in which the county commission had made a policy decision. The motion was unanimously carried. It was further agreed that the commission in the future would inform the manager of the majority's view on all proposed charter amendments.

Although Mr. McNayr is still Metro's most articulate spokesman, he may have to adopt a more cautious approach on those issues which tend to strongly divide the community. However, so long as he is able to capture the public's imagination and so long as an overwhelming balance of forces are in his favor, he will continue to be Metro's most important source of leadership and inspiration.

There is no doubt that an effective county manager must live dangerously yet cautiously. He must steer a delicate course between the Scylla of politics and the Charybdis of administrative nonpartisanship. Perhaps the most successful type of politics has been that which has robed itself in a nonpartisan or good-government mantle. ("It is politic for a politician to appear not as a politician when he engages in politics." [21]) If there are active pressures on the elective body and if the commission is a dynamically functioning group (not a submissive school-board type of legislative body), there is no reason to believe that the "political administrator" is incompatible with a democratic society.

# 19

# Metropolitan Miami in Perspective

WHAT WERE THE conditions—environmental and political—that made the experiment in metropolitan government in Dade County successful? Which, if any, experiences can be applied to other areas trying to form a metropolitan government? What are the fundamental problems that confronted Metropolitan Miami in 1962 that must be solved if metropolitan government is to succeed in Dade County?

Although Greater Miami has some unique characteristics, many other metropolitan areas are similar in size and are likewise confined to a single county. The problems confronting Miami in creating a metropolitan government were different from those of such complex and heterogeneous metropolitan areas as, for example, St. Louis and Cleveland. Large heterogeneous areas do not have the political and social cohesion characteristic of small- and medium-sized metropolitan areas, but they are, nevertheless, confronted by similar economic, ecological, and functional problems. And even though these giant metropolitan areas may at first drift into a patchwork kind of metropolitan government to meet their dilemmas, in time there will arise some demand for an overall plan to coordinate the activities of the many authorities, special districts, commissions, boards, and other local government units.

## THE MIAMI EXPERIENCE: A SUMMARY

Miami was able to create a metropolitan government with the very type of support that failed elsewhere in the nation because of a combination of characteristics peculiar to the area. Among the more important factors were the mobility of the population, the tourist atmosphere, the no-party system, the weak position of labor and minority groups, the vulnerable past of the central city, and the strong dependency of the population on the area-wide newspapers for political leadership.

In addition, Dade County's early success with consolidation of health, hospital, school, and Port Authority matters paved the way for greater public understanding of the necessity for more extensive political integration. The near victory in 1953 of a proposed merger of the City of Miami with Dade County convinced City of Miami officials that they could avoid total consolidation only by making some basic concessions. Thus, ironically, the initial steps to establish a metropolitan government stemmed from the efforts of the localists, who obtained a $50,000 allotment from the City of Miami to create the Metropolitan Miami Municipal (3M) Board. The 20-man Board, which included 8 members of the Dade League of Municipalities, was directed to draft "a plan for consolidation, merger, federation or reorganization of the municipal and county governments in Dade County." The 3M Board early achieved consensus on the basic principle of *federalism* for county-city relations.

Any attempt to reorganize the government structure of metropolitan Miami had to be approved by the Florida Legislature. The Dade County delegation to the state legislature, under the astute leadership of Senator R. ("Bunn") Gautier, induced the legislature to pass both the enabling resolution for the home rule amendment and the acts to create the first and second charter boards. The charter board acts provided, as was the intention of the Dade delegation, that funds be appropriated by the county to support charter board activities until such time as a home rule charter was adopted. The Dade delegation, which in these matters cooperated closely with the Miami-Dade Chamber of Commerce, the *Miami Herald,* the *Miami News,* and the League of Women Voters, was a highly significant force in providing the machinery needed to lay the foundation for metropolitan government.

The principal recommendations for establishing a metropolitan government were made by Public Administration Service in its report, *The Government of Metropolitan Miami.* The PAS recommendations served as guides for the 3M Board and the first and second charter boards. PAS consultants drafted the first version of the home rule charter and continued to consult with the charter board members until the final draft was completed. Not only did the consultants help to educate the members of the charter boards, the newspapers, and interested civic organizations, but their imprimatur was of great importance in molding public opinion. In effect, PAS put the "Good Housekeeping Seal of Approval" on Miami's experiment in metropolitan government.

The charter board members also had the respect of the community. The board was composed primarily of professional persons and owner-entrepreneurs who were neither second-line leaders nor ambassadors of special interests. At no time were they regarded by the public as representatives of either special economic groups or particular geographical areas. Indeed, nonpartisanship and *noblesse oblige* so permeated the thinking of the board members that they were able to transcend the provincialism of the areas in which they resided and the influence of the economic groups with which they were associated.

Other groups that helped to initiate and promote Metro were the Dade County Research Foundation, the Miami-Dade Chamber of Commerce, the Junior Chamber of Commerce, and the League of Women Voters. In opposition to metropolitan government were a majority of city officials and municipal employees, the Dade League of Municipalities, the beneficiaries of city contracts and purchases, most local chambers of commerce, a number of suburban newspapers, some civic organizations, and the less than legitimate business interests that had worked out a *modus vivendi* with the police and other officials of some municipalities.

Robert C. Wood, in his study *Suburbia: Its People and Their Politics* observes that metropolitan reform is usually espoused by a thin rank of ineffective "agitators"—editorial writers, planners, professors, civic association leaders, and others who rarely have the influence to sway public opinion. Professor Wood concludes that even the Miami reforms are surprising accomplishments for such "an ill-assorted collection of interests and personalities." [1]

The success achieved by these disparate groups must be attributed to the unique character of the Miami area, although the positive leadership forces, which in the final analysis put Metro across, should not be discounted. All things considered, it appears that some lessons in initiating a metropolitan reform movement can be learned from the Miami experience:

1. Bring together the moderate proponents and the ardent opponents of consolidation in a 3M type board.
2. Use the impartial expertise of a Public Administration Service type of organization and other professionals.
3. Appoint a charter board of prestigious civic leaders who are first-line leaders and not representatives of special interest groups.
4. Capitalize on the "good government" support of newspapers.
5. Use winning tags such as "home rule amendment" and "home rule charter."
6. Create a federal type of government as a compromise between localists and consolidationists.

## PERSPECTIVE

To what extent can the lessons learned from the Miami experience be applied to other metropolitan areas? Scott Greer in a study on metropolitics [2] observes that the metropolitan plans for Miami, St. Louis, and Cleveland were revolutions in that each plan was intended to bring about a radical change in the division of powers, rewards, and esteem. The revolutionary implications were probably less true for Miami than for the other two areas. The Miami situation was not so much a revolution as an attempt to have the formal political structure coincide more rationally with the informal community power structure.

In other metropolitan areas there were many centers of power or independent pyramids like labor, racial groups, political parties, giant corporate interests, and others, each with its sphere of influence but none with sufficient resources to exercise dominant influence over the major areas of policy. In Miami, aside from the office holders and municipal and county employees, there were no other strongly organized power groups to oppose the loose coalition of central city businessmen, area-wide newspapers, and "do-good" organizations that supported Metro. Similar coalitions have, of course, been found in every organized attempt to create metropolitan government. But elsewhere in the nation they invariably met with defeat because of the entrenched position of the countervailing groups who did not want to jettison the status quo for an unproved product. Ironically, it may be the lack of countervailing forces in Miami which has created the feeling of complacency within the coalition of businessmen, newspapers and "do-good" organizations. This complacent feeling has generally resulted in the coalition depending far more upon informal than on formal processes. Undoubtedly the absence of formalized action has at times been an advantage. The moment abstract concepts of good government become associated with special interests, the more do the good government goals become suspect.

Some political observers have at times expressed amazement at how little the average citizen knows of the particulars of metropolitan plans which are submitted for his approval. Yet, as Scott Greer notes, "Americans routinely make value judgments on public policies which they fail to understand in the most minimal sense." Only a relatively small number of Miami voters knew the provisions of the McLeod amendment, for example, but a large number voted for the amendment because of the belief that Metro was attempting to place an increased economic burden on their backs. The felt need (government by indignation, if you will) may be more meaningful than mere intellectual awareness. The majority of voters in the nation's metropolitan areas may be convinced that metropolitan government is an instrument for the well-to-do at the expense of the lower socioeconomic groups. There are some knowledgeable persons who feel that the people's intuition is not completely misguided.

The successful creation of Miami's metropolitan government cannot be ascribed to any crisis situation. Nor could Dade County be described as one of the nation's "governmentally most backward communities." [3] Health facilities, schools, hospitals, and the Port Authority had all been consolidated prior to Metro. Although the knowledgeable, the sensitive, and the reformers like to speak of unbearable conditions, the average citizen is made of sterner stuff. He is generally adjustable and has a high tolerance point. In Miami there was no empirical evidence to substantiate anything resembling a crisis. Indeed, one might say that there was less of a crisis in Greater Miami than in most metropolitan areas. At best, Dade's citizens may have been convinced that something had to be done to avert a future crisis which might result from Dade's population explosion. The leadership situation in Miami is also deserving of special attention. Miami leadership, as noted earlier, is a loose coalition of businessmen, newspapers, and civic groups. It has been suggested, however, that this group seek a wider membership base and a more formal organizational structure. Although there have been times when the absence of a strong leadership organization has been advantageous, Miami's loosely constituted coalition has not been able to provide the new metropolitan government with consistent support and continuous leadership. To be sure, the Government Research Council of the Miami-Dade Chamber of Commerce has manifested a fairly sober and realistic approach to many of Metro's problems and has been an important influence on Metro. But even though the council is composed of a number of responsible and capable persons, it is suspect by the very fact that it is under the roof of a particular interest group. An independent research organization with a broader base would have wider public support than the Research Council as presently constituted.

A closer relationship between Metro and the community "leaders" could also be achieved through other channels. Some observers, for example, believe that the University of Miami is in the position to foster an exclusive "civic club." University sponsored seminars (discussions and lectures by outstanding national experts) would bring Miami's problems to the fore and personally involve the "influentials" of the community. Invitations to the seminars would confer a mark of distinction upon those receiving them. In conjunction with these "informational" seminars there might also be "research seminars" led by reputable scholars.

If a broad-gauged leadership organization had existed in 1962 (where the members of the Crandon Committee and other community leaders could have met and exchanged views), this writer believes that the challenge posed by the Crandon Committee could have been avoided. The Crandon Committee proposals might have been compromised and settled by discussion within the group rather than by a special referendum election. The members of the Crandon Committee are honorable men who have made significant contributions to the community. One finds it difficult to ascribe their actions to purely economic motives, as implied by some of the committee's opponents. Indeed, if it were a question of a Marxist or Freudian explanation, this observer would be inclined to favor the latter. When the committee's dissatisfaction remained unresolved, the Crandon amendments through the *initiative process* were placed on the ballot. (Petitions for referenda, as previously observed, are not to be equated with the voice of the people.)

The recommendation for a new civic leadership group is not intended to either create or perpetuate any ruling oligarchy. A democratic society must encourage the formation of countervailing powers and, in time, countervailing groups in Miami may be expected to appear. In the interim period, however, a single civic fraternity by incorporating different leadership views would provide a more democratic consensus than that presently existing in Greater Miami. Such an organization might also contribute to the creation of a more stable political setting.

Another issue deserving special attention is the feasibility of a federal form of government as a solution to the complex problems of the modern metropolis. The significance of the federal formula in Miami can be appreciated only if we remember that it was through the combined efforts of the city-oriented officials, the federalists, and the ultra-consolidationists, a sort of political tossed salad, that a new metropolitan government ultimately emerged.

The federal principle may do violence to the theories of the "economy and efficiency" purists whose sole remedy for the problems arising from the proliferation of local government units is total consolidation. Yet the municipalities in Miami, as observed by Norton Long, "represent units of social capital that have taken a long time to build. They are, so to speak, going concerns and must not be lightly junked." He also remarked that the strong civic identification of the residents of a number of municipalities are precious assets "in an area which all too often seems rootless and lacking in dedicated citizenry." Professor Long concluded that it would be "plain folly to scrap these elements of solid good government for some theoretic, abstract game by putting the eggs in a single omelette." [4]

Federalism may be open to the charge that it is a tactical subterfuge deliberately lacking in clarity and tending to be all things to all people. Yet it is precisely because of these characteristics that federalism offers a partial solution in terms of both efficiency and human values. It combines, so to speak, some important features of both gargantua (the efficiency of a single consolidated government) and grass roots (the participation of small-town democracy).[5]

The federalism of the eighteenth century, "federalism emergent" as it has been characterized by Arthur W. MacMahon, placed primary emphasis upon the legal guarantees of exclusive powers among previously independent communities.[6] Early federalism was a device to give special protection to interests geographically based. Federalism of the twentieth century, "federalism mature," is predicated upon an already united community and shifts the emphasis from exclusive power to cooperative power.[7] Necessarily, modern federalism is informal and pragmatic by nature and it generally gives rise to enhanced cooperation, as well as competition, among the component units of the system.

According to Paul Ylvisaker, the geographical divisions of government should be designed as instruments to stimulate debate and transcend communities of interest among areal units. His criteria for sound intergovernmental relations include four things: a process of last resort to settle intergovernmental disputes and questions of jurisdiction; a process or processes of intergovernmental cooperation; a process by which the several governments may act separately and independently as well as in cooperation; and a process of organic change which can be neither dictated nor stopped by a minority of components.[8] The home rule amendment and the home rule charter would seem to embrace all four processes, or at least to make them possible.

Metro has reached its fifth birthday and the citizens of Greater Miami can look back with pride at its accomplishments and with relief at its survival. The struggle is not over; Metro will be confronted with more crises in the future. Neither the Greater Miami area nor its government has yet come of age. Yet the youthfulness which has plagued Miami has also been its greatest asset, for Miami, unlike most other metropolitan areas, is not shackled to the past.

The Miami metropolitan experiment has contributed to the maturity of the public and its officials. Municipal officials, in general, had had their fears of Metro quieted because of the experience of the past five years. They no longer fear the abolition of the cities by indirection. They also feel they can work with County Manager McNayr, who holds no dogmatic views regarding the division of powers between Metro and the municipalities. Mr. McNayr believes in coexistence and is enough of a pragmatist to realize that division of functions will depend on needs, resources, and talent, and not upon any doctrinaire philosophy. Indeed, Mr. McNayr represents the spirit of compromise that led to the successful creation of the nation's first metropolitan government.

Metro's biggest problem is in the area of finance. If Metro, under its present tax structure, attempts to improve and expand county-wide services, and at the same time improve municipal-type services for the unincorporated areas, it may be courting disaster. In the long run the energy and capability to cope with area-wide needs can be dissipated if the county becomes too absorbed in catering to the increased demands of the now well-urbanized unincorporated areas. Furthermore, city residents cannot be expected to blandly sit by and acquiesce in such expenditures. A community schism may develop between the incorporated and unincorporated areas—the signs have already begun to appear.

The needs of the unincorporated areas cannot be ignored, however. It is the responsibility of the Metro Commission, the county manager, and the county attorney, despite legal complications, to act upon this problem. These Metro officials will have to utilize existing revenue techniques, such as special districts, as well as improvise new techniques, if the financial ills of the metropolitan dilemma are to be solved.

Metro in 1962 is in a better position to progress than in any year since its inception. Certain pitfalls such as alienating the lower socio-economic groups or overextending itself in the unincorporated areas must be avoided. Despite a great many obstacles, Metro has made significant progress.

## APPENDIX A

# Metropolitan Dade County
# Population Increases*

| Area | 1950 | 1955 | 1960 | % Increase 1950–1960 |
|---|---|---|---|---|
| Metropolitan Dade County | 495,084 | 703,777 | 935,047 | 88.9 |
| Unincorporated Areas | 109,859 | 222,488 | 352,247 | 220.6 |
| By Municipalities: | | | | |
| Miami | 249,276 | 259,035 | 291,688 | 17.0 |
| Miami Beach | 46,282 | 50,891 | 63,145 | 36.4 |
| Hialeah | 19,676 | 43,135 | 66,972 | 240.4 |
| Coral Gables | 19,837 | 29,210 | 34,793 | 75.4 |
| North Miami | 10,734 | 23,463 | 28,708 | 167.4 |
| North Miami Beach | 2,129 | 12,161 | 21,405 | 905.4 |
| Miami Springs | 5,108 | 10,138 | 11,229 | 114.8 |
| South Miami | 4,809 | 7,600 | 9,846 | 104.7 |
| Opa-locka | 5,271 | 9,392 | 9,810 | 86.1 |
| Homestead | 4,573 | 6,848 | 9,152 | 100.1 |
| Miami Shores | 5,086 | 7,839 | 8,865 | 74.3 |
| West Miami | 4,043 | 5,158 | 5,296 | 31.0 |
| Florida City | 1,547 | 3,037 | 4,114 | 165.9 |
| Bay Harbor Islands | 296 | 1,716 | 3,249 | 997.6 |
| Surfside | 1,852 | 2,592 | 3,157 | 70.5 |
| Biscayne Park | 2,009 | 2,833 | 2,911 | 44.9 |
| Virginia Gardens | 235 | 1,554 | 2,159 | 818.7 |

* See U. S., Bureau of Census, *Census of the United States: 1950–1960, passim;* Special census of *Dade, Broward and Palm Beach Counties: 1955.*

|  |  |  |  | % In-crease 1950– |
|---|---|---|---|---|
| AREA | 1950 | 1955 | 1960 | 1960 |
| El Portal | 1,371 | 1,994 | 2,079 | 51.6 |
| North Bay Village | 198 | 1,249 | 2,006 | 913.1 |
| Bal Harbour | 224 | 334 | 727 | 224.6 |
| Sweetwater | 230 | 327 | 645 | 180.5 |
| Golden Beach | 156 | 249 | 413 | 164.7 |
| Hialeah Gardens |  | 188 | 172 | — |
| Medley | 106 | 132 | 112 | 5.9 |
| Pennsuco | 133 | 110 | 117 | −12.0 |
| Indian Creek | 44 | 56 | 60 | 36.4 |

# Membership of the County Commission and the City of Miami Commission, 1945–1962

| THE CITY OF MIAMI COMMISSION | THE COUNTY COMMISSION |
|---|---|
| *1943–1945*<br>Leonard K. Thomson, Mayor<br>J. A. Dunn<br>R. C. Gardner<br>Fred W. Hosea<br>C. H. Reeder | |
| *1945–1947*<br>Perrine Palmer, Jr., Mayor<br>J. A. Dunn<br>R. C. Gardner<br>Fred W. Hosea<br>Leonard K. Thomson | *1945–1948*<br>Charles H. Crandon, Chairman<br>Preston B. Bird<br>Val C. Cleary<br>N. P. Lowrey [2]<br>I. D. MacVicar [2]<br>Hugh Peters, Sr. |
| *1947–1949*<br>Robert L. Floyd, Mayor<br>William W. Charles<br>R. C. Gardner<br>Perrine Palmer, Jr.<br>H. Leslie Quigg | |
| *1949–1951*<br>William M. Wolfarth, Mayor<br>Louis Bandel<br>William W. Charles<br>Robert L. Floyd [1]<br>Cecil Kerby [1]<br>Perrine Palmer, Jr. | *1949–1952*<br>I. D. MacVicar, Chairman<br>Preston B. Bird<br>Hugh Peters, Sr.<br>Louis F. Snedigar [3]<br>Harold Turk [3]<br>Jesse H. Yarborough |

1. Floyd resigned in November, 1950, and Kerby was appointed in February, 1951, to complete the term of office.
2. Lowrey died while in office and was succeeded by MacVicar who was elected at a special election in 1946.
3. Snedigar died in December, 1951, and Harold Turk was appointed by the Governor in February, 1952, to complete the term of office.

THE CITY OF MIAMI COMMISSION
(Cont'd)
1951–1953
Chelsie J. Senerchia, Mayor
Robert H. Givens, Jr.
Perrine Palmer, Jr.
H. Leslie Quigg
William M. Wolfarth

THE COUNTY COMMISSION
(Cont'd)
1953–1956
I. D. MacVicar, Chairman
Jesse H. Yarborough, Chairman
Preston B. Bird
Hugh Peters, Sr.
Grant Stockdale

1953–1955
Abe Aronovitz, Mayor [4]
Randall N. Christmas
B. E. Hearn
H. Leslie Quigg
Chelsie J. Senerchia

1957–1958
Ralph A. Fossey, Chairman
Faris N. Cowart, Chairman
Charles F. Hall
Edwin Lee Mason
John B. McLeod

1955–1957
Randall N. Christmas, Mayor
George W. DuBreuil [4]
B. E. Hearn
James W. High
Otis W. Shiver

1957–1959
Robert K. High, Mayor
George W. DuBreuil
B. E. Hearn
James W. High [5]
Otis W. Shiver
Fred C. Davant [5]

1958–1960
Walter Weiss, Chairman
Ben C. McGahey, Chairman
Joseph A. Boyd, Jr.
Faris N. Cowart
Ralph A. Fossey
Alexander S. Gordon
Charles F. Hall
Robert M. Haverfield
Alexander Charles Kittel [6]
Edwin Lee Mason [6]
John B. McLeod
Arthur H. Patten, Jr.
Milton E. Thompson [7]

4. Aronovitz resigned from a four-year term of office in November, 1955, and DuBreuil was appointed to complete his term of office.
5. James W. High resigned in March, 1959, and Davant was appointed to complete the term of office.
6. Mason resigned in December, 1959, and Kittel was appointed to complete the term of office.
7. Thompson was elected to the County Commission on August 23, 1960, as a representative from Hialeah and sworn in on August 30, 1960. The City of Miami Beach elected Harold B. Spaet as its representative on November 22, 1960, but Mr. Spaet did not take office until January 3, 1961. Both of these cities qualified for representation on the commission as a result of the 1960 census.

THE CITY OF MIAMI COMMISSION
(*Cont'd*)
*1959–1961*
Robert K. High, Mayor
Henry L. Balaban
Joseph X. DuMond, Jr.
George W. DuBreuil
B. E. Hearn

*1961–1963*
Robert K. High, Mayor
Henry L. Balaban
Joseph X. DuMond, Jr.
David T. Kennedy
Alice C. Wainwright

THE COUNTY COMMISSION
(*Cont'd*)
*1961–1962*
Robert M. Haverfield, Chairman
Alexander S. Gordon, Chairman
James H. Allen [8]
Jack H. Beckwith [8]
Joseph A. Boyd, Jr.
Charles F. Hall [8]
Ben C. McGahey
Arthur H. Patten, Jr.
Frank O. Pruitt [8]
Harold B. Spaet [7,8]
Milton Thompson [8]
Walter Weiss
Winston W. Wynne [8]

*1962–1964*
Alexander S. Gordon, Chairman [9]
James H. Allen
Jack H. Beckwith
Joseph A. Boyd, Jr. [9]
Robert Brake [9]
Charles F. Hall
Hughlan Long [9]
Arthur H. Patten, Jr. [9]
Frank O. Pruitt
Tom Sasso [9]
Harold B. Spaet
Milton Thompson
Winston W. Wynne

8. The terms of office of Allen, Beckwith, Hall, Pruitt, Spaet, Thompson, and Wynne will end on the second Tuesday next succeeding the date of the second primary in 1964.
9. The terms of office of Boyd, Brake, Gordon, Long, Patten, and Sasso will end on the second Tuesday next succeeding the date of the second primary in 1966.

# APPENDIX C

# The Dade Delegations to
# the Florida Legislature, 1945–1961 [1]

| | 1945 | 1947 | 1948 | 1949 | 1951 | 1953 | 1955 | 1956 | 1957 | 1959 | 1961 |
|---|---|---|---|---|---|---|---|---|---|---|---|
| **SENATE** | | | | | | | | | | | |
| D. C. Coleman | X | X | | | | | | | | | |
| R. Bunn Gautier, Jr. | | | | X | X | X | X | X | X | | |
| Joe Eaton [2] | | | | | | | | | | X | |
| W. C. Herrell | | | | | | | | | | | X |
| **HOUSE** | | | | | | | | | | | |
| George S. Okell, Sr. | X | X | X | | | | | | | | |
| Richard Oelkers, Jr. [3] | X | X | X | X | | | | | | | |
| C. W. Peters | X | | | | | | | | | | |
| R. Bunn Gautier, Jr. | | X | X | | | | | | | | |
| William C. Lantaff | | X | X | X | | | | | | | |
| Grant Stockdale [3] | | | | X | | | | | | | |
| Dante B. Fascell | | | | | X | X | | | | | |
| Robert L. Floyd | | | | | X | | | | | | |
| John B. Orr, Jr. | | | | | X | | | | | | |
| W. C. Herrell | | | | | | | X | X | | | |
| George L. Hollahan, Jr. | | | | | | | | | X | X | X |
| David C. Eldredge | | | | | | | | | | | X |
| Carey Matthews | | | | | | | | | | | X |

1. 1948 and 1956 were the only even-numbered years during the period covered in which extraordinary sessions were held.
2. Joe Eaton resigned on September 30, 1959, but the office remained vacant until after the general election in November, 1960.
3. Richard Oelkers, Jr., died after the general election held in November, 1948. Grant Stockdale assumed office following a special election.

## APPENDIX D

## Election Statistics

### 1. Significant Election Returns *

a. May 25, 1948 —Amendment to the Florida Constitution consolidating Dade County, the City of Miami and other municipalities (county election only)—Defeated.

| | |
|---|---:|
| Total vote in Dade County | 51,334 |
| For | 23,513 |
| Against | 27,821 |

b. November 4, 1952 —Permissive state-wide home rule amendment (state-wide election)—Defeated.

| | |
|---|---:|
| Total vote in Florida | 407,858 |
| For | 175,117 |
| Against | 232,741 |
| Total vote in Dade County | 98,426 |
| For | 53,830 |
| Against | 44,596 |

c. June 9, 1953 —Referendum on the abolition of the City of Miami and transfer of its functions to the county (city election only)—Defeated.

| | |
|---|---:|
| Total vote in City of Miami | 54,292 |
| For | 26,692 |
| Against | 27,600 |

d. November 6, 1956 —Dade County Home Rule Amendment (state-wide election)—Adopted.

| | |
|---|---:|
| Total vote in Florida | 461,269 |
| For | 322,839 |
| Against | 138,430 |

---

* The state-wide election returns were gathered from *Report of the Secretary of State of the State of Florida, passim.* The statistics on the county and city elections were obtained from the Office of the Supervisor of Registration for Dade County, Florida.

Total vote in Dade County            121,049
For                                  86,612
Against                              34,437

e. May 21, 1957          —Home Rule Charter (county election only)
                         —Adopted.
Total vote in Dade County            87,024
For                                  44,404
Against                              42,620

f. September 30, 1958—Autonomy Amendment to the Home Rule
                         Charter (county election only)—Defeated.
Total vote in Dade County            124,313
For                                  48,893
Against                              74,420

g. November 3, 1959     —Home Rule Charter Amendment pertaining
                         to the election of the Sheriff (county election
                         only)—Defeated.
Total vote in Dade County            95,627
For                                  42,278
Against                              53,349

h. November 3, 1959     —Home Rule Charter Amendment pertaining
                         to the election of the Tax Assessor (county
                         election only)—Defeated.
Total vote in Dade County            92,697
For                                  38,781
Against                              53,916

i. November 3, 1959     —Home Rule Charter Amendments pertaining
                         to the size and method of electing the County
                         Commission (county elections only)
                         1. Five-man Commission to be elected on a
                         county-wide basis—Defeated.
Total vote in Dade County            85,633
For                                  15,687
Against                              69,946
                         2. Seven-man Commission to be elected on a
                         county-wide basis—Defeated.
Total vote in Dade County            81,066
For                                  10,865
Against                              70,201
                         3. Nine-man Commission to be elected on a
                         district basis—Defeated.
Total vote in Dade County            82,937
For                                  12,210
Against                              70,727

j. August 15, 1961       —Abolition of mandatory reassessment as re-
                         quired by home rule charter (county election
                         only)—Adopted.

|  |  |  |
|---|---|---|
| | Total vote in Dade County | 126,953 |
| | For | 115,026 |
| | Against | 11,297 |

k. October 17, 1961 — McLeod Amendment pertaining to autonomy, popular election of tax assessor and sheriff, and other drastic changes (county election only)—Defeated.

| | Total vote in Dade County | 202,267 |
|---|---|---|
| | For | 97,170 |
| | Against | 105,097 |

l. May 8, 1962 — Amendment to repeal the Metro ordinance authorizing the issuance of $9,000,000 transit system revenue bonds (county election only) —Defeated.

| | Total vote in Dade County | 129,662 |
|---|---|---|
| | For | 47,268 |
| | Against | 82,394 |

m. May 29, 1962 — Home Rule Charter Amendments pertaining to dual office holding, filing for office and competitive bidding (county election only)

1. Prohibition of dual office holding for county officials—Adopted.

| | Total vote in Dade County | 55,451 |
|---|---|---|
| | For | 49,168 |
| | Against | 6,283 |

2. Requirement for commission candidates to qualify for office within same period as other county offices—Adopted.

| | Total vote in Dade County | 57,519 |
|---|---|---|
| | For | 52,245 |
| | Against | 5,274 |

3. Requirement of competitive bidding for county transactions involving $1,000 or more—Adopted

| | Total vote in Dade County | 58,204 |
|---|---|---|
| | For | 53,371 |
| | Against | 4,833 |

n. August 21, 1962 — Home Rule Charter Amendments (county election only)

1. Divide the county into 9 districts and provide for the election of one commissioner from each district—Defeated.

| | Total vote in Dade County | 64,325 |
|---|---|---|
| | For | 29,415 |
| | Against | 34,910 |

2. Provide that appointment of major department heads by the county manager shall be subject to approval by the county commission—Adopted.

Total vote in Dade County          63,649
For                                32,845
Against                            30,804

3. Provide that no administrative order creating, merging, or combining departments shall become effective until approved by the county commission—Adopted.

Total vote in Dade County          63,124
For                                32,272
Against                            30,852

4. Create an independent Port Authority Board which shall have exclusive jurisdiction, power and control over Port Authority property, subject to approval of the annual budget by the county commission —Defeated.

Total vote in Dade County          63,330
For                                29,235
Against                            34,095

5. Establishment for each municipality having a population in excess of 2,500 of a Metropolitan-Municipal Court with jurisdiction to try offenses under county ordinances occurring within the boundaries of such municipality—Defeated.

Total vote in Dade County          63,838
For                                30,315
Against                            33,523

## 2. Voting Percentages by Assessed Residential Value *

| Residence Value Group ** | Unincorporated Area | City of Miami | Miami Beach & Adjacent Municipalities | Other Municipalities | All |
|---|---|---|---|---|---|
| HOME RULE AMENDMENT 1956 % FOR | | | | | |
| I | 78.1 | 79.1 | 63.0 | 63.8 | 69.8 |
| II | 72.9 | 76.7 | 65.4 | 72.2 | 73.2 |
| III | 73.1 | 73.9 | 64.2 | 69.7 | 72.1 |
| IV | 68.8 | 72.2 | 56.5 | 69.6 | 70.6 |
| All | 74.1 | 74.4 | 63.0 | 68.3 | 71.6 |
| CHARTER ADOPTION 1957 % FOR | | | | | |
| I | 62.0 | 69.7 | 46.6 | 67.2 | 56.6 |
| II | 48.4 | 63.4 | 37.1 | 40.2 | 52.1 |
| III | 46.0 | 54.6 | 33.2 | 40.2 | 48.4 |
| IV | 39.0 | 54.3 | 23.5 | 37.9 | 47.3 |
| All | 49.1 | 56.4 | 40.7 | 46.0 | 51.0 |
| AUTONOMY AMENDMENT 1958 % AGAINST | | | | | |
| I | 77.5 | 73.9 | 38.6 | 51.7 | 59.4 |
| II | 69.6 | 72.1 | 34.9 | 66.4 | 67.6 |
| III | 67.1 | 64.4 | 28.5 | 50.7 | 58.9 |
| IV | 56.0 | 62.8 | 23.9 | 44.6 | 55.2 |
| All | 66.0 | 65.8 | 34.7 | 52.8 | 59.9 |
| ELECTIVE SHERIFF 1959 % AGAINST | | | | | |
| I | 66.6 | 66.3 | 59.1 | 67.2 | 65.1 |
| II | 54.9 | 60.3 | 45.2 | 60.3 | 57.2 |
| III | 51.6 | 55.2 | 44.0 | 49.3 | 52.2 |
| IV | 42.8 | 54.3 | 35.2 | 44.2 | 49.4 |
| All | 55.8 | 56.9 | 52.6 | 55.6 | 55.9 |
| FIVE-MAN COMMISSION 1959 % AGAINST | | | | | |
| I | 87.9 | 85.0 | 82.9 | 87.5 | 86.2 |
| II | 83.1 | 81.9 | 76.2 | 86.2 | 83.2 |
| III | 79.1 | 80.1 | 66.5 | 83.2 | 79.9 |
| IV | 68.9 | 77.9 | 62.7 | 82.6 | 77.5 |
| All | 81.8 | 80.3 | 78.5 | 84.9 | 81.7 |

* Based on block analyses by the Bureau of Business and Economic Research, University of Miami, from data in *1958 Real Estate Directory* of Florida Realty Service, Inc. Statistics were compiled by Dr. Thomas J. Wood, Professor of Government, University of Miami.
** When assessed values are used, the county's voting precincts may be divided into four categories: I ($10,000 and above), 30 precincts; II ($6,000–$9,900), 22 precincts; III ($4,500–$5,900), 50 precincts; and IV (0–$4,400), 43 precincts.

## 2. Voting Percentages by Assessed Residential Value (Cont'd)

| Residence Value Group | Unincorporated Area | City of Miami | Miami Beach & Adjacent Municipalities | Other Municipalities | All |
|---|---|---|---|---|---|
| McLeod Amendment 1961 % Against | | | | | |
| I | 65.6 | 64.9 | 54.2 | 62.9 | 62.2 |
| II | 55.3 | 55.4 | 50.5 | 57.8 | 55.8 |
| III | 51.0 | 50.3 | 40.3 | 44.2 | 48.2 |
| IV | 33.7 | 46.3 | 32.3 | 42.7 | 42.5 |
| All | 53.0 | 50.9 | 48.3 | 51.5 | 52.0 |
| Crandon Amendment No. 1 1962 % Against District Elections | | | | | |
| I | 61.1 | 63.5 | 64.5 | 53.9 | 59.3 |
| II | 53.6 | 58.6 | 65.9 | 57.2 | 55.9 |
| III | 54.2 | 52.2 | 56.0 | 47.5 | 51.6 |
| IV | 46.6 | 53.1 | 52.9 | 44.7 | 49.7 |
| All | 55.4 | 54.5 | 61.7 | 51.0 | 54.3 |
| Crandon Amendment No. 2 1962 % Against County Commission Approval of County Manager Appointments | | | | | |
| I | 58.5 | 59.5 | 50.3 | 49.8 | 53.9 |
| II | 49.1 | 53.5 | 52.9 | 49.9 | 50.2 |
| III | 49.2 | 46.7 | 44.6 | 41.3 | 45.6 |
| IV | 39.1 | 45.8 | 39.1 | 37.9 | 42.6 |
| V | 51.1 | 48.8 | 48.2 | 45.2 | 48.3 |

## 3. County Wide Referendum Concerning Local Government Structure *

| Year | Issue | Per Cent For | Against | Turnout |
|---|---|---|---|---|
| 1945 | Consolidation of School Districts | 94.4 | | 12.7 |
| 1948 | Merger of Miami and County (plus 4 small cities) | 45.8 | | 32.7 |
| 1952 | Constitutional Amendment—Permissive Home Rule | 54.7 | | 37.6 |
| 1953 | Consolidation—Miami and County | 49.7 | | 40.8 |
| 1956 | Constitutional Amendment—Dade Home Rule | 71.6 | | 35.3 |
| 1957 | Home Rule Charter | 51.0 | | 26.0 |

* Statistics were compiled by Dr. Thomas J. Wood, Professor of Government, University of Miami.

|      |                                        | PER CENT |         |         |
| YEAR | ISSUE                                  | FOR  | AGAINST | TURNOUT |
|------|----------------------------------------|------|---------|---------|
| 1958 | Autonomy Amendment                     |      | 59.9    | 34.2    |
| 1959 | Elective Sheriff                       |      | 55.9    | 25.5    |
| 1959 | Elective Assessor                      |      | 58.2    | 24.9    |
| 1959 | Five-Man Commission                    |      | 81.7    | 23.1    |
| 1959 | Seven-Man Commission                   |      | 86.6    | 21.8    |
| 1959 | Nine-Man Commission                    |      | 85.3    | 22.3    |
| 1961 | Abolition of Mandatory Reassessment    | 90.6 |         | 30.6    |
| 1961 | McLeod Amendment                       |      | 52.0    | 48.7    |
| 1962 | Bus Purchase                           |      | 63.5    | 32.9    |
| 1962 | County Dual-Office Holding             | 88.7 |         | 14.0    |
| 1962 | Qualifying Periods For County Commission Offices | 90.8 |   | 14.6    |
| 1962 | Competitive Bids For County Purchases  | 91.7 |         | 14.7    |
| 1962 | Election of Metro Commission by Districts Only |  | 54.3 | 16.2   |
| 1962 | Commission Approval of County Manager Appointments | 51.6 | | 16.0 |
| 1962 | Commission Approval of County Department Reorganization | 51.1 | | 15.9 |
| 1962 | Independent Port Authority             |      | 53.8    | 15.9    |
| 1962 | Return of Traffic Courts to Municipalities |  | 52.5    | 16.0    |

# APPENDIX E

# The Home Rule Amendment*

### Constitution of the State of Florida

SECTION 11. Dade County, home rule charter. (1) The electors of Dade County, Florida, are granted power to adopt, revise and amend from time to time a home rule charter of government for Dade County, Florida, under which the Board of County Commissioners of Dade County shall be the governing body. This charter:

(a) Shall fix the boundaries of each county commission district, provide a method for changing them from time to time, and fix the number, terms and compensation of the commissioners, and their method of election.

(b) May grant full power and authority to the Board of County Commissioners of Dade County to pass ordinances relating to the affairs, property and government of Dade County and provide suitable penalties for the violation thereof; to levy and collect such taxes as may be authorized by general law and no other taxes, and to do everything necessary to carry on a central metropolitan government in Dade County.

(c) May change the boundaries of, merge, consolidate, and abolish and may provide a method for changing the boundaries of, merging, consolidating and abolishing from time to time all municipal corporations, county or district governments, special taxing districts, authorities, boards, or other governmental units whose jurisdiction lies wholly within Dade County, whether such governmental units are created by the Constitution or the Legislature or otherwise, except the Dade County Board of County Commissioners as it may be provided for from time to time by this home rule charter and the Board of Public Instruction of Dade County.

---

* This amendment was originally contained in Senate Joint Resolution 1046, Gen. Laws of Florida, 1955. Only the numbering and lettering of the various subsections of the resolution have been changed to conform with the Florida Constitution.

(d) May provide a method by which any and all of the functions or powers of any municipal corporation or other governmental unit in Dade County may be transferred to the Board of County Commissioners of Dade County.

(e) May provide a method for establishing new municipal corporations, special taxing districts, and other governmental units in Dade County from time to time and provide for their government and prescribe their jurisdiction and powers.

(f) May abolish and may provide a method for abolishing from time to time all offices provided for by Article VIII, Section 6, of the Constitution or by the Legislature, except the Superintendent of Public Instruction and may provide for the consolidation and transfer of the functions of such offices, provided, however, that there shall be no power to abolish or impair the jurisdiction of the Circuit Court or to abolish any other court provided for by this Constitution or by general law, or the judges or clerks thereof although such charter may create new courts and judges and clerks thereof with jurisdiction to try all offenses against ordinances passed by the Board of County Commissioners of Dade County and none of the other courts provided for by this Constitution or by general law shall have original jurisdiction to try such offenses, although the charter may confer appellate jurisdiction on such courts, and provided further that if said home rule charter shall abolish any county office or offices as authorized herein, that said charter shall contain adequate provision for the carrying on of all functions of said office or offices as are now or may hereafter be prescribed by general law.

(g) Shall provide a method by which each municipal corporation in Dade County shall have the power to make, amend or repeal its own charter. Upon adoption of this home rule charter by the electors this method shall be exclusive and the Legislature shall have no power to amend or repeal the charter of any municipal corporation in Dade County.

(h) May change the name of Dade County.

(i) Shall provide a method for the recall of any commissioner and a method for initiative and referendum, including the initiation of and referendum on ordinances and the amendment or revision of the home rule charter, provided, however, that the power of the Governor and Senate relating to the suspension and removal of officers provided for in this Constitution shall not be impaired, but shall extend to all officers provided for in said home rule charter.

(2) Provision shall be made for the protection of the creditors of any governmental unit which is merged, consolidated, or abolished or whose boundaries are changed or functions or powers transferred.

(3) This home rule charter shall be prepared by a Metropolitan Charter Board created by the Legislature and shall be presented to the

electors of Dade County for ratification or rejection in the manner provided by the Legislature. Until a home rule charter is adopted the Legislature may from time to time create additional Charter Boards to prepare charters to be presented to the electors of Dade County for ratification or rejection in the manner provided by the Legislature. Such Charter, once adopted by the electors, may be amended only by the electors of Dade County and this charter shall provide a method for submitting future charter revisions and amendments to the electors of Dade County.

(4) The County Commission shall continue to receive its prorata share of all revenues payable by the state from whatever source to the several counties and the state of Florida shall pay to the Commission all revenues which would have been paid to any municipality in Dade County which may be abolished by or in the method provided by this home rule charter; provided however, the Commission shall reimburse the comptroller of Florida for the expense incurred if any, in the keeping of separate records to determine the amounts of money which would have been payable to any such municipality.

(5) Nothing in this section shall limit or restrict the power of the Legislature to enact general laws which shall relate to Dade County and any other one or more counties in the State of Florida or to any municipality in Dade County and any other one or more municipalities of the state of Florida, and the home rule charter provided for herein shall not conflict with any provision of this Constitution nor of any applicable general laws now applying to Dade County and any other one or more counties of the State of Florida except as expressly authorized in this section nor shall any ordinance enacted in pursuance to said home rule charter conflict with this Constitution or any such applicable general law except as expressly authorized herein, nor shall the charter of any municipality in Dade County conflict with this Constitution or any such applicable general law except as expressly authorized herein, provided however that said charter and said ordinances enacted in pursuance thereof may conflict with, modify or nullify any existing local, special or general law applicable only to Dade County.

(6) Nothing in this section shall be construed to limit or restrict the power of the Legislature to enact general laws which shall relate to Dade County and any other one or more counties of the state of Florida or to any municipalities in Dade County and any other one or more municipalities of the State of Florida relating to county or municipal affairs and all such general laws shall apply to Dade County and to all municipalities therein to the same extent as if this section had not been adopted and such general laws shall supersede any part or portion of the home rule charter provided for herein in conflict therewith and shall supersede any provision of any ordinance enacted pursuant to said charter and in conflict

therewith, and shall supersede any provision of any charter of any municipality in Dade County in conflict therewith.

(7) Nothing in this section shall be construed to limit or restrict the power and jurisdiction of the Railroad and Public Utilities Commission or of any other state agency, bureau or commission now or hereafter provided for in this Constitution or by general law and said state agencies, bureaus and commissions shall have the same powers in Dade County as shall be conferred upon them in regard to other counties.

(8) If any section, subsection, sentence, clause or provisions of this section is held invalid as violative of the provisions of Section 1 of Article XVII of this Constitution the remainder of this section shall not be affected by such invalidity.

(9) It is declared to be the intent of the Legislature and of the electors of the State of Florida to provide by this section home rule for the people of Dade County in local affairs and this section shall be liberally construed to carry out such purpose, and it is further declared to be the intent of the Legislature and of the electors of the State of Florida that the provisions of this Constitution and general laws which shall relate to Dade County and any other one or more counties of the State of Florida or to any municipality in Dade County and any other one or more municipalities of the State of Florida enacted pursuant thereto by the Legislature shall be the supreme law in Dade County, Florida, except as expressly provided herein and this section shall be strictly construed to maintain such supremacy of this Constitution and of the Legislature in the enactment of general laws pursuant to this Constitution.

## APPENDIX F

# Names and Occupations of the Members of the 3M Board and First and Second Charter Boards

THE ORIGINAL 3M BOARD

George E. Holt, Chairman
Senior Circuit Court Judge
Abe Aronovitz, Attorney
James A. Cox, Landscaping
†Angus W. Graham, Realtor
and School Board Member
†W. C. Herrell, Manager of
Sanitarium and Mayor of
Miami Springs
William Imand, Plumber
Donald R. Larson, Professor of
Government, University of
Miami
†Robert M. Morgan, Account-
ant
†Joseph J. Orr, General Con-
tractor
E. Albert Pallot, Attorney
†William L. Pallot, Attorney
Perrine Palmer, Jr., Investment
Counselor
S. D. Phillips, Jr., Mover and
Mayor of Miami Shores
†W. Keith Phillips, Insurance
Agent and Mayor of Coral
Gables

FIRST CHARTER BOARD

*George E. Holt, Chairman
Mrs. John A. Baker, Former
President of League of
Women Voters
†George H. Cooper, Grower
J. Abney Cox, Agriculture
Charles H. Crandon, Whole-
sale Druggist
William Grogan, Labor official
*Donald R. Larson
E. B. Leatherman, Circuit
Court Clerk
†I. D. MacVicar, Lumber dealer
and County Commissioner
†*Robert M. Morgan
†Max Orovitz, Business Entre-
preneur
†*Joseph J. Orr
†*William L. Pallot
†Franklin Parson, Attorney
*S. D. Phillips, Jr.
†*W. Keith Phillips, Jr.
J. D. Ryan, Town Adminis-
trator of Miami Springs
†Leonard Usina, Banker

THE ORIGINAL 3M BOARD
Thomas Sasso, Roofing and
Mayor of North Miami
Chelsie J. Senerchia, Engineer
and Mayor of Miami
Harold Shapiro, Attorney and
Mayor of Miami Beach
Ray T. Sterling, Mortgages
Frank J. Wead, Realtor and
Mayor of Opa-locka
Walter Weiss, Overseas Trans-
portation and Mayor of
Homestead

FIRST CHARTER BOARD
†Mitchell Wolfson, Owner of
Motion Picture Theaters
and Television Station
WTVJ

SECOND CHARTER BOARD
**S. D. Phillips, Jr., Chairman
**Mrs. John A. Baker
†**George H. Cooper
**Charles H. Crandon
**William Grogan
Mrs. Seymour B. Liebman,
Educator
†George S. Okell, Sr., Attorney
†**Max Orovitz
†**Joseph J. Orr
†**William L. Pallot
**Franklin Parson
Kurt Peiser, Ford Store Execu-
tive
†**W. Keith Phillips
**J. D. Ryan
†William D. Singer, Restau-
rants
H. Franklin Williams, Vice
President, University of Mi-
ami
†**Mitchell Wolfson

† Members of Miami-Dade Chamber of Commerce (prior to February, 1955,
known as the Miami Chamber of Commerce).
* Carried over from the 3M Board.
** Carried over from the first Charter Board.

# APPENDIX G

# Significant Sections of the Home Rule Charter

## PREAMBLE

We, the people of this County, in order to secure for ourselves the benefits and responsibilities of home rule, to create a metropolitan government to serve our present and future needs, and to endow our municipalities with the rights of self determination in their local affairs, do under God adopt this home rule Charter.

ARTICLE I

## Board of County Commissioners

*Section 1.01. Powers.*

A. The Board of County Commissioners shall be the legislative and the governing body of the county and shall have the power to carry on a central metropolitan government. This power shall include but shall not be restricted to the power to:

1. Provide and regulate arterial, toll, and other roads, bridges, tunnels, and related facilities; eliminate grade crossings; provide and regulate parking facilities; and develop and enforce master plans for the control of traffic and parking.

2. Provide and operate air, water, rail, and bus terminals, port facilities, and public transportation systems.

3. License and regulate taxis, jitneys, limousines for hire, rental cars and other passenger vehicles for hire operating in the unincorporated areas of the county.*

---

* In *Dade County* v. *Mercury Radio Service,* 134 So. 2d 791 (Fla. 1961), the Florida Supreme Court held that Dade County Ordinance No. 58–35, which provided for the licensing and regulation of all taxicabs and other vehicles for hire operating in the unincorporated areas, was unconstitutional in that it con-

4. Provide central records, training, and communications for fire and police protection; provide traffic control and central crime investigation; provide fire stations, jails, and related facilities; and subject to Section 1.01 A(18) provide a uniform system for fire and police protection.

5. Prepare and enforce comprehensive plans for the development of the county.

6. Provide hospitals and uniform health and welfare programs.

7. Provide parks, preserves, playgrounds, recreation areas, libraries, museums, and other recreational and cultural facilities and programs.

8. Establish and administer housing, slum clearance, urban renewal, conservation, flood and beach erosion control, air pollution control, and drainage programs and cooperate with governmental agencies and private enterprises in the development and operation of these programs.

9. Provide and regulate or permit municipalities to provide and regulate waste and sewage collection and disposal and water supply and conservation programs.

10. Levy and collect taxes and special assessments, borrow and expend money and issue bonds, revenue certificates, and other obligations of indebtedness in such manner, and subject to such limitations, as may be provided by law.

11. By ordinance, establish, merge, and abolish special purpose districts within which may be provided police and fire protection, beach erosion control, recreation facilities, water, streets, sidewalks, street lighting, waste and sewage collection and disposal, drainage, and other essential facilities and services. All county funds for such districts shall be provided by service charges, special assessments, or general tax levies within such districts only. The Board of County Commissioners shall be the governing body of all such districts and when acting as such governing body shall have the same jurisdiction and powers as when acting as the Board.

12. Establish, coordinate, and enforce zoning and such business regulations as are necessary for the protection of the public.

13. Adopt and enforce uniform building and related technical codes and regulations for both the incorporated and unincorporated areas of the county; provide for examinations for contractors and all parties engaged in the building trades and for the issuance of certifi-

flicted with the general statutes of the State of Florida. The ordinance was declared invalid both as to the taxicab companies holding master permits issued by the Florida Railroad and Public Utilities Commission, and as to the taxicab companies regulated by ordinances of the various municipalities in Dade County. (Sections 323.05 (1) and 323.05 (3), Florida Statutes). The County Attorney, Darrey Davis, believed that the Court's opinion in effect nullified and invalidated Section 1.01 A (3) of the Home Rule Charter.

cates of competency and their revocation after hearing. Such certificates shall be recognized and required for the issuance of a license in all municipalities in the county. No municipality shall be entitled to require examinations or any additional certificate of competency or impose any other conditions for the issuance of a municipal license except the payment of the customary fee. The municipality may issue building permits and conduct the necessary inspections in accordance with the uniform codes and charge fees therefor.

14. Regulate, control, take over, and grant franchises to, or itself operate gas, light, power, telephone, and other utilities, sanitary and sewage collection and disposal systems, water supply, treatment, and service systems, and public transportation systems, provided, however, that:

(a) Franchises under this subsection may only be granted by a two-thirds vote of the members of the Board present and approved by a majority vote of those qualified electors voting at either a special or general election.

(b) The county shall not operate a light, power, or telephone utility to serve any territory in the county which is being supplied with similar service except by a majority vote of those qualified electors voting in an election held not less than six months after the Board has passed an ordinance to that effect by a two-thirds vote of the members of the Board present. Such ordinance shall contain information on cost, method of financing, agency to regulate rates, agency to operate, location, and other information necessary to inform the general public of the feasibility and practicability of the proposed operation.

15. Use public funds for the purposes of promoting the development of the county, including advertising the area's advantages.

16. Establish and enforce regulations for the sale of alcoholic beverages in the unincorporated areas and approve municipal regulations on hours of sale of alcoholic beverages.

17. Enter into contracts with other governmental units within or outside the boundaries of the county for joint performance or performance by one unit in behalf of the other of any authorized function.

18. Set reasonable minimum standards for all governmental units in the county for the performance of any service or function. The standards shall not be discriminatory as between similar areas. If a governmental unit fails to comply with such standards, and does not correct such failure after reasonable notice by the Board, then the Board may take over and perform, regulate, or grant franchises to operate any such service. The Board may also take over and operate, or grant franchises to operate any municipal service if:

(a) In an election called by the Board of County Commissioners within the municipality a majority of those voting vote in favor of turning the service over to the county; or

(b) The governing body of the municipality requests the county to take over the service by a two-thirds vote of its members, or by referendum.

19. By ordinance, abolish or consolidate the offices of Sheriff, Constables, or any county office created by the Legislature, or provide for the consolidation and transfer of any of the functions of such officers, provided, however, that there shall be no power to abolish the Superintendent of Public Instruction or to abolish or impair the jurisdiction of the Circuit Court or to abolish any other court provided by the Constitution or by general law, or the judges or clerks thereof.

20. Make investigations of county affairs, inquire into the conduct, accounts, records, and transactions of any department or office of the county, and for these purposes require reports from all county officers and employees, subpoena witnesses, administer oaths, and require the production of records.

21. Exercise all powers and privileges granted to municipalities, counties and county officers by the Constitution and laws of the state, and all powers not prohibited by the Constitution or by this Charter.

22. Adopt such ordinances and resolutions as may be required in the exercise of its powers, and prescribe fines and penalties for the violation of ordinances.

23. Perform any other acts consistent with law which are required by this Charter or which are in the common interest of the people of the county.

24. Supersede, nullify, or amend any special law applying to this county, or any general law applying only to this county, or any general law where specifically authorized by the Constitution.

B. No enumeration of powers in this Charter shall be deemed exclusive or restrictive and the foregoing powers shall be deemed to include all implied powers necessary and proper to carrying out such powers. All of these powers may be exercised in the incorporated and unincorporated areas, subject to the procedures herein provided in certain cases relating to municipalities.

C. . . . The Board shall also provide for . . . the protection of pension rights of affected employees of any governmental unit which is merged, consolidated, or abolished or whose boundaries are changed or functions or powers transferred.

D. The Board shall be entitled to levy in the unincorporated areas all taxes authorized to be levied by municipalities and to receive from the state any revenues collected in the unincorporated areas on the same basis as municipalities.

.    .    .    .    .    .    .    .    .    .    .    .    .    .    .

*Section 1.03.  Districts.*

A. There shall be five County Commission districts. The initial boundaries of these districts shall be identical with the boundaries of the five county commission districts existing at the time of the 1956 general election.

B. The Board may by ordinance adopted by two-thirds vote of the members of the Board change the boundaries of the districts from time to time. The boundaries shall be fixed on the basis of the character, population, and geography of the districts.

*Section 1.04.  Composition of the Board.*

A. From each of the districts there shall be:

1. A County Commissioner who shall be a qualified elector residing within the district for six months before qualifying who shall be elected by the qualified electors of his district. Beginning with the state primary elections in 1958 such Commissioners shall be elected for a term of four years.

2. A County Commissioner who shall be a qualified elector residing within the district for six months before qualifying who shall be elected by the qualified electors of the county at large. Beginning with the state primary elections in 1964 such Commissioners shall be elected for a term of four years.

B. From each municipality in this county which shall have a population of 60,000 inhabitants or more according to latest federal census, there shall be a County Commissioner who shall be a qualified elector residing within the municipality for six months before qualifying who shall be elected by the qualified electors of such municipality. Such Commissioners shall serve for a term of four years.

.   .   .   .   .   .   .   .   .   .   .   .   .   .   .

ARTICLE 3

The County Manager

*Section 3.01.  Appointment and Removal.*

The Board of County Commissioners shall appoint a County Manager who shall be the chief executive officer and head of the administrative branch of the county government. The Board shall fix the Manager's compensation, and he shall serve at the will of the Board. .

*Section 3.02.  Qualifications.*

The Manager shall be chosen by the Board on the basis of his executive and alministrative qualifications. At the time of his appointment he need not be a resident of the state. No County Commissioner shall be eligible for the position of Manager during or within two years after the expiration of his latest term as Commissioner.

Section 3.03.   Absence of Manager.

The Board may designate a qualified administrative officer of the county to assume the duties and authority of the Manager during periods of temporary absence or disability of the Manager.

Section 3.04.   Powers and Duties.

A. The Manager shall be responsible to the Board of County Commissioners for the administration of all units of the county government under his jurisdiction and for carrying out policies adopted by the Board. The Manager, or such other persons as may be designated by resolution of the Board, shall execute contracts and other instruments, sign bonds and other evidences of indebtedness, and accept process.

B. The Manager shall have the power to appoint and remove all administrative officers and employees of the county subject to the provisions of this Charter and civil service rules and regulations.*

Section 3.05.   Restriction on Board Members.

Neither the Board nor any of its members shall direct or request the appointment of any person to, or his removal from, office by the Manager or any of his subordinates, or take part in the appointment or removal of officers and employees in the administrative services of the county. Except for the purpose of inquiry, as provided in Section 1.01 A(20), the Board and its members shall deal with the administrative service solely through the Manager and neither the Board nor any members thereof shall give orders to any subordinates of the Manager, either publicly or privately. Any wilful violation of the provisions of this Section by a member of the Board shall be grounds for his removal from office by an action brought in the Circuit Court by the State Attorney of this county.

ARTICLE 4

Administrative Organization and Procedure

Section 4.01.   Departments.

There shall be departments of finance, personnel, planning, law, and such other departments as may be established by administrative order of the Manager. All functions not otherwise specifically assigned to others by this Charter shall be performed under the supervision of the Manager.

---

* On August 21, 1962 Section 3.04 was amended to provide that appointment of major department heads by the County Manager shall be subject to approval by the County Commission.

*Section 4.02. Administrative Procedure.*

The Manager shall have the power to issue and place into effect administrative orders, rules, and regulations. The organization and operating procedure of departments shall be set forth in administrative regulations which the Manager shall develop, place into effect by administrative orders, and submit to the Board. The Board may, by ordinance, modify such orders, rules or regulations.*

. . . . . . . . . . . . . . . . . .

*Section 4.04. Assessment and Collection of Taxes.*

A. Beginning with the tax year 1961, the county tax rolls prepared by the county shall be the only legal tax rolls in this county for the assessment and collection of county and municipal taxes. Thereafter no municipality shall have an assessor or prepare an ad valorem tax roll. Each municipality shall continue to have the right to adopt its own budget, fix its own millage, and levy its own taxes. Each municipality shall certify its levies to the County Manager not later than 30 days after the county tax rolls have been finally approved by the Board. Any municipality may obtain a copy of this tax roll upon payment of the cost of preparing such a copy, and copies of the tax rolls shall be available for public inspection at reasonable times. Maps showing the assessed valuation of each parcel of property may be prepared and made available for sale to the public at a reasonable price.

B. All county and municipal taxes for the tax year beginning January 1, 1961, and all subsequent tax years, shall be collected by the county on one bill prepared and sent out by the county. The amounts of county and municipal taxes shall be shown as separate items, and may be paid separately.

. . . . . . . . . . . . . . . .

*Section 4.05. Department of Personnel.*

A. The Board of County Commissioners shall establish and maintain personnel and civil service, retirement, and group insurance programs. The personnel system of the county shall be based on merit principles in order to foster effective career service in county employment and to employ those persons best qualified for county services which they are to perform.

B. The County Manager shall appoint a personnel director who shall head the department of personnel and whose duty it shall be to administer the personnel and civil service programs and the rules governing them. The standards of such programs shall not be less than those prevailing at the time of the effective date of this Charter.

---

* On August 21, 1962 Section 4.02 was amended to provide that no administrative order, rules or regulations creating, merging or combining departments shall become effective until approved by resolution of the County Commission.

C. Except as provided herein, Chapter 30255, General Laws, 1955, as it exists on the effective date of this Charter, shall remain in effect until amended or changed by ordinance of the Board of County Commissioners adopted by two-thirds vote of the members present after recommendation from either the Personnel Advisory Board or the County Manager.

D. Employees of municipalities who, by merger, transfer, or assignment of governmental units or functions become county employees, shall not lose the civil service rights or privileges which have accrued to them during their period of employment with such municipality, and the county shall use its best efforts to employ these employees within the limits of their capabilities. However, if because of the merger of a department or division of a municipality with the county, all of the employees of such department or division are unable to be employed by the county either because of lack of funds or lack of work, the employee possessing the greater amount of service shall be retained in accordance with civil service rules and regulations. Those employees who are not retained shall be placed on a priority list for employment by the county subject to seniority. Any nonretained employee shall have the option, if a vacancy occurs or exists in another department, and if he is qualified to render the service required, to either accept such employment or remain on the priority list until such time as employment shall be available for him in his own or similar classification.

E. The pension plan presently provided by the state for county employees shall not be impaired by the Board. Employees of municipalities, who by merger, transfer, or assignment of governmental units or functions become county employees shall not lose their pension rights, or any reserves accrued to their benefit during their period of employment with such municipality. The Board of County Commissioners shall provide a method by which these employees' rights and reserves shall be protected, and these employees shall continue until retirement, dismissal, or death in a pension status no less beneficial than the status held by them at the time of merger or assignment.

F. The Board of County Commissioners shall provide and place into effect a practical group insurance plan for all county employees.

*Section 4.06.   Department of Law.*

There shall be a county attorney appointed by the Board of County Commissioners who shall serve at the will of the Board and who shall head the department of law. He shall devote his full time to the service of the county and shall serve as legal counsel to the Board, Manager, and all county departments, offices, and agencies, and perform such other legal duties as may be assigned to him. With the approval of the Board, he may appoint such assistants as may be necessary in order that his duties may be performed properly. The Board may employ special counsel for specific needs.

.    .    .    .    .    .    .    .    .    .    .    .    .    .

ARTICLE 5

Municipalities

Section 5.01.    Continuance of Municipalities.

The municipalities in the county shall remain in existence so long as their electors desire. No municipality in the county shall be abolished without approval of a majority of its electors voting in an election called for that purpose. The right of self determination in local affairs is reserved and preserved to the municipalities except as otherwise provided in this Charter.

Section 5.02.    Municipal Powers.

Each municipality shall have the authority to exercise all powers relating to its local affairs not inconsistent with this Charter. Each municipality may provide for higher standards of zoning, service, and regulation than those provided by the Board of County Commissioners in order that its individual character and standards may be preserved for its citizens.

Section 5.03.    Municipal Charters.

A. Except as provided in Section 5.04, any municipality in the county may adopt, amend, or revoke a charter for its own government or abolish its existence in the following manner. . . .

Section 5.04.    Changes in Municipal Boundaries.

A. The planning director shall study municipal boundaries with a view to recommending their orderly adjustment, improvement, and establishment. Proposed boundary changes may be initiated by the Planning Advisory Board, the Board of County Commissioners, the governing body of a municipality, or by a petition of any person or group concerned.

B. The Board of County Commissioners, after obtaining the approval of the municipal governing bodies concerned, after hearing the recommendations of the Planning Advisory Board, and after a public hearing, may by ordinance effect boundary changes, unless the change involves the annexation or separation of an area of which more than 250 residents are electors, in which case an affirmative vote of a majority of those electors voting shall also be required. Upon any such boundary change any conflicting boundaries set forth in the charter of such municipality shall be considered amended.

C. No municipal boundary shall be altered except as provided by this Section.

Section 5.05.    Creation of New Municipalities.

The Board of County Commissioners and only the Board may authorize the creation of new municipalities in the unincorporated areas of the county after hearing the recommendations of the Planning Advisory Board, after a public hearing, and after an affirmative vote of a majority of the electors voting and residing within the proposed boundaries. The Board of County Commissioners shall appoint a charter commission, consisting of five electors residing within the proposed boundaries, who shall propose a charter to be submitted to the electors in the manner provided in Section 5.03. The new municipality shall have all the powers and rights granted to or not withheld from municipalities by this Charter and the Constitution and general laws of the State of Florida.

*Section 5.06. Contracts with Other Units of Government.*

Every municipality in this county shall have the power to enter into contracts with other governmental units within or outside the boundaries of the municipality or the county for the joint performance or performance by one unit in behalf of the other of any municipal function.

*Section 5.07. Franchise and Utility Taxes.*

Revenues realized from franchise and utility taxes imposed by municipalities shall belong to municipalities.

## Article 6

## Metropolitan Court

*Section 6.01. Metropolitan Court Established.*

A. A court is hereby established, the name of which shall be the Metropolitan Court. There shall be as many judges of this Court as the Board shall deem necessary to administer promptly and expeditiously the business of the Court.

B. The judges shall be appointed by the Board by vote of two-thirds of the members of the Board to serve for six years. Terms of office of judges may be staggered. The senior judge shall be the administrative officer of the Court. All judges shall be attorneys who have been qualified for five years to practice law in the State of Florida. The compensation of the judges and all Court employees shall be fixed by ordinance.

C. Any judge may be removed for malfeasance, misfeasance, or nonfeasance by vote of two-thirds of the members of the Board after public hearing.

*Section 6.02. Jurisdiction and Procedure.*

A. The Court shall have jurisdiction to try all cases arising under ordinances adopted by the Board.

B. The clerk of the Metropolitan Court shall be appointed by the Board. The clerk may appoint deputy clerks upon approval of the Manager. The Court may hold sessions in such places as the Board may designate.

C. Arrests, complaints, prosecutions, and convictions shall be instituted and processed in the manner provided by the rules of the Court. When the complaint is made in the name of the county, a formal complaint shall not be necessary to give the Court jurisdiction of offenses triable in such Court, but the accused may be tried for the offense for which he is docketed, provided such docket entry is sufficient to put the accused upon notice of the offense with which he is charged.

D. No person shall upon conviction for the violation of any county ordinance be punished by a fine exceeding $1,000 or imprisonment in the county jail for more than one year or by both such fine and imprisonment. If the offense is punishable by a fine exceeding $500 or imprisonment in the county jail for more than 60 days, the accused shall be entitled to a trial by jury upon demand.

E. All prosecutions for violations of any ordinance punishable by fine or imprisonment shall be conducted by the State Attorney of this county, if he be willing, and, if not, by the department of law. The Board may by ordinance provide for a public defender.

F. Appeals will lie to the Circuit Court of this county from any final judgment. All such appeals shall be taken within 20 days from the entry of the judgment in the manner provided by the rules of the Circuit Court. The decision of the Circuit Court shall be subject to review in the same manner and within the same time as any other decision of the Circuit Court.

G. The judges of the Metropolitan Court are hereby empowered to adopt rules of procedure governing the Court to punish for contempt of court including imprisonment not in excess of 48 hours, to issue search warrants, and to fix the amount of bail and appeal bonds. The judges and the clerks or their deputies may administer oaths, issue witness subpoenas, and warrants for arrest.

. . . . . . . . . . . . .

ARTICLE 8

General Provisions

. . . . . . . . . . . .

Section 8.03. Tort Liability.*

The County shall be liable in actions of tort to the same extent that municipalities in the State of Florida are liable in actions in tort. However, no suit shall be maintained against the county for damages to persons or property or for wrongful death arising out of any tort unless written notice of claim shall first have been given to the county in the manner and within the time provided by ordinance, except that the time

---

* This section was declared unconstitutional in *Kaulakis* v. *Boyd*, 138 So. 2d 505 (Fla. 1962). The Florida Supreme Court held that tort liability was not a matter of local concern but must conform to the general statutes of the State of Florida.

fixed by ordinance for notice shall be not less than 30 days nor more than 120 days.

### Section 8.04. Supremacy Clause.

A. This Charter and the ordinances adopted hereunder shall in cases of conflict supersede all municipal charters and ordinances, except as herein provided, and where authorized by the Constitution, shall in cases of conflict supersede all special and general laws of the state.

B. All other special and general laws and county ordinances and rules and regulations not inconsistent with this Charter shall continue in effect until they are superseded by ordinance adopted by the Board pursuant to this Charter and the Constitution.

. . . . . . . . . . . . . . . . .

### Section 8.06. Effect of the Charter.

A. This Charter shall be liberally construed in aid of its declared purpose, which is to establish effective home rule government in this county responsive to the people. If any Article, Section, subsection, sentence, clause, or provision of this Charter or the application thereof shall be held invalid for any reason the remainder of the Charter and of any ordinances or regulations made thereunder shall remain in full force and effect.

B. Nothing in this Charter shall be construed to limit or restrict the power and jurisdiction of the Florida Railroad and Public Utilities Commission.

### Section 8.07. Amendments.

Amendments to this Charter may be proposed by a resolution adopted by the Board of County Commissioners or by petition of electors numbering five percent of the number voting in the county for the office of Governor in the last preceding gubernatorial general election. The Board shall call an election not less than 60 nor more than 120 days after it adopts the resolution or receives a petition certified in the manner required for an initiatory petition for an ordinance. The result shall be determined by a majority of the electors voting on the amendment.

### Section 8.08. Effective Date.

This Charter shall become effective 60 days after it is ratified by a majority of the qualified electors of the county voting on the Charter.

### ARTICLE 9

## Transitory Provisions

. . . . . . . . . . . . . . .

### Section 9.02. Appointment of County Manager.

The County Manager shall be appointed no later than October 31, 1957.

*Section 9.03.   Reassessment.*

A. On or before May 1, 1958, the Board of County Commissioners shall provide for the reassessment according to law of all real and tangible personal property within the incorporated and unincorporated areas of the county exclusive of property assessed by the state. The cost of this reassessment shall be paid out of the general funds of the county or any other funds that might be available. This reassessment shall be completed as expeditiously as possible but in no event later than January 1, 1961.*

B. After this reassessment has been completed and made official by the Board, county tax rolls reflecting this reassessment shall be completed and promptly made available to each municipality. Beginning with the 1961 tax year, no other real and tangible personal property tax rolls than those prepared by the county shall be legal or in any manner used for the assessment of taxes within the incorporated and unincorporated areas, except as provided in 9.03 D.*

C. Prior to January 1, 1961, each municipality shall conform its fiscal year to that of the county, and to accomplish this may levy taxes for less or more than one year but for not more than two years at once.

D. Upon petition from any municipality on grounds of hardship caused by use of the county tax rolls or prescribed fiscal year, the Board may from year to year grant that municipality an exemption, but no such exemption shall extend beyond January 1, 1966.

.   .   .   .   .   .   .   .   .   .   .   .   .   .

*Section 9.06.   Transition.*

In order that there may be no interruption of the business of the county, all persons holding office at the time this Charter takes effect shall continue in the performance of their functions and duties until their successors are appointed, or until their functions and duties are transferred, altered, or abolished in accordance with this Charter. All laws in force when this Charter becomes effective and not inconsistent therewith shall continue in force until they are superseded by ordinances adopted by the Board in pursuance of this Charter. All ordinances and resolutions of the county in force when this Charter becomes effective, and all lawful rights, claims, actions, orders, obligations, proceedings, and contracts shall continue until modified, amended, repealed, or superseded in accordance with this Charter.

*Section 9.07.   Termination of this Article.*

After January 1, 1967, this Article 9 shall cease to be a part of this Charter.

---

* An amendment to the charter enacted by referendum on August 15, 1961 eliminated sections 9.03 A and 9.03 B.

# Bibliographical Data

## I. Primary Sources

### A. DOCUMENTS

Florida, *Constitution* (1885).
Metropolitan Dade County, Home Rule Charter (1957).

### B. STATE LEGISLATION

1. *Codified Laws*

Florida, *Statutes* (1959), secs. 165.01, 165.03, 165.04, 165.08. (Municipal incorporation under general law.)
Florida, *Statutes* (1959), secs. 167.43, 167.43 (1), 210.03 (1), 210.02 (7). (Municipal taxing powers.)
Florida, *Statutes* (1959), c. 186. (Model traffic code.)
Florida, *Statutes* (1959), cc. 776–965. (Penal Code.)
Florida, *Statutes* (1959), c. 367 (Water and Sewer System Regulatory Law.)
Florida, *Statutes* (1959), sec. 550.13. (Racing taxes.)
Florida, *Statutes* (1959), Sec. 205.02. (Concerning county and city occupational taxes.)

2. *Uncodified Laws*

Laws of Florida, *passim.* (Incorporation of Municipalities in Dade County by special act.)
Special Acts of Florida (1941), c. 21388. (Creation of Department of Water and Sewers of the City of Miami.)
General Acts of Florida (1943), c. 21871. (Creation of county-wide health department.)
Special Acts of Florida (1943), c. 22303. (Creation of Greater Miami Port Authority.)
General Acts of Florida (1945), c. 22963. (Creation of Dade County Port Authority.)
Special Acts of Florida (1945), c. 23225. (Authorization to Dade County to construct and operate hospitals.)
Special Acts of Florida (1945), c. 23226. (Consolidation of Dade County School districts.)

Special Acts of Florida (1945), c. 23300. (Abolition of Greater Miami Port Authority.)

Special Acts of Florida (1945), c. 23404. (Authorization to the City of Miami to lease or sell Jackson Memorial Hospital.)

Special Acts of Florida (1947), cc. 24467, 24468. (Provisions with regard to H.J.R. 407 dealing with consolidation of Dade County, the City of Miami, and four small municipalities.)

Special Acts of Florida (1949), c. 25758. (Foreclosure of further municipal incorporation in Dade County under the general law.)

General Acts of Florida (1951), c. 26614. (Creating the Interama Authority.)

Special Acts of Florida (1953), cc. 29280, 29281. (Merger of City of Miami with Dade County.)

General Acts of Florida (1955), c. 30255. (Larger counties civil service law.)

Special Acts of Florida (1955), c. 30686. (Creation of the first Charter Board.)

Laws of Florida, Extraordinary Session (1956), c. 31420. (Creation of the second Charter Board.)

General Acts of Florida (1957), c. 57–912. (Ratification of Charter Board actions.)

3. *Joint Resolutions*

General Laws of Florida (1943), H.J.R. 786. (Consolidation of tax assessing and tax collecting offices and of certain court offices in Dade and Orange Counties.)

*Florida House Journal* (1945) pp. 274, 722, H.J.R. 440. (Permissive consolidation of cities and county governments or of their officers or functions anywhere in the state by a majority referendum vote.)

*Florida House Journal* (1945), pp. 768, 889, H.J.R. 975. (Consolidation of city and county governments or of their agencies anywhere in the state by legislative act to be followed by a referendum.)

General Laws of Florida (1947), H.J.R. 407. (Consolidation of Dade County, the City of Miami, and four small municipalities.)

General Laws of Florida (1951), S.J.R. 117. (Permissive statewide home rule amendment.)

General Laws of Florida (1955), S.J.R. 1046. (Dade County Home Rule Amendment.)

4. *Acts and Resolutions proposed in 1959 session of the Florida Legislature*

S.B. No. 440 (1959). (Retention of cigarette taxes collected in Dade County.)

S.B. No. 606, H.B. No. 840 (1959). (Regulation of water and sewage rates.)
H.B. No. 1310 (1959). (Duval County special districts.)
S.J.R. 797 (1959). (Permissive county gasoline tax.)

C. ORDINANCES

1. *Early Drafts of Metro Ordinances*
Metropolitan Court Ordinance. Undated.
Public Works Department Ordinance. Public Hearings, August 16, 1957.
Zoning and Building Department Ordinance. Proposed, July, 1957.
Traffic Ordinance. Public Hearings, September 17, 1957.
Contractors Examination Code. Undated.

2. *Metro Ordinances as Enacted*
Metro (Dade County, Florida) Ordinance No. 57-2. (Public Works Department.)
Metro (Dade County, Florida) Ordinance No. 57-11. (Authorizing County Manager to enter into contracts with municipalities.)
Metro (Dade County, Florida) Ordinance No. 57-12. (Metropolitan Traffic Code.)
Metro (Dade County, Florida) Ordinance No. 57-16. (Amending Larger Counties Civil Service Act.)
Metro (Dade County, Florida) Ordinance No. 57-19. (Zoning Code, Part I—unincorporated areas.)
Metro (Dade County, Florida) Ordinance No. 57-20. (Zoning Code, Part II—municipalities.)
Metro (Dade County, Florida) Ordinance No. 57-21. (Zoning Code, Part III—Air Force Base.)
Metro (Dade County, Florida) Ordinance No. 57-22. (South Florida Building Code.)
Metro (Dade County, Florida) Ordinance No. 57-23. (Relating to election for abolishing City of Miami.)
Metro (Dade County, Florida) Ordinance No. 57-25. (Examination and Qualification of Contractors.)
Metro (Dade County, Florida) Ordinance No. 57-26. (Repealing ordinance relating to election for abolishing City of Miami.)
Metro (Dade County, Florida) Ordinance No. 57-27. (Deferring effective date of Metropolitan Traffic Code.)
Metro (Dade County, Florida) Ordinance No. 57-28. (Traffic and Transportation Department.)
Metro (Dade County, Florida) Ordinance No. 57-30. (Subdivision regulations.)
Metro (Dade County, Florida) Ordinance No. 57-31. (Department of Zoning and Building.)
Metro (Dade County, Florida) Ordinance No. 57-32. (Deferring effective date of Metropolitan Traffic Code.)

Metro (Dade County, Florida) Ordinance No. 58-2. (Deferring
effective date of Building and Zoning Ordinance.)
Metro (Dade County, Florida) Ordinance No. 58-8. (Extending
effective date for auto inspections by county under Traffic Code.)
Metro (Dade County, Florida) Ordinance No. 58-10. (Deferring
effective date of Building and Zoning Ordinance.)
Metro (Dade County, Florida) Ordinance No. 58-25. (Amend-
ing Public Works Department Ordinance.)
Metro (Dade County, Florida) Ordinance No. 58-26. (Deferring
effective date of Building and Zoning Ordinance.)
Metro (Dade County, Florida) Ordinance No. 58-28. (Depart-
ment of Traffic and Transportation.)
Metro (Dade County, Florida) Ordinance No. 58-33. (Deferring
effective date of Building and Zoning Ordinance.)
Metro (Dade County, Florida) Ordinance No. 58-39. (Repealing
Building and Zoning Ordinance and Zoning Code, Part II.)
Metro (Dade County, Florida) Ordinance No. 58-46. (Providing
for Special Purpose Districts.)
Metro (Dade County, Florida) Ordinance No. 59-8. (Providing
for Special Taxing Districts.)
Metro (Dade County, Florida) Ordinance No. 59-23. (Adopting
Homestead Penal Ordinances.)
Metro (Dade County, Florida) Ordinance No. 59-25. (Adopting
Florida City Penal Ordinances.)
Metro (Dade County, Florida) Ordinance No. 59-28. (Adopting
Hialeah Penal Ordinances.)
Metro (Dade County, Florida) Ordinance No. 59-29. (Adopting
Opa-locka Penal Ordinances.)
Metro (Dade County, Florida) Ordinance No. 59-34. (Adopting
Biscayne Park Penal Ordinances.)
Metro (Dade County, Florida) Ordinance No. 59-36. (Amending
Special Purpose District Ordinance.)
Metro (Dade County, Florida) Ordinance No. 59-40. (Review of
municipal sales of publicly owned real property.)
Metro (Dade County, Florida) Ordinance No. 60-6. (Creating a
metropolitan Dade County Urban Renewal Ordinance.)
Metro (Dade County, Florida) Ordinance No. 60-7. (Creating a
metropolitan Special Taxing District Ordinance.)
Metro (Dade County, Florida) Ordinance No. 60-14. (Zoning
Appeals Board for unincorporated areas.)
Metro (Dade County, Florida) Ordinance No. 60-20. (Creating a
metropolitan Dade County Water and Sewer Board.)
Metro (Dade County, Florida) Ordinance No. 60-23. (Creating a
metropolitan Dade County Transit Authority.)
Metro (Dade County, Florida) Ordinance No. 60-42. (Concern-
ing municipal boundaries.)

Metro (Dade County, Florida) Ordinance No. 60–45. (Creating Islandia, a new municipality.)
Metro (Dade County, Florida) Ordinance No. 62–2. (Concerning loan arrangement with the First National Bank.)
Metro (Dade County, Florida) Ordinance No. 62–12. (Concerning recognition of municipal certificates of competency.)
Metro (Dade County, Florida) Ordinance No. 62–14. (Concerning specific zoning requirements.)

D. RESOLUTIONS

Metro (Dade County, Florida) Resolution No. 2521, December, 1958. (Concerning financial assistance to launch Interama.)
Metro (Dade County, Florida) Resolution No. 3609, July 21, 1959. (Concerning transfer of Coral Gables traffic police to Metro.)
Metro (Dade County, Florida) Resolution No. 4830, April 5, 1960. (Concerning Metro construction of Dodge Island seaport.)
Metro (Dade County, Florida) Resolution Nos. 4966, 4967, April 21, 1960. (Concerning radio communication services to municipalities.)
Metro (Dade County, Florida) Resolution No. 6542, May 9, 1961. (Concerning approval of purchase contract for buses.)
Metro (Dade County, Florida) Resolution No. 6639, June 8, 1961. (Concerning referendum election on mandatory reassessment.)
Metro (Dade County, Florida) Resolution No. 7047, October 13, 1961. (Concerning rental credit to City of Miami on proposed City-County building.)
Metro (Dade County, Florida) Resolution No. 7333, February 20, 1962. (Concerning exclusive use of franchise funds for the unincorporated area.)

E. LITIGATION AND ADVISORY OPINIONS

1. *United States Supreme Court*
   *Ocean Beach Heights, Inc.* v. *Brown-Crummer Investment Co.*, 302 U. S. 614 (1939).
2. *Florida Supreme Court*
   *Adams* v. *Housing Authority of the City of Daytona Beach*, 60 So. 2d 663 (Fla. 1952).
   In re *Advisory Opinions to the Governor*, 76 Fla. 417, 418, 79 So. 874 (1918).
   *Attorney General* v. *Connors*, 27 Fla. 339, 9 So. 7 (1891).
   *Blitch* v. *Buchanan*, 100 Fla. 1202, 131 So. 151 (1930).
   *Chase* v. *Cowart*, 102 So. 2d 147 (Fla. 1957).
   *City of Coral Gables* v. *Gray*, 154 Fla. 881, 19 So. 2d 318 (1944).
   *City of Fort Lauderdale* v. *Carter*, 71 So. 2d 260 (Fla. 1954).
   *City of Miami* v. *Aronovitz*, 114 So. 2d 784 (Fla. 1959).

*City of Miami* v. *Kenton,* 115 So. 2d 547 (Fla. 1959).
*City of Miami Beach* v. *County of Dade,* 122 So. 2d 84 (Fla. 1960), rehearing denied, 129 So. 2d 413 (Fla. 1960), cert denied, 82 Sup. Ct. 45, rehearing denied, 82 Sup. Ct. 192 (1961).
*City of Miami Beach* v. *Cowart,* 116 So. 2d 432 (Fla. 1959).
*City of Miami Beach* v. *Crandon,* 35 So. 2d 285 (Fla. 1948).
*Dade County* v. *Dade County League of Municipalities,* 104 So. 2d 512 (Fla. 1958).
*Dade County* v. *Mercury Radio Service,* 134 So. 2d 791 (Fla. 1961).
*Dade County* v. *Young Democratic Club of Dade County,* 104 So. 2d 636 (Fla. 1958).
*Fisher* v. *Board of Commissioners of Dade County,* 84 So. 2d 572 (Fla. 1956).
*Florida ex rel Glyn* v. *McNayr,* 133 So. 312 (Fla. 1961).
*Gray* v. *Golden,* 89 So. 2d 785 (Fla. 1956).
*Grubstein* v. *Urban Renewal Agency of City of Tampa,* 115 So. 2d 745 (Fla. 1959).
*Klemm* v. *Davenport,* 100 Fla. 627, 129 So. 904 (1930).
*Leatherman* v. *Alta Cliff Co.,* 114 Fla. 305, 153 So. 845 (1934).
*Manhood* v. *State ex rel. Davis,* 101 Fla. 1254, 133 So. 90 (1931).
*Miami Shores Village* v. *Cowart,* 108 So. 2d 468 (Fla. 1958).
*State* v. *Alsop,* 120 Fla. 628, 163 So. 80 (1935).
*State* v. *County Commissioners,* 23 Fla. 483, 3 So. 193 (1887).
*State* v. *Grable,* 72 Fla. 61, 72 So. 460 (1916).
*State* v. *County of Dade,* 125 So. 2d 833 (Fla. 1960).
*Whisnant* v. *Stringfellow,* 50 So. 2d 885 (Fla. 1951).
3. *Florida Circuit Courts*
*Aronovitz* v. *City of Miami,* No. 59C1239A (Dade Cir. Ct. Fla. 1959).
*Burgin* v. *City of Coral Gables,* No. 59L3738E (Dade Cir. Ct. Fla. 1959).
*Chase* v. *Board of County Commissioners,* 11 Fla. Supp. 36 (Dade Cir. Ct. 1957).
*Cicero and Girtman* v. *Dade County,* No. 58C482 (Dade Cir. Ct. Fla. 1958).
*City of Miami* v. *County of Dade,* No. 206817 (Dade Cir. Ct. Fla. 1957).
*City of Miami Beach* v. *Cowart,* No. 58C5895 (Dade Cir. Ct. Fla. 1959).
*County of Dade* v. *State,* No. 60C447 (Dade Cir. Ct. Fla. 1960).
*Dade County* v. *Miami Beach,* No. 59C6004 (Dade Cir. Ct. Fla. 1959).
*Dade County* v. *City of Miami Beach,* No. 59C6606 (Dade Cir. Ct. Fla. 1960).

*DeLoach* v. *City of Miami,* No. 59L402 (Dade Cir. Ct. Fla. 1959).
*Florida* ex rel. *Glynn* v. *McNayr,* No. 61L2784 (Dade Cir. Ct. Fla. 1961).
*Golden* v. *Gray,* 9 Fla. Supp. 17 (Leon Cir. Ct. 1956).
*High* v. *City of Miami,* No. 59C10098A (Dade Cir. Ct. Fla. 1960).
*Keton* v. *City of Miami,* 14 Fla. Supp. 68 (Dade Cir. Ct. 1959).
*Miami Shores Village* v. *County Commissioners,* 12 Fla. Supp. 168 (Dade Cir. Ct. 1958).
*Wolff* v. *Dade League of Municipalities,* No. 58C7450 (Dade Cir. Ct. Fla. 1958).
*Young Democratic Club of Dade County* v. *Dade County,* Nos. 58C2522, 58C3454 (Dade Cir. Ct. Fla. 1958).

4. *Other Litigation*
In re *Petition of Auditor General,* 226 Mich. 170, 197 N. W. 552 (1924).

5. *Florida Attorney General Opinions*
Florida, *Biennial Report of Attorney General* (1951–1952), p. 258.
Florida, *Biennial Report of Attorney General* (1957–1958), p. 368.

F. OFFICIAL REPORTS

Campbell, O. W. *The First Annual Report on the Progress of Metropolitan Dade County, Florida.* Miami: 1958. (Mimeographed.)
The Commission on Intergovernmental Relations. *A Report to the President for Transmittal to the Congress.* Washington: June, 1955.
*Final Report of the Grand Jury* in the Circuit Court of the Eleventh Judicial Circuit of Florida in and for the County of Dade. (Filed 1939).
*Final Report of the Grand Jury* in the Circuit Court of the Eleventh Judicial Circuit in and for the County of Dade. (Filed Nov. 12, 1958).
*Final Report of the Grand Jury* in the Circuit Court of the Eleventh Judicial Circuit of Florida in and for the County of Dade. (Filed Nov. 10, 1959).
Metropolitan Dade County Planning Department. *Planning Review Report of the Miami Seaport Location.* Miami: July, 1959. (Mimeographed.)
Metropolitan Dade County Planning Department. *Preliminary Land Use Plan, Draft of Summary Report.* Miami: Nov., 1960. (Mimeographed.)
Morgan, Altemus & Barrs, CPA. *Statement of Funds Available and Disbursed for Period August 9, 1956, through December 31, 1956.*
Morgan, Altemus & Barrs, CPA. *Statement of Funds Available and Disbursed for Period January 1, 1957, through June 25, 1957.*
*Report of the Comptroller, State of Florida, For the Fiscal Year Ended June 20, 1958.*

260 BIBLIOGRAPHICAL DATA

*Reports of the Secretary of State of Florida, passim.*

Toulmin, Harry T. *Metropolitan Dade County, Florida: A Report on Administrative Improvement Through February,* 1959. Miami: 1959. (Mimeographed.)

U. S. Bureau of the Census, *Census of the United States:* 1920–1950, *passim.*

U. S. Bureau of the Census, *Special Census of the State of Florida:* 1945.

U. S., Congress, House, Subcommittee of the Committee on Government Operations. *Hearings on Federal-State-Local Relations, Dade County (Florida) Metropolitan Government.* 85th Cong., 1st sess., Nov. 21 and 22, 1957.

U. S. Congress, Senate, Subcommittee of the Committee on the Judiciary. *Hearings on Confirmation of Nomination of James L. Guilmartin, of Florida, to be United States Attorney for the Southern District of Florida.* 83rd Cong., 1st sess., June 18 and 19, 1953.

G. OTHER PRIMARY MATERIALS

American Bar Association Traffic Court Program. *Preliminary Report and Recommendations for the Metropolitan Court of Dade County.* Miami: May 12, 1959. (Mimeographed.)

Beiler, Ross C. *Public Opinion Polls:* Beiler Survey No. 10 (1957–58), Beiler Survey No. 12 (Sept., 1958), Beiler Survey No. 13 (Nov. and Dec. 1959).

Campbell, O. W. *Memorandum to County Commission: Financing Neighborhood Services.* Miami: February 18, 1959. (Mimeographed.)

*City of Miami Beach Annual Fiscal Report, Fiscal Year Ending September 30, 1959.*

Dubbin, Blatt & Schiff. *The Sixth Draft of the Home Rule Bill.* Miami: 1955. (Mimeographed.)

Florida, *House Journal, passim.*

Florida, *Senate Journal, passim.*

*Joint Resolution Proposing an Amendment to Article VIII to the Constitution of the State of Florida Relative to Cities and Counties.* 1945. (Mimeographed.)

Memorandum to the Board of County Commissioners from Darrey A. Davis, County Attorney, Jan. 6, 1959. (Dade County, Florida.)

Memorandum to E. A. Evans, City Manager, from William L. Pallot, City Attorney, Dec. 24, 1958. (City of Miami, Florida.)

Metropolitan Dade County, Florida. *Budget, Fiscal Year 1958–1959.*

Metropolitan Dade County, Florida. *Budget, Fiscal Year 1959–1960.*

Metropolitan Dade County, Florida. *Budget, Fiscal Year 1960–1961.*

*Metro (Dade County, Florida) Commission Minutes,* July 22, 1957, to Aug. 24, 1962.

Metropolitan Miami Municipal Board. *History and Objectives of the 3M Board as of March 1, 1955.* Miami: 1955. (Mimeographed.)
*Minutes of the Metropolitan Charter Boards.* June 27, 1955, to June 28, 1957. Dade County, Florida.
*Minutes of the Metropolitan Miami Municipal Board.* Miami, Florida.
*Operational Plan for Dade County Fire Service: Mutual Aid Organization.* Dade County, Florida: Oct. 3, 1957. (Mimeographed.)
Paul, Daniel P. S. *Draft of the Home Rule Amendment.* Miami, Florida: 1955. (Mimeographed.)
Public Administration Service. *Working Draft for a Proposed Charter, Dade County, Florida.* Chicago: Dec. 1, 1955. (Mimeographed.)
Rader and Associates. *Survey and Report on Privately Owned Water and Sewerage Utilities in Metropolitan Dade County, Florida.* Miami: November, 1958.

## II. Secondary Sources

A. Books

Adrian, Charles R. *Governing Urban America.* New York: McGraw-Hill Co., 1955.
Babb, Jervis J. *Guiding Metropolitan Growth.* New York: Committee for Economic Development, 1960.
Bollens, John C. *The States and the Metropolitan Problem.* Chicago: The Council of State Governments, 1956.
Burns, James MacGregor. *Congress on Trial.* New York: Harper & Brothers, 1949.
Dade County Development Department. *Economic Survey of Metropolitan Miami.* Miami, Dade County Development Department, 1959.
Dahl, Robert A. *Who Governs?* New Haven: Yale University Press, 1961.
Dauer, Manning J., Carleton, William G., Baker, W. Freeman, and Pettengill, Dwynal B. "Florida," in Paul Theodore David, Malcolm Moos, and Ralph M. Goldman (eds.), *Presidential Nominating Politics in 1952: The South.* Baltimore: The Johns Hopkins Press, 1954, pp. 116–144.
Doyle, Wilson Keyser, Laird, Angus McKenzie, and Weiss, S. Sherman. *The Government and Administration of Florida.* New York: Thomas Y. Crowell Co., 1954.
Fiser, Webb S. *Mastery of the Metropolis.* Englewood Cliffs, New Jersey: Prentice Hall, Inc., 1962.
Galbraith, John K. *The Affluent Society.* Boston: Houghton Mifflin Co., 1958.
Government Affairs Foundation, Inc., *Metropolitan Surveys: A Digest.* Chicago: Public Administration Service, 1958.
Greene, Lee S. "The Problem of Government in Metropolitan Areas,"

in John M. Claunch (ed.), *The Problem of Government in Metro-politan Areas: A Symposium*. Dallas: Arnold Foundation, Southern Methodist University, 1958, pp. 3–23.

Greer, Scott. *Governing the Metropolis*, New York: John Wiley & Sons, 1962.

Gunther, John. *Inside U. S. A.* New York: Harper & Brothers, 1955.

Heldt, Henning, "Heaven or Honky-Tonk?" in Robert S. Allen (ed), *Our Fair City*. New York: The Vanguard Press, Inc., 1947, pp. 77–99.

Jones, Victor. "Local Government in Metropolitan Areas: Its Relation to Urban Development," in Coleman Woodbury (ed.), *The Future of Cities and Urban Redevelopment*. Chicago: University of Chicago Press, 1953, pp. 497–605.

————. *Metropolitan Government*. Chicago: University of Chicago Press, 1942.

Kafka, Franz. *The Castle*. New York: Alfred A. Knopf, Inc., 1956.

Key, V. O., Jr. *Southern Politics*. New York: Alfred A. Knopf, Inc., 1950.

Kneier, Charles Maynard. *City Government in the United States*. New York: Harper & Brothers, 1947.

Long, Norton E. *The Polity*. Chicago: Rand McNally and Co., 1962.

MacCorkle, Stuart Alexander. *American Municipal Government and Administration*. Boston: D. C. Heath, 1948.

MacMahon, Arthur W. (ed.). *Federalism: Mature and Emergent*. New York: Doubleday and Co., 1956.

Maas, Arthur (ed.). *Area and Power: A Theory of Local Government*. Glencoe, Ill.: The Free Press, 1958.

Michels, Robert. *Political Parties*. Glencoe, Ill.: The Free Press, 1949.

Nolting, Orin F., and Arnold, David S. (eds.). *The Municipal Year Book, 1958*. Chicago: The International City Managers Association, 1958.

Price, Hugh Douglas. *The Negro and Southern Politics*. New York: New York University Press, 1957.

Public Administration Service. *The Government of Metropolitan Miami*. Chicago: Public Administration Service, 1954.

Riker, William H. *The Study of Local Politics*. New York: Random House, Inc., 1959.

Sayre, Wallace S., and Kaufman, Herbert. *Governing New York City*. New York: Russell Sage Foundation, 1960.

Scammon, Richard M. (ed.), Government Affairs Institute. *American Votes, I*. New York: Macmillan Company, 1956.

————. Government Affairs Institute. *America Votes, 1956–57*. New York: Macmillan Company, 1958.

Schmandt, Henry J., Steinbicker, Paul G., and Wendel, George D.

*Metropolitan Reform in St. Louis.* New York: Holt, Rinehart and Winston, 1961.
Schulz, Ernst B. *Essentials of Government.* Englewood Cliffs, New Jersey: Prentice-Hall, Inc., 1958.
Snider, Clyde Frank. *American State and Local Government.* New York: Appleton-Century-Crofts, 1950.
Truman, David Bicknell. *The Governmental Process.* New York: Alfred A. Knopf, Inc., 1951.
University of Miami Bureau of Business and Economic Research. *Economic Almanac of Southeastern Florida, 1959.* Coral Gables: 1959.
Vernon, Raymond. *The Changing Economic Function of the Central City.* New York: Committee for Economic Development, April, 1959.
Webster, Donald H. *Urban Planning and Municipal Public Policy.* New York: Harper & Bros., 1958.
Wood, Robert C. *Metropolis Against Itself.* New York: Committee for Economic Development, March, 1959.
————. *Suburbia: Its People and Their Politics.* Boston: Houghton Mifflin Co., 1959.
Wolff, Reinhold P. *Miami Metro: The Road to Urban Unity.* Coral Gables: Bureau of Business and Economic Research, University of Miami, 1960.

B. ARTICLES

Adrian, Charles R. "A Study of Three Communities," *Public Administration Review,* XVIII (Summer, 1958), 208–13.
Banfield, Edward C. "The Politics of Metropolitan Area Organization," *Midwest Journal of Political Science,* I (May, 1957), 77–91.
Bromage, Arthur W. "Political Representation in Metropolitan Areas," *American Political Science Review,* LII (June, 1958), 406–18.
Christenson, Reo. M. "The Power of the Press: The Case of 'The Toledo Blade,'" *Midwest Journal of Political Science,* III (Aug., 1959), 227–40.
Corcoran, John D. "Seeking Better Government for Metropolitan Areas," *Public Management,* XL (Apr., 1958), 82–85.
Derge, David R. "Metropolitan and Outside Alignment in Illinois and Missouri Legislative Delegations," *American Political Science Review,* LII (Dec., 1958), 1051–65.
Doherty, Herbert J., Jr. "Liberal and Conservative Voting Patterns in Florida," *The Journal of Politics,* XIV (Aug., 1952), 403–18.
Eliot, Thomas H. "Dilemmas in Metropolitan Research," *Midwest Journal of Political Science,* II (Feb., 1958), 26–39.
Frost, Richard T. "On Derge's Metropolitan and Outside Legislative Delegations," *American Political Science Review,* LIII (Sept., 1959), 792–95.

Heard, Alexander. "Interviewing Southern Politicians," *American Political Science Review*, XLIV (Dec., 1950), 886–97.
Prothro, James W., Campbell, Ernest Q., and Grigg, Charles M. "Two-Party Voting in the South," *American Political Science Review*, LII (Mar., 1958), 131–40.
Sayre, Wallace S. "The General Manager Idea for Large Cities," *Public Administration Review*, XIV (Autumn, 1954), 253–58.
Sofen, Edward. "Problems of Metropolitan Leadership: The Miami Experience," *Midwest Journal of Political Science*, V (Feb., 1961), 18–38.
————. "Financial Dilemma Miami-Dade Style," *National Civic Review* (April, 1962), pp. 220–22.
Sours, James K. "Some Observations on Management of Large Cities," *University of Wichita Bulletin*, Wichita, Kans. (August, 1957).
"What the Cities are Doing," *Public Management*, (July, 1958), 172–73.
Wilmott, John F. "The Truth About City-County Consolidation," *Miami Law Quarterly*, II (Dec., 1947), 127–79.
Wood, Robert C. "The New Metropolis," *American Political Science Review*, LII (Mar., 1958), 108–22.

C. NEWSPAPERS AND MAGAZINES

*Miami Herald*. 1945–1948 (special events); 1953–1962. *passim*.
*Miami News*. 1945–1948 (special events); 1953–1962. *passim*.
*Miami Beach Sun*. 1954–1959 (special events).
*Time Magazine*, Sept. 29, 1958.

D. RADIO AND TELEVISION PROGRAMS

Drew Pearson, NBC radio network. 6:00 P.M., Apr. 19, 1959.
"Important," television station WSPT (Channel 10, Miami), 6:00 P.M., Sept. 12, 1958, May 17, 1959, 1960–1962, *passim*.
Ralph Renick, television station WTVJ (Channel 4, Miami), 6:30 P.M., Monday–Friday, 1957–1962, *passim*.
"University of Miami Round Table Discussion," radio station WGBS (Miami), 9:30 P.M., Oct. 2, 1958.

E. OTHER MATERIAL

Adrian, Charles A. *The Role of the City Council in Community Policy-Making*. Michigan State University: 1959. (Mimeographed.) (Paper delivered at the 1959 Annual Meeting of the American Political Science Association, at Washington, D. C., Sept. 10–12, 1959.)
Beiler, Ross C. *Memorandum to the Greater Miami Foundation for Civic Education*. Coral Gables: May 17, 1953. (Mimeographed.)
Beiler, Ross C., and Wood, Thomas J. *Metropolitan Politics of Greater Miami*. Coral Gables: 1958. (Mimeographed.) (Address

delivered at the Annual Meeting of the Southern Political Science
Association, at Gatlinburg, Tenn., Nov. 6–8, 1958.)
Campbell, O. W. *The Dade County Experiment in Metropolitan
Government to Date.* Los Angeles: 1958. (Mimeographed.)
(Speech delivered at Metropolitan Government Symposium, at
Los Angeles, Calif., Apr. 8, 1958.)
————. Speech delivered at the Annual Conference of the League
of California Cities, Los Angeles, Calif., Oct. 26–29, 1958.
(Mimeographed.)
Citizens' "Vote No" Committee. *Report to Miami-Dade Chamber
Board Meeting.* Miami: Oct. 13, 1958. (Mimeographed.)
City of Miami and Metropolitan Dade County. *Magic City Center:
Economic Appraisal and Projections.* Miami: Mar., 1960. (Mimeo-
graphed.)
Coke, James C. *Metropolitan Government Structure: Some Critical
Determinants of Proposed Metropolitan Solutions.* University of
Pennsylvania: 1958. (Mimeographed.) (Address delivered at the
Annual Meeting of the American Political Science Association at
St. Louis, Mo., Sept. 4–6, 1958.)
*The Crime Commission of Greater Miami.* Miami. (Undated pam-
phlets.)
Dade County Research Foundation. *A Commentary on the Proposed
Metropolitan Ordinances.* Miami: Aug., 1957. (Mimeographed.)
————. *Pre-election Questionnaire.* Miami: June, 1958. (Mimeo-
graphed.)
————. "What's the Proposition?" *Consolidation Story No. 1.* Miami:
April, 1953. (Mimeographed.)
————. *Newsletters.* Miami: 1947–1958, *passim.* (Mimeographed.)
Department of Water and Sewers, City of Miami, Florida. *Pure Water
for the Magic City.* Miami: 1957–58.
————. *Semi-autonomous Status of the Department of Water and
Sewers of the City of Miami.* Miami: 1958. (Mimeographed.)
Downing, Rondal G. *The Reapportionment Amendment of 1959.*
Gainesville, Fla: Public Administration Clearing Service, Univer-
sity of Florida, 1959. (Pamphlet.)
Gray, Kenneth E. *A Report on Politics in St. Louis.* Cambridge: Cen-
ter for Urban Studies, Harvard University, 1959. (Mimeographed.)
Heuson, W. G., Slotts, M. F., and Wolff, Reinhold P. *A Study of
Florida's Miscellaneous Taxes, Licenses and Fees Prepared for the
Florida Legislative Interim Committee on Finance and Taxation.*
Coral Gables, Fla., University of Miami: 1960. (Mimeographed.)
Jensen, James R. *The Politics of Metropolitan Integration: An Interim
Report from Houston.* Houston: 1958. (Mimeographed.) (Address
delivered at the Annual Meeting of the Southern Political Science
Association, at Gatlinburg, Tenn., Nov. 6–8, 1958.)
Milwaukee Citizens Government Research Bureau. *Report on Meet-*

266                                    BIBLIOGRAPHICAL DATA

*ing of the Milwaukee Delegation with Dade County Officials on the New Metropolitan Miami Government Plan.* Milwaukee, 1958. (Mimeographed.)

National Municipal League. *Digest of County Manager Charters and Laws.* 5th ed. New York: 1958. (Mimeographed.)

O'Harrow, Dennis. *Metropolitan Planning for Dade County.* Miami: 1958. (Mimeographed.)

Pallot, William L. *An Open Letter to the Chairman of the Board of Dade County Commissioners and to all the Mayors of the Municipalities in the Greater Miami Area.* Miami: June 16, 1953. (Mimeographed.)

Sales Management. *Survey of Buying Power.* New York: May 10, 1950.

Serino, Gustave R. *Miami's Metropolitan Experiment.* Gainesville, Fla.: Public Administration Clearing Service, University of Florida, 1958. (Pamphlet.)

Sofen, Edward, Committee on Municipal Research, Department of Government, University of Miami. *Comparative Basic Costs of Home Ownership in Dade County.* Coral Gables: 1960. (Mimeographed.)

―――. *Comparative Services and Expenditures in Dade County.* Coral Gables: 1960. (Mimeographed.)

―――. *A Report on Politics in Greater Miami.* Cambridge: Center for Urban Studies, Harvard University, 1961. (Mimeographed.)

Toulmin, Harry T. *Miami Metro and the Voters.* Miami: 1959. (Mimeographed.) (Speech delivered at National Planning Conference, Minneapolis, Minn., May 13, 1959.)

Willmott, John F. "City-County Consolidation," *Governmental Research Association: Notes & References.* Vol. 4, No. 9, New York: Sept. 1948.

Wood, Robert C. *Metropolitan Government, 1975: An Extrapolation of Trends—The New Metropolis: Green Belts, Grass Roots or Gargantua?* Massachusetts 1957. (Mimeographed.) (Paper presented at the American Political Science Association, New York, Sept., 1957.)

―――. *Some Implications of Metropolitan Growth for Government.* Massachusetts: Aug. 1, 1958. (Mimeographed.)

Wood, Thomas J., and Sofen, Edward. *Municipal Finance in Dade County for the Fiscal Year 1960.* Coral Gables: Committee on Municipal Research, Government Department, University of Miami, 1961. (Mimeographed.)

# Notes

## Introduction

1. Herbert J. Doherty, Jr., "Liberal and Conservative Voting Patterns in Florida," 14 *Journal of Politics* 403–15 (Aug., 1952).
2. V. O. Key, Jr., *Southern Politics* (New York: Alfred A. Knopf, 1955), Chapter 5.
3. Richard M. Scammon (ed.), Government Affairs Institute, *America Votes, I* (New York: Macmillan, 1956), p. 57.
4. Richard M. Scammon (ed.), Government Affairs Institute, *America Votes, 1956–57* (New York: Macmillan, 1958), p. 67.
5. James W. Prothro, Ernest Q. Campbell, and Charles M. Grigg, "Two Party Voting in the South: Class vs. Party Identification," 52 *American Political Science Review* 132 (Mar., 1958).
6. Key, *Southern Politics*, pp. 83–87.
7. *Ibid.*, p. 99, n. 15.
8. Henning Heldt, "Heaven or Honky-Tonk?" in Robert S. Allen (ed.), *Our Fair City* (New York: Vanguard Press, 1947), pp. 77–99.
9. Abe Aronovitz died on July 11, 1960, but the legend of "honest Abe" lives on.
10. Individual members of the Dade County Development Committee, an organization whose primary interest is to promote capital improvements for the Greater Miami area, also contributed to the achievement of Metro. The committee is composed of 75 members who are among the area's most influential businessmen and civic leaders. While the sentiments of many of these persons were overwhelmingly in favor of the home rule charter, the organization as such took no official stand on this issue. However, individual members worked with the Charter Board, the Miami-Dade Chamber of Commerce, and other pro-Metro civic organizations.

## 1  Metropolitan Miami

1. In this study the terms Metropolitan Miami, Greater Miami, the Miami area, and Dade County are used interchangeably to describe the

entire area involved in the Miami metropolitan experiment. This area includes 26 municipalities and the unincorporated areas of Dade County, Florida. To avoid confusion, the core city of Miami, the largest of Dade's municipalities, will be designated as the City of Miami.

2. Public Administration Service, *The Government of Metropolitan Miami* (Chicago: Public Administration Service, 1954), p. 1.

3. In 1920, 42,753 persons resided in Greater Miami and, in 1945, 315,060 persons. See U. S., Bureau of the Census, *Census of the United States: 1920–1960, passim; Special Census of the State of Florida: 1945.*

4. A six-month record, from January through June, 1960, of the Mayflower Transit Company, one of the largest interstate moving concerns operating in the Greater Miami area, reveals that 410 families moved into the Miami area and 320 moved out. Although one cannot conclude without additional data that this is a fixed ratio of in- to out-migration, the figures nonetheless indicate a possible pattern. The data further show that the geographical regions that send Miami the greatest number of new residents also receive the greatest number of outgoing families. Edward Sofen, *A Report on Politics in Greater Miami* (Cambridge: Center for Urban Studies, Harvard University, 1961. Mimeographed).

5. Dade County Development Department, *Economic Survey of Metropolitan Miami* (Miami: Dade County Development Department, 1959), sec. 16, p. 4.

6. Projection made in October, 1958, by Dr. Reinhold P. Wolff of the University of Miami's Bureau of Business and Economic Research. The United States Bureau of the Census on July 29, 1960, however, designated the Ft. Lauderdale-Hollywood area as a separate and distinct metropolitan area. See *Miami Herald*, July 30, 1960, p. 1A.

7. Dennis O'Harrow, *Metropolitan Planning for Dade County: A Summary Report* (Dade County: Dec., 1958. Mimeographed), p. 49. In noting the existence of 31 governmental units in Dade County, O'Harrow seems to have been referring to the 26 municipalities, the county government, the Dade County Board of Public Instruction, the Dade County Port Authority, the Central and Southern Florida Flood Control District, and the Little River Valley Drainage District. All exercise some taxing powers. For other possibilities, see Public Administration Service, *Metropolitan Miami*, pp. 124–26.

8. Albany-Schenectady-Troy; Atlanta; Birmingham; Cincinnati; Columbus; Dallas; Denver; Houston; Kansas City; Louisville; Milwaukee; New Orleans; Portland, Oregon; Providence; San Antonio; San Diego; Seattle; and Youngstown. See O'Harrow, *Metropolitan Planning*, p. 50.

9. A charter for Dade's twenty-seventh municipality, Islandia, a series of isolated and undeveloped islands to the south of the Dade County mainland, was approved by the voters of the new city on June 20, 1961. Its 14 registered voters own property in the new community but most

reside elsewhere. Islandia is a paper city with a great potential because of its 17 miles of ocean front. However, since Islandia as a political entity was nonexistent during the struggle over Metropolitan government, it will not be dealt with in the study.

10. Edward Sofen, Department of Government, University of Miami, *Comparative Basic Costs of Home Ownership in Dade County* (Coral Gables: 1960. Mimeographed), p. 5.

11. When the term of office of Judge L. E. Thomas, Negro judge for the Negro municipal precinct court, expired on January 5, 1962, the City Commission did not reappoint Judge Thomas nor appoint any other Negro to fill the position. As of February, 1962, the other municipal judges took turns in presiding at this court.

12. Except for Coral Gables, all the cities included in the category of "self-conscious" communities voted either against the pro-Metro home rule charter or for the "anti-Metro" autonomy amendment. In most cases they embraced both of these voting positions. The position of Coral Gables will be examined and analyzed in a later part of this study.

13. Florida, *Constitution* (1885), Art. VIII, sec. 8. See *State v. Grable*, 72 Fla. 61, 72 So. 460 (1916) and *State v. County Commissioners*, 23 Fla. 483, 3 So. 193 (1887). Florida, *Constitution* (1885), Art. III, sec. 24, incorporating an amendment adopted in 1934, contemplated putting an end to the establishment of municipalities by special legislation. See *State v. Alsop*, 120 Fla. 628, 163 So. 80 (1935). However, the legislature has remained unaffected by the provisions of Article III, section 24.

14. Florida, *Statutes* (1957), sec. 165.01.

15. Florida, *Statutes* (1957), secs. 165.03, 165.04, 165.08.

16. *Ocean Beach Heights, Inc. v. Brown-Crummer Investment Co.*, 302 U. S. 614 (1939); *Leatherman v. Alta Cliff Co.*, 114 Fla. 305, 153 So. 845 (1934); *Manhood v. State ex. rel. Davis*, 101 Fla. 1254, 133 So. 90 (1931).

17. Public Administration Service, *Metropolitan Miami*, pp. 5, 6, 11.

18. Special Acts of Florida (1949), c. 25758. The underlying reason for this legislation was the creation or attempted creation of a number of municipalities in substandard areas, sometimes as devious schemes of land promoters.

19. Information obtained from former members of the 1953 Dade delegation to the state legislature.

## 2 Functional Cooperation and Consolidation

1. As of November, 1958, there were 57 private water and sewer service companies in the Miami area with widely varying rate structures. Rader and Associates, *Survey and Report on Privately-Owned Water and Sewerage Utilities in Metropolitan Dade County, Florida* (Miami: Nov.,

1958), pp. 3–59. During 1958 there were numerous complaints about the water rates of the Consumers Water Company, which services the cities of South Miami and Coral Gables and the adjacent unincorporated areas. As a result the City of South Miami took action which led to a reduction in water rates within the city. In *Consumers Water Company v. City of South Miami*, No. 58C5168 (Dade Cir. Ct. Fla. 1961), the Dade Circuit Court held that the rates fixed by the South Miami City Commission were reasonable and not confiscatory. The decision was appealed.

2. Department of Water and Sewers, City of Miami, Florida, *Pure Water for the Magic City* (Miami: 1957–58), p. 2. On December 3, 1961, Metro unveiled its twin master plans for water and sewer development. Both plans called for long-range development aimed at a unified water and sewer service for Dade County. See Department of Water and Sewers, City of Miami, Florida, *Report on Master Plan for Water Facilities* (Miami: 1961); and Greely and Hanson, and Maurice H. Connel Associates, *Metropolitan Dade County Master Plan for Sanitary Sewerage* (Miami: 1961).

3. In April, 1960, Metro purchased the North Miami system and provided radio communication services to the member cities on a contractual basis. Since that time, Metro has created an extensive Metropolitan Police Radio Communications Department at a cost of some $500,000—$200,000 of which was obtained from federal Civil Defense. The Department presently serves 9 cities. The independent communication systems of the cities of Miami, Hialeah, Miami Beach, and Coral Gables are still maintained as in the pre-Metro period. On February 13, 1962, these four systems through a mutual agreement installed a "flip-the-switch" system which permits a dispatcher in one system in an emergency to reach simultaneously the police cars of all four systems.

4. In the pre-Metro period, the City of Miami had both a police academy and a fire college, whereas Dade County had only a police academy. Since October 1, 1960, Dade County has also established a fire academy and has expanded its police training program. The latter is formulated, directed, and supervised by the Dade County Public Safety Department in cooperation with the Adult Division of the Dade County Board of Public Instruction.

5. Information from City of Miami Fire Chief N. O. Wheeler, chairman of the Mutual Aid Organization.

6. Despite the relative dearth of long-range planning, the County Commission displayed exceptional foresight in acquiring potential sites for beaches and parks.

7. Public Administration Service, *Metropolitan Miami*, pp. 136–38.

8. Metro (Dade County, Florida) Ordinance No. 57–22.

9. *City of Coral Gables* v. *Gray*, 154 Fla. 881, 19 So. 2d 318 (1944). The issue involved a proposed amendment to the Florida Constitution which provided for the consolidation in Dade County and in Orange

County of municipal and county tax assessing and collecting offices and of certain court offices (General Laws of Florida (1943), H. J. R. 786). Orange County had been included in the proposal to win support in the state legislature. Ironically, the proposed amendment was ruled unconstitutional on the grounds that it embraced more than one county and also affected more than one article of the Florida Constitution.

10. General Acts of Florida (1943), c. 21871.

11. Special Acts of Florida (1945), c. 23226.

12. *Ibid.*, secs. 2, 5. See also Florida, *Constitution* (1885), Art. XII, secs. 8, 10.

13. Florida, *Constitution* (1885), Art. XII, sec. 8.

14. *Ibid.*, sec. 10.

15. Interview with John D. Pennekamp, associate editor of the *Miami Herald*.

16. The Dade County electorate cast 13,800 votes for consolidation and 821 votes against. The official election returns were obtained from the office of the Dade County Board of Public Instruction.

17. Professor Reinhold P. Wolff, formerly of the University of Miami's Bureau of Business and Economic Research, contends that Dade County does not receive a proportionate share of the funds it contributes to the state. For example, state income from horse and dog tracks and jai-alai frontons was $24.9 million in the fiscal year ending June 30, 1957. Of this amount, Dade County establishments contributed $13.6 million, but the county in return received only $175,000. Another example is the state tax on alcoholic beverages, which yielded nearly $40 million, of which Dade contributed approximately $7.8 million. The state sales and use tax from Dade amounted to $8.4 million. Despite these substantial contributions to the state, Dade received only slightly more than $1 million in direct benefits from the State Treasury along with indirect benefits from such state-wide services as education, hospitals, penal institutions, and state promotional activities. Wolff concludes that most of these services are provided in proportion to Dade's population but do not compensate for Dade's contributions to the State Treasury. Reinhold P. Wolff, *Miami Metro: The Road to Urban Unity* (Coral Gables: Bureau of Business and Economic Research, University of Miami, 1960), p. 153.

This point of view should be compared with that expressed in a 1959 report specially prepared by the Legislative Reference Bureau for Dade Representative W. C. Herrell, former chairman of the Legislative Council. The report estimated that the total state tax collection from Dade County for the fiscal year ending June 30, 1959, was $159,530,143 or 24 per cent of the state total. The county received almost $24 million in school funds, $6½ million in public assistance, more than $21 million in road funds, and some $4⅓ million from other sources. All told, these expenditures amounted to $56,243,289. A variety of other services and functions emanating from the governor's office, the legislature, the judicial system, general governmental agencies, the Board of Health, the correctional system and a $1,000 grant-system for each state university student prorated for the Greater Miami area yielded an additional total of $46,918,601 in state revenue spent in Dade County. On the basis of this latter figure, plus the aforementioned $56,243,289, Dade received the sum of $103,161,890 or 15.77 per cent of the state's total expenditures.

18. City of Miami Beach, *Annual Fiscal Report, Fiscal Year Ending September 30, 1959*, p. 43. Miami Beach, like all the other cities in Dade County, benefits from a county health department, county welfare department, county hospitals, county parks, and the state court system for the county. However, even if Miami Beach residents were to use their proportionate per capita share of county services the return they would receive from the county would be a substantially lower percentage than the county receives from the state.

19. Special Acts of Florida (1943), c. 22303.

20. Special Acts of Florida (1945), c. 23300; General Acts of Florida (1945), c. 22963.

21. Most City of Miami business groups, as exemplified by their actions in the Miami-Dade Chamber of Commerce, have supported every move for functional and geographical consolidation in the area. See below, pp. 79–80. Although there is no evidence that the central city businessmen constituted the moving force behind the transfer of the Port Authority to the county, the consensus of informed observers is that the move received the blessing of these businessmen.

22. The local oil companies reflected the ambivalence of a group which generally preferred city control (e.g., the City of Miami Seaport), but were nevertheless willing to support county control where it would redound to the companies' benefit. The idea for a county Port Authority bill was first mentioned to a member of the Dade delegation by an oil company representative.

23. *Miami Herald*, Sept. 29, 1945, p. 1B.

24. The Department of Water and Sewers of the City of Miami was created by Special Acts of Florida (1941), c. 21388. This semiautonomous agency was patterned after recommendations made to the City Commission in 1940 by the City of New York Fund Council and by investment bankers. Department of Water and Sewers of the City of Miami, *Semi-autonomous Status of the Department of Water and Sewers of the City of Miami* (Miami: 1958. Mimeographed), p. 1.

25. *Final Report of the Grand Jury* in the Circuit Court of the Eleventh Judicial Circuit of Florida in and for the County of Dade filed on May 8, 1939), p. 3. Grand jury reports are not confined to discussions of violations of the law, but may examine, criticize, and make recommendations concerning any issue under investigation.

26. Special Acts of Florida (1945), c. 23225.

27. *Ibid.*, c. 23404.

28. Information from the Office of County Clerk, Board of County Commissioners, Dade County.

29. *Miami Herald*, Jan. 31, 1947, p. 1B; Apr. 3, 1948, p. 1B.

30. *Ibid.*, June 7, 1946, p. 1B. For a list of the members of the County Commission and of the City of Miami Commission see Appendix B.

31. The investigating committee was composed of E. C. Allen, Abe Aronovitz, Beverly Benson, Raymond Miller, and William D. Singer.

32. City Commissioners Robert L. Floyd, Perrine Palmer, Jr., and H. Leslie Quigg voted for the measure and Commissioners William W. Charles and R. C. Gardner voted against it. *Miami Herald*, June 3, 1948, p. 8A.

33. The vote was 53,003 for and 10,593 against. Information from the Office of the Supervisor of Registration for Dade County, Florida.


3   Moves for Governmental Consolidation

1. *Joint Resolution* Proposing an Amendment to Article VIII to the Constitution of the State of Florida Relative to Cities and Counties (1945. Mimeographed). A copy of this proposal may be found in the files of the University of Miami's Department of Government.

2. Mayor Thomson's files were made available to the Ford study group.

3. *Miami Herald*, Mar. 4, p. 1A, and Mar. 11, 1945, p. 5B.

4. *Ibid.*, Mar. 6, 1945, p. 6A.

5. *Ibid.*, Mar. 16, 1945, p. 1B. Golden Beach, Indian Creek Village, Homestead, and Florida City were not represented at the meeting. The City of Miami was not invited.

6. *Miami Herald*, Apr. 4, 1945, p. 4A.

7. *Ibid.*, Mar. 14, 1945, p. 1B.

8. *Ibid.*, Apr. 5, 1945, p. 6A.

9. H. J. R. 440 (1945). See Florida, *House Journal* (1945), pp. 274, 722.

10. See Florida, *Senate Journal* (1945), p. 745.

11. Flagler City is no longer in existence.

12. General Laws of Florida (1947), H.J.R. 407.

13. Special Acts of Florida (1947), c. 24468.

14. Special Acts of Florida (1947), c. 24467.

15. General Laws of Florida (1947), H.J.R. 407, sec. 14 (e)2.

16. *Miami Herald*, Feb. 7, 1948, p. 1B.

17. See *ibid.*, Jan. 31, p. 1B; Feb. 7, p. 1B; Feb. 20, 1948, p. 1B.

18. *Ibid.*, Feb. 7, 1948, p. 1B.

19. *Ibid.*, Feb. 20, 1948, p. 1B.

20. *City of Miami Beach* v. *Crandon*, 35 So. 2d 285 (Fla. 1948), was the only one of the three cases dealing with the constitutionality of submitting the consolidation measure to the voters of Dade County. The other two cases, which challenged the constitutionality of the amendment itself, were dependent upon the outcome of the county referendum. See *Miami Herald*, May 8, 1948, p. 1A.

21. John F. Willmott, "City-County Consolidation," *Government Research Association: Notes & References*, Vol. 4, No. 9 (Sept. 1948), pp. 2–3. League of Women Voters records indicate that the organization took no official stand on the consolidation issue; many of its members, however, actively supported this move for consolidation. In 1948 there was only one league in Dade County, the League of Women Voters of the City of Miami, although some members were from other cities. Subsequently, leagues were formed in the cities of Coral Gables, Hialeah, and Miami Beach.

22. *Miami Herald*, Mar. 3, 1948, p. 1B.

23. The organization felt that no active work should be undertaken until pending litigation was disposed of in the courts. However, some of the litigation was still pending when the vote was taken on May 25, 1948. The Consolidation Committee folded a few weeks before the elections. Its work was taken over by a group of Miami Junior of Chamber of Commerce members who actively campaigned by making speeches and distributing pamphlets. Willmott, "City-County Consolidation," pp. 2–3.

24. The number of persons residing in the City of Miami in 1945 was 197,326, which was 63 per cent of Dade County's 315,060 population. By 1950 the city contained 249,276 persons who accounted for approximately 50 per cent of Dade County's 495,084 population. U. S., Bureau of the Census, *Census of the United States: 1950; Special Census of the State of Florida: 1945*.

25. Of the 28,800 votes from the City of Miami, 16,853 were for the proposal and 11,947 against. Information obtained from the Office of the Supervisor of Registration for Dade County, Florida.

26. Ross C. Beiler and Thomas J. Wood, *Metropolitan Politics of Greater Miami* (Coral Gables, Florida: 1958. Mimeographed), p. 2. (Paper delivered at Annual Meeting of Southern Political Science Association at Gatlinburg, Tenn., Nov. 6–8, 1958.)

27. Willmott, "City-County Consolidation," pp. 2–3.

28. General Laws of Florida (1951), S.J.R. 117.

29. It should be recalled that the City of Miami had been viewed as "the enemy" by its sister cities in the 1945 and 1948 consolidation attempts. Some City of Miami elected officials had taken the lead in promoting and supporting these early movements. What happened by 1951 to bring about a change of outlook by the city fathers? According to some observers, the City of Miami commissioners were no longer

business oriented but politically oriented (i.e., those receptive to other interests). There was a new type of commissioner who no longer catered to the business interests and who, in a number of instances, received financial support from the illegal gambling groups. It might also be noted that in 1945, for example, the City of Miami contained over 60 per cent of the population against approximately 50 per cent in 1952 which would mean that the city's relative strength in regard to the rest of the county had diminished by 1952.

Coral Gables voters approved the amendment by slightly more than the county average despite the opposition of the city council. The 1952 vote represented the beginning of a change in the attitude of Coral Gables voters on issues pertaining to metropolitan problems.

30. Miami Beach Councilman Melvin J. Richard claimed the action was illegal and refused to sign the letters.

31. S.B. No. 452, the initial consolidation bill, did not contain a referendum. See Florida, Senate Journal (1953), p. 168.

32. Information obtained from interviews with the four Dade delegates to the 1953 session of the Florida Legislature.

33. Miami Herald, Mar. 23, p. 6A, and Mar. 25, 1953, p. 6A; Miami News, Mar. 25, 1953, pp. 14A, 15A.

34. Miami Herald, Apr. 24, 1953, p. 1B.

35. Ibid., Mar. 19, 1953, p. 1A.

36. 48 yeas and 34 nays. See Florida, House Journal (1953), pp. 322–23.

37. Some students of Florida government maintain that the legislative tradition of noninterference with local bills supported by a majority of a county delegation does not apply when a dissenting delegate seeks to have a referendum attached to the bill. See Wilson Keyser Doyle, Angus McKenzie Laird, and S. Sherman Weiss, The Government and Administration of Florida, (New York: Thomas Y. Crowell, 1954), p. 72. Members of the Dade delegation, however, did not concur with this interpretation of legislative behavior.

38. Special Acts of Florida (1953), c. 29280, abolished the City of Miami and provided for a referendum; Special Acts of Florida, (1953), c. 29281, established a local government for the new City and County of Miami in the event of the approval of the referendum.

39. Ross C. Beiler, Memorandum to the Greater Miami Foundation for Civic Education (Coral Gables, Florida: May 17, 1953. Mimeographed). Many residents of the unincorporated areas felt they, too, should have been entitled to vote on the issue.

40. Dade County Research Foundation, "What's the Proposition?" Consolidation Story No. 1 (Miami: Apr. 18, 1953. Mimeographed), p. 3.

41. George S. Okell, Sr., quoted in Miami Herald, June 10, 1953, p. 10A.

4   Opening the Way for Metropolitan Government

1. *Miami Herald,* June 17, 1953, p. 6A.
2. *Ibid.,* July 1, 1953, p. 6C.
3. *Ibid.,* July 2, 1953, p. 1B.
4. U. S. Congress, House, Subcommittee of the Committee on Government Operations, *Hearings, Federal-State-Local Relations, Dade County (Florida) Metropolitan Government,* 85th Cong. 1st sess., Nov. 21 and 22, 1957, p. 6.
5. *Miami Herald,* July 26, 1953, p. 1B.
6. The Advisory Committee was composed of Judge George E. Holt, chairman of the 3M Board; Donald R. Larson, chairman of the Government Department of the University of Miami; William L. Pallot, attorney; and Joseph J. Orr, plumbing contractor. Larson, Pallot, and Orr emerged as the prime policy formulators of the 3M Board and later of the first Charter Board. See below, p. 82.
7. The University of Miami Committee on Municipal Research was composed of the following members of the Government Department: Professor Donald R. Larson, chairman, and Professors Gustave R. Serino, Edward Sofen, and Thomas J. Wood. Aside from Dr. Larson who was also a member of the 3M Board, it was more of an advisory than a supervisory committee.
8. Public Administration Service, *The Government of Metropolitan Miami* (Chicago: Public Administration Service, 1954), pp. 87–111.
9. The sixth draft of the home rule bill, which was written by the law firm of Dubbin, Blatt & Schiff, read: "The electors of Dade County, Florida, shall have and are hereby given the power and authority to establish, alter and *abolish a central county government* . . . in the place of any and all *county* and district governments. . . ." (Emphasis added.)
10. The sixth draft provided that ". . . no municipality may be *abolished* nor may its boundaries be reduced *except upon approval by a majority vote* of the qualified voters participating in an election and residing in the entire combined area affected. . . ." (Emphasis added.)
11. Paul's draft of the home rule amendment permitted the charter board to "provide a method by which any or all of the functions or powers of any municipal corporation or other governmental unit in Dade County may be transferred to the County Commission." See Florida, *Constitution* (1885), Art. VIII, sec. 11 (1) (d) for the provision as enacted (Appendix E).
12. *Metropolitan Charter Board Minutes,* Indoctrination Meeting of the New Charter Board Members, Dec. 5, 1956.
13. *Ibid.*
14. See General Laws of Florida (1955), S.J.R. 1046 and also

c. 31420, Laws of Florida, Extraordinary Session, 1956, which repealed c. 30686, Special Acts of Florida, 1955.

15. Florida, *Constitution* (1885), Art. III, sec. 27. For a judicial construction of this section, see *Blitch* v. *Buchanan*, 100 Fla. 1202, 131 So. 151 (1930).

16. In re *Advisory Opinions to the Governor*, 76 Fla. 417, 418, 79 So. 874 (1918); *Attorney General* v. *Connors*, 27 Fla. 339, 9 So. 7 (1891); Florida, *Biennial Report of the Attorney General* (1951–1952), p. 258.

17. Florida, *Constitution* (1885), Art. XVI, sec. 15.

18. George E. Holt, circuit judge; E. B. Leatherman, circuit court clerk; I. D. MacVicar, county commissioner; Robert M. Morgan, member of the State Board of Accountancy; J. Abney Cox, chairman of the Central and Southern Florida Flood Control Board.

19. General Laws of Florida (1955), S.J.R. 1046.

20. The distinction between the reorganization of the County Commission and its complete elimination, as advocated by the 3M Board, was probably more illusory than real.

21. Florida, *Constitution* (1885), Art. IX, sec. 15; Florida, *Statutes* (1957), sec. 550.13.

22. For the legal and constitutional technicalities of this problem, see Florida, *Biennial Report of the Attorney General* (1957–1958), p. 368.

23. Florida, *Report of the Comptroller, State of Florida, for the Fiscal Year Ended June 30, 1960*, pp. 298–302.

24. Compare the sixth draft, drawn up at an earlier date: "The central county government established under this section *may exercise all the powers of a municipality* created pursuant to State law. . . ." (Emphasis added.)

25. For an example of a violation of this provision, see General Acts of Florida (1957), c. 57912, and *Chase* v. *Cowart*, 102 So. 2d 147 (Fla. 1957).

26. *Golden* v. *Gray*, 9 Fla. Supp. 17 (Leon Cir. Ct. 1956).

27. *Gray* v. *Golden*, 89 So. 2d 785 (Fla. 1956).

28. The problem of inadequate taxing powers was to plague the new metropolitan government later. Some observers believe this inadequacy to be Metro's greatest shortcoming. This matter will be developed in subsequent chapters.


5   Allocation of Powers by the Charter


1. Public Administration Service, *Working Draft for a Proposed Charter, Dade County, Florida* (Chicago: Public Administration Service, 1955. Mimeographed).

2. Information on Charter Board meetings is taken from minutes of the meetings in the board files.

3. For example, the Public Administration Service draft did not include the equivalent of section 1.01 B or section 8.04.

4. Powers that normally belong to the county government or that refer only to the administrative functions of the county are not considered. They include the authority of the county to create and control other government units (including special districts), to investigate county affairs, and to exercise the power of eminent domain.

5. An amendment to the charter enacted by referendum on August 15, 1961, eliminated sections 9.03 A and 9.03 B. The former provided for county reassessment of all real and tangible personal property. The latter, as of the beginning of the 1961 tax year, made mandatory the employment of the tax rolls prepared by the county for the assessment of taxes within both the incorporated and unincorporated areas, except as provided in 9.03 D.

6. In *Dade County* v. *Mercury Radio Service*, 134 So. 2d 791 (Fla. 1961), the Florida Supreme Court held that Dade County Ordinance No. 58–35 which provides for the licensing and regulation of all taxicabs and other vehicles for hire operating in the unincorporated areas, was unconstitutional in that it conflicted with the general statutes of the State of Florida. The ordinance was declared invalid both as to the taxicab companies holding master permits issued by the Florida Railroad and Public Utilities Commission, and as to the taxicab companies regulated by ordinances of the various municipalities in Dade County. (Sections 323.05 (1) and 323.05 (3), Florida Statutes.) County Attorney Darrey Davis believed that the court's opinion in effect nullified and invalidated Section 1.01 A (3) of the home rule charter.

7. Since under the Home Rule Amendment the county was not permitted to receive cigarette taxes from the unincorporated areas on the same basis as the cities, the italicized phrase in Section 1.01 D above would appear to be inconsistent with the provisions of the amendment.

8. See note 6.

9. In commenting on the distinguishing features of federal systems of government, Ernest B. Schulz made the following observations: (1) "The principal earmark of a federal system is the guarantee by adequate constitutional arrangement, of some degree of autonomy for major local units. Neither the continued existence of these political subdivisions nor the retention of their right to govern themselves depends on the will of the central government." (2) "The central government and the major political subdivisions derive their discretionary powers from the same source, viz., the constitution." (3) There is also needed "a mode of amendment which is so devised that neither the central government nor the major political subdivisions possess the exclusive right to alter the constitution's provisions." *Essentials of Government* (Englewood Cliffs, N. J.: Prentice-Hall, 1958), p. 182.

10. The national government has exercised a similar type of control over the states through grants-in-aid and tax rebates.

## 6   Charter Board Decisions

1. In a September, 1958, poll in which 433 registered voters were interviewed (Beiler Survey No. 12), respondents were handed a list of factors "which may have been helpful to you in making up your mind how to vote on the Autonomy Amendment on September 30." Each was asked to name the factor that had been most helpful and then the second and third most helpful factors. First factors were weighted three points; second, two points; and third, one point.
The results were as follows:

| FACTOR | PERCENTAGE |
|---|---|
| Miami Herald | 24½ |
| Ralph Renick (WTVJ television newscaster) | 15 |
| Neighbors, miscellaneous friends | 13½ |
| Trusted political leaders | 10½ |
| Organizations, fellow members | 10 |
| Work Companions | 9½ |
| Family | 6 |
| Miami News | 5 |
| Television stations WCKT, WPST, WTVJ | 4 |
| WQAM, other radio stations | 2 |

Interviews with the principals who were most active in promoting or opposing metropolitan government indicated that these persons overwhelmingly believed the Herald to be the most important influence in molding public opinion.

2. E.g., Miami Herald, July 9, p. 6A, and Dec. 19, 1956, p. 6A.

3. Miami News, Dec. 26, 1956, p. 15A.

4. In any case, television today is helping to destroy the near monopoly of the Miami newspapers in molding political opinion.

5. The legislative and administrative aspects of Metro are recounted in Chapter 14.

6. Dade County government prior to Metro was of the commission type with each commissioner in charge of specific departments. The commissioners had been under attack by the newspapers and the Dade County Research Foundation. John F. Wilmott, executive director of the foundation, believed the commission form of government to be an anachronism.

7. On February 13, 1956, the first Charter Board, by a 13 to 2 vote, approved a motion to have a council-manager form of government with a commission composed of 5 commissioners from districts at large, 5 from, and elected by, districts, a chairman elected at large, and 1 commissioner from each city with 6 per cent or more of the total county population. Four Charter Board members were absent when the vote was taken.

8. General Acts of Florida (1955), c. 30255, sec. 13.

9. A few months after the creation of the metropolitan government, the Personnel Board, as provided in a new personnel ordinance, became a purely advisory body. See Metro (Dade County, Florida) Ordinance No. 57–16.

10. The earliest empirical evidence to substantiate such citizen reactions was a September, 1958, poll in which 433 registered voters were interviewed (Beiler Survey No. 12). When interviewees were asked what they believed Greater Miami or Dade County most needed, they gave the following answers:

| NEED | PERCENTAGE |
|------|------------|
| 1. Highway, expressway, traffic handling improvements | 22 |
| 2. Metro, better governmental organization and co-ordination | 15 |
| 3. Better official personnel, political improvements | 11 |
| 4. Improved recreational facilities, parks, planning and zoning | 5½ |
| 5. Improved public safety services (more hospitals) | 5 |
| 6. Sewage, drainage, water facilities, garbage collection | 5 |
| 7. Street repaving, sidewalks, street lighting | 4½ |
| 8. More jobs, industry, better pay | 4 |
| 9. Better bus transportation | 4 |
| 10. Improvements in schools | 2½ |
| 11. Economy in county government | 2 |

When asked "What appears to you to be the best way to get this," the replies were as follows:

| MEANS | PERCENTAGE |
|-------|------------|
| 1. Insignificant answers | 29 |
| 2. Metro, county government | 18 |
| 3. State or federal intervention | 14 |
| 4. Other local government | 3 |
| 5. Citizen action; governmental not specified | 11 |
| 6. By improving governmental officials (nonspecific) | 5 |
| 7. Improved system for taxing (or borrowing) | 1 |

## 7   For and Against the Charter

1. The press release, dated March 28, 1957, is from Charter Board files. The Dade League of Municipalities is an association of Dade municipalities created for the purpose of promoting mutual interests.

2. *Miami Herald*, April 30, 1957, p. 1C; *Miami News*, April 30, 1957, p. 8A.

3. *Miami News*, April 23, 1957, p. 4A.

4. See editorials, *Miami Beach Sun,* April 7, 9, 12, May 19, 1957.

5. In a state-wide election in November, 1942, Article VIII, Section 11 of the Florida Constitution was amended to read as follows: "The County Commissioners of Dade County who shall be elected at the general election in 1942 shall, immediately after the beginning of their terms of office, redistrict Dade County into 5 County Commissioners' Districts to be numbered by the said Commissioners from one to five respectively and delineate the boundaries of such Districts in such a manner as to include within the respective Districts territory as follows:

"One of the said Commissioners' Districts shall compromise the territory which was on the first day of April 1941, embraced within Election Precincts numbered 24 to 32, inclusive, and also such parts of Election Precincts numbered 10, 56, 60, and 61 as lie east of the Western shore of Biscayne Bay, all as established by a resolution of the County Commissioners of said County adopted November 14, 1939, designated as Resolution No. 1077. . . ."

This last paragraph defines the boundaries of District No. 5 so as to include all of Miami Beach. The home rule amendment superseded this section of the Florida Constitution.

6. *Miami News,* May 10, 1957, p. 8A.

7. *Miami Herald,* May 8, 1957, p. 22A.

8. The executive committee of the Citizens Committee Opposing Metropolitan Charter consisted of Dean R. Claussen, Robert G. Lovett, D. Richard Mead, George S. Okell, Sr., William Owens, and Dr. Ben J. Sheppard (*Miami News,* May 10, 1957, p. 8A).

9. Article X, Section 7 of the Florida Constitution provides that certain real property on which the owner or his dependents reside is exempt from general property taxes on the first $5,000 of the assessed valuation.

10. *Miami News,* May 16, 1957, p. 1A.

11. The 3M Board voted 14 to 1 to endorse the charter and work for its adoption. The only dissenter was a former Miami Beach councilman.

12. While the Charter Board performed yeoman work in preparing the charter, only a handful of its members took an active role in the charter campaign.

13. Information on the league is from Mrs. John Baker, a former president of the League of Women Voters of Miami, Mrs. John Lotz III and Mrs. Thomas J. Wood, members of the same league.

14. Mr. Herrell, former president of the Dade County League of Municipalities, adopted a neutral position.

15. *Miami Herald,* May 10, 1957, p. 11C.

16. The cost of the campaign was paid from Charter Board funds allocated by the county. The Citizens Committee Opposing Metropolitan Charter condemned the use of these funds for campaign purposes.

17. Morgan, Altemus, & Barrs, CPA, *Statement of Funds Available and Disbursed for Period August 9, 1956 through December 31, 1956;* Morgan, Altemus, & Barrs, CPA, *Statement of Funds Available and*

*Disbursed for Period January 1, 1957, through June 25, 1957, Metropolitan Charter Board, Miami, Florida.* Funds expended prior to August 9, 1956, were included in the first of the above reports.

18. Information from Charter Board files.

19. The League of Woman Voters assumed a large share of the responsibility for telephoning and for distributing brochures, postcards, and bumper strips. Leaders of some Negro organizations took charge of the distribution of campaign materials in Negro areas.

20. Precinct returns were obtained from the Supervisor of Registration, Dade County, Florida.

21. Since some precincts are within both incorporated and unincorporated areas, it is impossible to make a more exact computation.

22. A division of the county's voting precincts into four classes based on the assessed valuation of residences, ranging from category I, the highest, to category IV, the lowest, showed that categories I and II favored the charter and categories III and IV opposed it. Percentage-wise, the vote was as follows: in category I, 56.6 per cent approved the charter; in category II, 52.1 per cent; in category III, 48.4 per cent; and in category IV, 47.3 per cent.

23. Ross C. Beiler and Thomas J. Wood, *Metropolitan Politics of Miami*, Table II (Mimeographed), p. 18. (Paper delivered at the annual meeting of the Southern Political Science Association at Gatlinburg, Tenn., Nov. 7, 1958.)

24. See below, p. 120.

25. City Manager E. Arthur Evans of the central City of Miami, who subsequently led the battle in favor of the autonomy amendment, supported the charter in 1957.

26. A poll conducted in late 1957 and early 1958 (Beiler Survey No. 10) indicated that the anti-Metro forces were primarily concerned with preserving for the cities some constitutional prerogatives and their "rightful" areas of functioning.

27. See Chapter 6, "Charter Board Decisions," note 10.


8  Reflections on the Creation of Metro

1. A September, 1958, poll (Beiler Survey No. 12) indicated that the attitude of 433 registered voters towards the autonomy amendment, a pro-city amendment to the home rule charter, varied with the length of residence.
The statistics were as follows:

|  | 7 months to 5 years (88 persons) | 5 years to 13 years (144 persons) | 13 years and longer (201 persons) |
|---|---|---|---|
| For | 22.5% | 23.0% | 30.5% |
| Against | 60.0% | 53.5% | 50.0% |
| Uncertain | 17.0% | 23.5% | 19.5% |

2. U. S., Congress, House, Subcommittee of the Committee on Government Operations, *Hearings, Federal-State-Local Relations, Dade County (Florida) Metropolitan Government,* 85th Cong. 1st. sess., Nov. 21 and 22, 1957, p. 114.

3. The Crime Commission was founded on March 31, 1948. It was approved by 250 delegates representing some 90 Dade County civic, patriotic, and business organizations at a three-day law enforcement convention at the Mayfair Theater in the City of Miami. (*The Crime Commission of Greater Miami,* undated pamphlet.)

4. *Miami Herald,* Jan. 12, 1947, p. 1A. Businessmen were responsible for creating and financially supporting both the Crime Commission and the Research Foundation.

5. Regular elections are held in the Miami area in even-numbered years; special elections in odd-numbered years.

6. The localists insisted upon maintaining the autonomy of the municipalities.

7. The consolidationists espoused the abolition of the municipalities and the creation of a single government for the Greater Miami area.

8. Edward C. Banfield, "The Politics of Metropolitan Area Organization," 1 *Midwest Journal of Political Science* 86 (May, 1957).

9. Governmental Affairs Foundation, Inc., *Metropolitan Surveys: A Digest* (Chicago; Public Administration Service, 1958), p. 163.

10. Interview with Dr. Thomas J. Wood, Department of Government, University of Miami.

11. *Ibid.*

12. Kenneth E. Gray, *A Report on Politics in St. Louis* (Cambridge: Center for Urban Studies, 1959. Mimeographed), Ch. II, pp. 20–21; Ch. V, p. 5.

13. In 1958 only 13 per cent of Greater Miami's nonagricultural labor force were employed by manufacturing concerns, while approximately 30 per cent of the national labor force were so employed. See University of Miami Bureau of Business and Economic Research, *Economic Almanac of Southeastern Florida, 1959* (Coral Gables: University of Miami, 1959), p. 25; United States Department of Commerce, *Statistical Abstract of the United States, 1959* (Washington, D. C.: U. S. Government Printing Office, 1959), p. 210.

14. *Miami Herald,* Oct. 18, 1959, p. 1G.

15. The city-wide distribution of its members and the aggressive leadership of its secretary-treasurer have made this union the most active and effective interest group in St. Louis. Once a month, assemblies of union stewards are held to discuss city problems and implement requests that have arisen at ward meetings. Their actions are confined primarily to endorsements of candidates and of issues in city, state, and national elections. See Gray, *Report on Politics,* Chapter V, pp. 7–12.

16. Ross C. Beiler and Thomas J. Wood, *Metropolitan Politics,* p. 13.

17. The information was obtained from an interview with Dr.

Thomas J. Wood, professor of Government, University of Miami, December 31, 1959.

18. See above, p. 60.

19. Reo M. Christenson, "The Power of the Press: The Case of 'The Toledo Blade,'" 3 *Midwest Journal of Political Science* 227-28 (Aug., 1959).

20. In August, 1958, Don Shoemaker, former editor of the *Southern School News*, was appointed editor of the *Miami Herald's* editorial page. On January 17, 1962, Mr. Shoemaker became editor of the *Miami Herald*. Mr. Pennekamp continues as associate editor.

21. As of September, 1961, the daily circulation of the *Miami Herald* was 299,689 and that of the *Miami News*, 138,753; the Sunday circulation was 351,222 for the *Herald* and 117,716 for the *News*.

22. The information was obtained from an interview with Alfred Canel, executive vice-president of the Miami-Dade Chamber of Commerce.

23. In a late 1957 and early 1958 poll (Beiler Survey No. 10) respondents were asked what individuals or groups they would name as most influential in the decisions shaping the new county government. Out of 723 persons questioned (422 registered, 301 unregistered), only 5.5 per cent alluded to a category that included the Chamber of Commerce, the Junior Chamber of Commerce, neighborhood groups, clubs and fraternal organizations. The other responses were as follows:

| | |
|---|---|
| 1. No group indicated | 82.0 per cent |
| 2. Municipal (city commissioners, city officials, Dade League of Municipalities, police, municipal employee groups) | 3.5 per cent |
| 3. County Commission and Port Authority | 6.5 per cent |
| 4. Newspapers | 4.5 per cent |
| 5. Television | 1.0 per cent |
| 6. Charter Board and other advisory boards | 1.5 per cent |

The response to the question on which individuals were most influential was practically nil. One would have to conclude that the "average" resident was unaware of the identity of the decision makers in the Greater Miami area.

24. The position of executive director remained vacant until filled by Harry T. Toulmin on August 19, 1956.

25. There were actually four separate leagues at the time—City of Miami, Miami Beach, Hialeah and Coral Gables—with a total membership of 450. The information was obtained from an interview with Mrs. John Baker, former president of the League of Women Voters of (the City of) Miami. League activities in promoting the home rule amendment were previously mentioned in Chapter 4.

26. Mr. Gautier was a member of the Florida Legislature from 1947

through 1956. He served one term in the House and four in the Senate (Appendix C).

27. The information was obtained from interviews with members of the Miami-Dade Chamber of Commerce, with representatives of the *Miami Herald,* and with R. Bunn Gautier.

28. "It appears, then, that the group experiences and affiliations of an individual are the primary, though not the exclusive, means by which the individual knows, interprets, and reacts to the society in which he exists." David Bicknell Truman, *The Governmental Process* (New York: Alfred A. Knopf, 1951), p. 21.

29. James McGregor Burns, *Congress on Trial* (New York: Harper & Brothers, 1949), pp. 18–31.

30. Robert Michels, *Political Parties* (Glencoe, Ill.: The Free Press, 1949).

31. John D. Corcoran, "Seeking Better Government for Metropolitan Areas," 40 *Public Management* 82 (Apr., 1958).

32. James R. Jensen, *The Politics of Metropolitan Integration: An Interim Report from Houston* (Houston: Nov. 6–8, 1958. Mimeographed), p. 7. (Paper delivered at the annual meeting of the Southern Political Science Association at Gatlinburg, Tenn., Nov. 6–8, 1958.)

33. The information was obtained from Charter Board files. The memorandum was signed by Robert P. Daly, co-director of public information for the Metropolitan Charter Board.


9   Implementing the Charter

1. As mentioned earlier, pp. 72–73, the County Commission had been held in high esteem for many years. Beginning in May, 1954, the area-wide newspapers began to criticize the commissioners for alleged abuses in regard to both Port Authority and county business transactions. The closed-door conferences of the commission also came under attack. Four of the five incumbents ran for re-election in 1956 and were defeated.

2. *Miami Herald,* April 23, 1957, p. 1C.

3. *Miami News,* Mar. 22, p. 6A, and Apr. 23, 1957, p. 4A.

4. *Ibid.,* June 2, 1957, p. 12A.

5. As previously noted, the Board of County Commissioners was also the governing body of the Port Authority.

6. An opinion from the county attorney on August 21, 1958, declared that the entire commission was the fully authorized Port Authority. See *Miami Herald,* Aug. 22, 1958, p. 1C. Litigation instituted to test the constitutionality of the home rule charter provision pertaining to the election of additional commissioners was also unsuccessful. *Young Democratic Club of Dade County v. Dade County,* Nos. 58C2522, 58C3454 (Dade Cir. Ct. Fla. 1958). The Florida Supreme Court later upheld

286                                                  NOTES FOR PAGES 88–95

the constitutionality of all the provisions of the charter pertaining to the election of county commissioners. *Dade County* v. *Young Democratic Club of Dade County,* 104 So. 2d 636 (Fla. 1958).

7. The County Commissioners' terms of office were from January 1, 1957, to January 2, 1961. Metro went into effect on July 21, 1957.

8. The Metropolitan Charter Legal Committee included Thomas C. Britton, Joe Eaton, David P. Catsman, Edwin Lee Mason, William L. Pallot, Daniel P. S. Paul, Lucien C. Proby, Marion E. Sibley, and Edwin E. Strickland. The committee was established at a special meeting of the County Commission on May 27, 1957.

9. Florida, *Statutes* (1957), c. 186.

10. Florida, *Statutes* (1957), cc. 776–965.

11. Members of the committee, which was established at a special meeting of the County Commission on May 27, 1957, included Ralph A. Fossey, Harold O. Freeburg, E. B. Leatherman, Robert M. Morgan, William Melvin Monroe, William L. Pallot, Daniel P. S. Paul, Marion E. Sibley, Harry S. Sweeting, and David W. Walters.

12. Mr. Toulmin worked closely with members of the Metro Legal Committee, advising them on the organization of the new departments.

13. The drafts of ordinances examined in this chapter were early versions of those enacted.

14. Department of Building and Zoning Ordinance (Dade County, Florida), secs. 8.02, 8.06, 8.11, 8.17. (Proposed July, 1957.)

15. *Ibid.,* secs. 8.01, 8.19, 8.21.

16. Contractors Examination Code (Dade County, Florida, undated), sec. 17.01. An early draft was obtained from the county attorney's office.

17. Public Works Department Ordinance (Dade County, Florida), secs. 5.02, 5.04. (Public Hearings, Aug. 16, 1957.)

18. Traffic Ordinance (Dade County, Florida), secs. 2.01–2, 4.01, 6.02, 26.02. (Public Hearings, Sept. 17, 1957.) See also Metropolitan Court Ordinance (Dade County, Florida, undated), sec. 3.04. An early draft was obtained from the county attorney's office.

19. *Miami Herald,* July 12, 1958, p. 22A.

20. Traffic Ordinance (Dade County, Florida), sec. 25.03–2. (Public Hearings, Sept. 17, 1957.)

21. Dr. Thomas J. Wood, Department of Government, University of Miami, and Harry T. Toulmin, then executive director of the Dade County Research Foundation.

10   The Cities Declare War on Metro

1. *Miami Herald,* July 16, 1957, p. 1B.
2. *Ibid.,* July 17, 1957, p. 1C.
3. *Miami News,* July 19, 1957, p. 2A.
4. *Miami Herald,* July 17, 1957, p. 1C.

5. *Miami News*, Aug. 1, 1957, p. 14A.
6. *Miami Herald*, July 21, 1957, p. 7A.
7. John B. McDermott in *ibid.*, July 21, 1957, p. 3G.
8. *Miami News*, July 24, 1957, p. 4A.
9. *Ibid.*, July 29, 1957, p. 5A.
10. *Miami Herald*, July 27, 1957, p. 21A.
11. *Miami News*, July 27, 1957, pp. 1A, 3A.
12. *Ibid.*, Aug. 9, 1957, p. 1A; *Miami Herald*, Aug. 10, 1957, p. 4A.
13. *Miami Herald*, Aug. 13, 1957, p. 1B.
14. *Miami News*, Aug. 13, 1957, p. 8A.
15. *Ibid.*, Aug. 18, 1957, p. 4A.
16. *Ibid.*, Aug. 25, 1957, p. 11A.
17. *Ibid.*, Sept. 19, 1957, p. 4A.
18. *Miami Herald*, Sept. 25, 1957, p. 16A.
19. See below, p. 111. Assessments were based on a charge of 10 cents for each resident in the various cities (see *Miami Herald*, Oct. 23, 1957, p. 19A).
20. *Miami Herald*, Oct. 17, 1957, p. 1D.


## 11   Compromise Proves Chimerical

1. *Miami Herald*, Aug. 27, 1957, p. 1C.
2. *Miami News*, Aug. 25, 1957, p. 1A.
3. *Ibid.*
4. *Ibid.*, July 28, 1957, p. 5A; and information from interview with Mr. Campbell.
5. *Miami Herald*, Aug. 27, 1957, p. 1C.
6. *Ibid.*, Oct. 17, 1957, p. 1D.
7. *Ibid.*
8. On August 19, 1957, Mr. Sibley jolted the Dade County Bar Association with the proposal that the City of Miami abolish itself (*ibid.*, Aug. 20, 1957, p. 1C).
9. Hugh P. Emerson, an accountant, was chairman of the committee. Others were Joe Bernstein, John Newbauer, and Herman Rubin, jewelers; R. B. Carson, meteorologist; M. D. Chapman, owner of a parking lot chain; John E. Cicero, William W. Gibbs, and John Charles Girtman, attorneys; Byron B. Freeland, department store owner; Hiram Gates, stationer; Robert C. Hector, feed store owner; Jack Horsley, insurance agent; David Hume, advertising man; E. Nolan Johnson, Robert M. Morgan, and Hugh F. Purvis, accountants; E. W. Lane, occupation unlisted; Michael O'Neil, tire company owner; and F. G. (Pat) Railey, wholesale hardware store owner (*ibid.*, Oct. 26, 1957, p. 1B).
10. As a jurisdictional entity, the City of Miami would not have been abolished.
11. See Metro (Dade County, Florida) Ordinance No. 57–23.

12. *Miami Herald,* Oct. 29, 1957, p. 1C.
13. *Miami Herald,* Oct. 25, 1957, p. 1A; *Miami News,* Oct. 25, 1957, p. 6A; *Miami Herald,* Oct. 26, 1957, p. 1B.
14. *Miami Herald,* Nov. 1, 1957, p. 1B.
15. The information was obtained from an interview with Mr. Campbell.
16. *Miami Herald,* Nov. 1, 1957, p. 1B.
17. *Ibid.*
18. *City of Miami* v. *County of Dade,* No. 206817 (Dade Cir. Ct. Fla. 1957).
19. *Miami Herald,* Nov. 6, 1957, p. 1B. The Miami Citizens and Taxpayers League was an *ad hoc* group created to meet the threat to abolish the City of Miami. Alex M. Balfe and Admiral Charles D. Leffler were cochairmen of the group.
20. Copy obtained from the Miami-Dade Chamber of Commerce.
21. Metro (Dade County, Florida) Ordinance No. 57–26.
22. *Miami Herald,* Nov. 7, 1957, p. 16A; *Miami News,* Nov. 7, 1957, p. 1A.
23. *Miami News,* Nov. 6, 1957, p. 1A.
24. The office of county attorney was created by the home rule charter, sec. 4.06. Mr. Davis was appointed county attorney on August 1, 1957.
25. *Miami News,* Dec. 10, 1957, p. 1C.
26. *Ibid.*
27. *Miami Herald,* Dec. 13, 1957, p. 1C.
28. The information concerning this meeting was obtained from interviews with the county manager and with representatives from the Miami-Dade Chamber of Commerce and the Dade League of Municipalities.
29. *Miami Herald,* Dec. 14, 1957, p. 1B.
30. *Miami News,* Dec. 14, 1957, p. 3A.
31. *Ibid.*
32. *Ibid.*
33. *Ibid.*
34. *Ibid.,* Dec. 10, 1957, p. 1C.
35. Home Rule Charter, sec. 8.07 (see Appendix G), requires that a proposal to amend the charter must be approved at least 60 days before it appears on the ballot.
36. Abe Aronovitz had opposed the home rule charter in 1957, but saw no inconsistency in his support of Metro against the autonomy amendment. He maintained that he had taken issue with the charter only because of the defects in its structure, not because of his opposition to a metropolitan government.
37. *Miami Herald,* Dec. 17, 1957, p. 1B.
38. *Ibid.,* Jan. 22, 1958, p. 1C.
39. *Ibid.,* Jan. 26, 1958, p. 1B.

40. *Cicero and Girtman* v. *Dade County*, No. 58C482 (Dade Cir. Ct. Fla. 1958). The Supreme Court later concurred in the temporary delay (*Miami Herald*, Feb. 8, 1958, p. 1A).

41. Judge Holt, as chairman of the 3M Board and the first Charter Board, was a staunch supporter of metropolitan government.

42. *Miami Herald*, Feb. 8, 1958, p. 1A.

43. *Ibid.*, March 11, 1958, p. 1B.

44. Mr. Gautier and Mr. Anderson were on the subcommittee but not on the full committee. The latter included Abe Aronovitz, Alex M. Balfe, Shepard Broad, O. W. Campbell, Dean R. Claussen, Faris N. Cowart, George W. DuBreuil, E. Arthur Evans, Ralph A. Fossey, B. E. Hearn, Otis W. Shiver, Dr. Robert T. Spicer, Harry T. Toulmin, and Mitchell Wolfson.

45. *Dade County* v. *Dade County League of Municipalities*, 104 So. 2d 512 (Fla. 1958).

## 12 The Autonomy Amendment Defeated

1. *Miami News*, June 6, 1958, p. 1C.

2. *Ibid.*

3. *Dade County* v. *Dade County League of Municipalities*, 104 So. 2d 512 (Fla. 1958).

4. *Ibid.* at 515.

5. The autonomy amendment, *inter alia*, gave municipalities the right to exercise all powers granted by *Special Act* (text of autonomy amendment on p. 97). The Supreme Court believed that this part of the amendment was in contravention of the provisions of the home rule amendment to the Florida Constitution.

6. *Dade County* v. *Dade County League of Municipalities*, 104 So. 2d 512, 515 (Fla. 1958).

7. *Miami News*, July 31, 1958, p. 1A.

8. *Final Report of the Grand Jury* in the Circuit Court of the Eleventh Judicial Circuit of Florida in and for the County of Dade (filed Nov. 12, 1958), p. 3.

9. *Miami News*, Sept. 23, 1958, p. 1C.

10. *Miami Beach Record*, Sept., 1958.

11. *Miami Herald*, Sept. 17, 1958, p. 18A.

12. *Time*, Sept. 29, 1958, p. 17.

13. Citizens' "Vote No" Committee, *Report to Miami-Dade Chamber Board Meeting* (Miami: Oct. 13, 1958. Mimeographed), p. 3.

14. *Miami Herald*, Aug. 3, 1958, p. 1B.

15. The information was obtained from interviews with members of the Miami-Dade Chamber of Commerce.

16. *Miami Herald*, Sept. 21, 1958, p. 13B.

17. *Ibid.*, Sept. 25, 1958, p. 1B.

18. A content analysis of the mass media for the 30-day period before the autonomy amendment election was conducted by Professor Ross C. Beiler, with the aid of Fred Perlove, student assistant.

19. *Miami Herald*, Sept. 13, 1958, p. 13A.

20. *Miami News*, Dec. 19, 1957, p. 16B.

21. *Miami Herald*, Aug. 31, 1958, p. 1B.

22. On September 12, 1958, Mr. Campbell appeared on "Important," a weekly television program on station WPST.

23. *Miami Herald*, Sept. 29, 1958, p. 1C.

24. General Acts of Florida (1955), c. 30255, sec. 18(e), as amended by the Board of County Commissioners, Dade County, Florida, April 26, 1958. See home rule charter, sec. 4.05 C (Appendix G).

25. The information was obtained from various interviews.

26. *Miami Herald*, Sept. 30, 1958, p. 12A.

27. O. W. Campbell, *The First Annual Report on the Progress of Metropolitan Dade County, Florida* (Dade County, Florida, Sept. 1958. Mimeographed).

28. There were a few employees in the county manager's office who actively cooperated with the pro-Metro forces, and, in particular, with the League of Women Voters.

29. *Miami Herald*, Oct. 1, 1958, p. 1A. Public indignation forced the commission to change its position later. The commissioners who voted in favor of gambling maintained that they were concerned only with giving the public an opportunity to air its views on the subject.

30. *Ibid.*, Sept. 3, 1958, p. 17A.

31. *Wolff* v. *Dade League of Municipalities*, 58C7450 (Dade Cir. Ct. Fla. 1958).

32. One might note that Charter Board expenditures for the campaign for the home rule amendment and the home rule charter were far in excess of expenditures by the Dade League of Municipalities in the autonomy amendment campaign. The dollar cost of services by municipal employees in the autonomy campaign was not computed, however.

33. E. g., *Miami News*, Sept. 12, p. 1C, and Sept. 17, 1958, p. 1D; *Miami Herald*, Sept. 25, p. 1B, and Sept. 29, 1958, p. 1C.

34. *Miami Herald*, Sept. 21, 1958, p. 2F.

35. *Miami News*, Sept. 14, 1958, p. 3B.

36. "UM Round Table Discussion" on radio station WGBS, 9:30 P.M., October 2, 1958, with Dr. H. Franklin Williams, moderator, and Winston W. Wynne, Ray T. Sterling, and Edward Sofen participating.

37. Registered voters in the county totaled 360,973 as of August 8, 1958; 145,297 voted in the legislative race. (The information was obtained from the office of the Supervisor of Registration for Dade County, Florida.)

38. A total of 126,475 persons voted: 30,760 in District 1; 47,062 in District 2; 23,542 in District 3; 10,982 in District 4; 14,129 in

District 5. (The information was obtained from the office of the Supervisor of Registration for Dade County, Florida.)

39. Of the 114,411 persons who voted on the question, 79,277 opposed the name change and 35,134 favored it. (The information was obtained from the office of the Supervisor of Registration for Dade County, Florida.)

40. The number of votes in each city was estimated by Dr. Thomas J. Wood. Official county election returns are recorded only by precincts which do not necessarily correspond with municipal boundaries.

41. *Ibid.*

42. U. S., Congress, House, Subcommittee of the Committee on Government Operations, *Hearings, Federal-State-Local Relations, Dade County (Florida) Metropolitan Government,* 85th Cong., 1st sess., Nov. 21 and 22, 1957, p. 27.

43. Anti-Metro cities are all those which voted either against the home rule charter or for the autonomy amendment. In most cases cities in this category adopted both these voting positions.

## 13    The Fate of the Ordinances

1. Metro (Dade County, Florida) Ordinance No. 57–22.
2. Metro (Dade County, Florida) Ordinance No. 57–19.
3. Metro (Dade County, Florida) Ordinance No. 57–20. This ordinance was repealed by Metro (Dade County, Florida) Ordinance No. 58–39.
4. Metro (Dade County, Florida) Ordinance No. 57–21.
5. Metro (Dade County, Florida) Ordinance No. 57–30.
6. Metro (Dade County, Florida) Ordinance No. 57–31. This ordinance was repealed by Metro (Dade County, Florida) Ordinance No. 58–39.
7. Metro (Dade County, Florida) Ordinance No. 57–31, sec. 8.19.
8. *Ibid.,* sec. 8.29.
9. Metro (Dade County, Florida) Ordinance Nos. 58–2, 58–10.
10. Metro (Dade County, Florida) Ordinance Nos. 58–26, 58–33.
11. Metro (Dade County, Florida) Ordinance No. 58–39.
12. See pp. 132–133 for ways in which the controversy over the ordinances might have been mitigated.
13. *Miami Herald,* May 9, 1958, p. 6A.
14. *Miami News,* July 29, 1957, p. 1A.
15. Metro (Dade County, Florida) Ordinance No. 57–25.
16. Some contractors maintain they have paid more in fees since the advent of Metro than they did before. See Reinhold P. Wolff, *Miami Metro: The Road to Urban Unity* (Coral Gables: Bureau of Business and Economic Research, University of Miami, 1960), p. 114.
17. *Miami Shores Village v. Cowart,* 108 So. 2d 468 (Fla. 1958).

18. *Miami Herald*, Nov. 11, 1959, p. 10A.

19. Legal action to compel Coral Gables to recognize the Metro license was upheld in *Burgin* v. *City of Coral Gables*, No. 59L3738E (Dade Cir. Ct. Fla. 1959). An appeal was denied in *City of Coral Gables* v. *Burgin*, 135 So. 2d 771 (Fla. App. 1961). The appellate decision was affirmed by the Florida Supreme Court in September, 1962.

20. Metro (Dade County, Florida) Ordinance No. 62–12.

21. Metro (Dade County, Florida) Ordinance No. 57–12.

22. *Ibid.*, sec. 26.08.

23. Metro (Dade County, Florida) Ordinance No. 57–27, sec. 4.

24. Metro (Dade County, Florida) Ordinance No. 57–32, sec. 2.

25. Metro (Dade County, Florida) Ordinance No. 58–8, sec. 1.

26. U. S., Congress, House, Subcommittee of the Committee on Government Operations, *Hearings, Federal-State-Local Relations, Dade County (Florida) Metropolitan Government*, 85th Cong., 1st sess., Nov. 21 and 22, 1957, pp. 99–100.

27. Metro (Dade County, Florida) Ordinance No. 57–12, sec. 4.01.

28. *Ibid.*, sec. 4.01.1.

29. *Ibid.*, sec. 21.07. As of 1962, this section was still "on the books" and was still unenforced.

30. Milwaukee Citizens Government Research Bureau, *Report on the Meetings of the Milwaukee Delegation with Dade County Officials on the New Metropolitan Miami Government Plan* (Week of April 21, 1958. Mimeographed), p. 56.

31. Metro (Dade County, Florida) Ordinance No. 57–12, sec. 26.05.

32. Information obtained from Miss Mary Ann Cardoso of the Motor Vehicle Division of the Public Safety Department, Dade County, Florida.

33. See below, Chapter 15.

34. *Miami Herald*, Mar. 5, 1959, p. 1B.

35. Metro (Dade County, Florida) Ordinance No. 57–12, secs. 2.01–2, 26.01, 26.02.

36. Some cities have even turned over penal code cases to the Metro courts—Homestead, Florida City, Hialeah, Opa-locka, and Biscayne Park. Metro (Dade County, Florida) Ordinances No. 59–23, 59–25, 59–28, 59–29, 59–34.

37. Metro (Dade County, Florida) Ordinance No. 57–2, sec. 5.04.

38. Metro (Dade County, Florida) Ordinance No. 58–25, sec. 4.

39. *Miami Shores Village* v. *County Commissioners*, 12 Fla. Supp. 168, 179–80 (Dade Cir. Ct. 1958).

40. *Miami Herald*, June 28, 1958, p. 1B.

41. *Miami Shores Village* v. *Cowart*, 108 So. 2d 468, 471 (Fla. 1958).

42. *Miami News*, Sept. 15, 1957, p. 1A.

43. Dade County Research Foundation, *A Commentary on the Proposed Metropolitan Ordinances* (Miami: Aug., 1957. Mimeographed), p. 10.

44. *Miami Herald*, Aug. 1, 1957, p. 1A.
45. Milwaukee Citizens Government Research Bureau, *Report on the Meetings*, p. 44.
46. O. W. Campbell, *The First Annual Report on the Progress of Metropolitan Dade County, Florida* (Miami: Sept., 1958. Mimeographed), p. 40.

## 14 Sundry Problems of the New Government

1. The County Commission which held office until 1956 had fallen into disrepute as a result of a series of exposés by the area-wide newspapers, and the five commissioners who succeeded them had all been strongly endorsed by the *Miami Herald*. Four of the five had also been endorsed by the *News*.
2. On May 27, 1959, George M. McSherry, $30,000-a-year director of the Port Authority, was dismissed by the County Commission.
3. The county manager can hire and fire all county administrative officers and employees without interference from the county commissioners who, except for the purpose of inquiry, may deal with such officers and employees only through the manager. (Home Rule Charter, secs. 3.04 B and 3.05; see Appendix G.) In contrast, the County Commission sits as both the administrative and governing body of the Port Authority with no limits placed upon its administrative discretion.
4. A ruling of the county attorney disqualifying one of the commissioners from voting on the causeway issue subsequently led to the defeat of plans for submitting a $60.3 million airport-causeway bond issue to the voters.
5. *Miami News*, Mar. 20, 1959, p. 1C.
6. Mr. Toulmin singled out Commissioner Alexander S. Gordon as the principal culprit who was responsible for attempting to discredit the administration.
7. *Miami Herald*, Apr. 21, 1959, p. 1C.
8. Metro (Dade County, Florida) *Commission Minutes*, Apr. 28, 1959, p. 17.
9. The division within the commission, particularly between some of the "old" and "new" commissioners, made it difficult for any administrator to work with them. The "old" commissioners felt they had more experience and, in addition, they continued to receive $15,000 salaries (as provided by the charter) as against $6,000 received by the new commissioners.
10. *Miami News*, May 29, 1959, p. 6A.
11. The *Miami Herald*, in particular, kept hammering away at the need for rapid action.
12. *Miami Herald*, Dec. 2, 1958, p. 10.

294                           NOTES FOR PAGES 139–147

13. *Final Report of the Grand Jury* in the Circuit Court of the Eleventh Judicial Circuit of Florida in and for the County of Dade, pp. 7–8.

14. Metro (Dade County, Florida) Ordinance No. 60–23.

15. Metro (Dade County, Florida) *Commission Minutes*, Jan. 17, 1961, pp. 7–9.

16. Metro (Dade County, Florida) Resolution No. 6542.

17. *Miami News*, Nov. 7, 1961, p. 1C.

18. An act of the 1959 Florida Legislature apparently gave the Florida Railroad and Public Utilities Commission jurisdiction over all private water and sewerage companies. Florida, *Statutes* (1959), c. 367, the Water and Sewer System Regulatory Law.

19. *Miami Herald*, Oct. 2, p. 19A; Oct. 3, p. 6C; and Oct. 4, 1960, p. 16A. A bond issue of $7.1 million was validated in *County of Dade v. State of Florida*, No. 60C10499 (Dade Cir. Ct. Fla. 1960).

20. Metro (Dade County, Florida) *Commission Minutes*, Mar. 7, 1961, pp. 29–33.

21. Metro (Dade County, Florida) Ordinance No. 60–20.

22. *Grubstein v. Urban Renewal Agency of City of Tampa*, 115 So. 2d 745 (Fla. 1959). As of 1962, the state legislature had still refused to enact a state-wide urban renewal act.

23. Metro (Dade County, Florida) Ordinance No. 60–6.

24. Metropolitan Dade County Planning Department, *Preliminary Land Use Plan, Draft of Summary Report* (Miami: 1960. Mimeographed). See also *Existing Land Use Study* (Miami: Metropolitan Dade County, 1961).

25. City of Miami and Metropolitan Dade County, *Magic City Center: Economic Appraisal and Projections* (Miami: Mar. 1960. Mimeographed).

26. Harry T. Toulmin, *Metropolitan Dade County, Florida: A Report on Administrative Improvement through February, 1959* (Miami: 1959. Mimeographed); O. W. Campbell, *The First Annual Report on the Progress of Metropolitan Dade County, Florida* (Miami: Sept., 1958. Mimeographed), p. 17.

27. The Department of Traffic and Transportation, created by ordinance on September 6, 1960, was abolished on August 1, 1961, and most of its functions transferred to the Public Works Department.

28. Metro (Dade County, Florida) Resolution No. 7333.

29. *Miami Herald*, Aug. 19, 1959, p. 1B.

30. *Miami News*, Aug. 14, 1959, p. 1C.

31. See Appendix D.

32. The incumbent sheriff and tax assessor had been elected in 1956 and were entitled under the charter to serve through 1960. After July, 1957, both these department heads were responsible to the county manager.

## 15  Metro and the Cities

1. It should be noted that the Cleveland charter also met with opposition on the ground that the charter did not go far enough toward creating a unified metropolitan government. Although all charters are bound to meet with such criticism, in Cleveland a group of consolidationists formally organized to defeat what they characterized as "a timid and tragically inadequate district proposal." Henry J. Schmandt, Paul Steinbecker, and George D. Wendel, *Metropolitan Reform in St. Louis* (New York: Holt, Rinehart and Winston, 1961), p. 37.

2. The Illinois Commission on Urban Problems visited Miami on April 17 and 18; the Milwaukee Metropolitan Study Commission from April 21 to 25.

3. *Miami News,* Aug. 25, 1957, p. 1A.

4. See above, pp. 100–101.

5. O. W. Campbell, *Speech* delivered at Annual Conference, League of California Cities, Los Angeles, Oct. 26–29, 1958 (Mimeographed), p. 6.

6. Milwaukee Citizens Government Research Bureau, *Report on the Meetings of the Milwaukee Delegation with Dade County Officials on the New Metropolitan Miami Government Plan* (week of April 21, 1958. Mimeographed), p. 16.

7. Mr. Campbell frequently used the analogy of the county as a wholesaler and the municipalities as retailers.

8. *Miami Shores Village v. Cowart,* 108 So. 2d 468, 471 (Fla. 1958).

9. *Ibid.*

10. *Miami Herald,* Oct. 15, 1958, p. 7A.

11. *Ibid.,* Dec. 31, 1958, p. 4A.

12. County Attorney Davis declared that the practical effect of the decision was to eliminate "minimum standards" as a limitation on the power of the County Commission over the cities. This interpretation may have been correct as applied to the traffic code but hardly as applied to every one of the county's powers. The interpretations of the decision by Mr. Pallot and Mr. Davis are in separate memoranda. (*Memorandum* to the Board of County Commissioners from Darrey A. Davis, County Attorney, Jan. 6, 1959; and *Memorandum* to E. A. Evans, City Manager, from William L. Pallot, City Attorney, Dec. 24, 1958.)

13. *Miami Herald,* Jan. 16, 1959, p. 6A.

14. *DeLoach v. City of Miami,* No. 59L402 (Dade Cir. Ct. Fla. 1959).

15. The city later withdraw the charges against the traffic violator rather than let the Metro court take jurisdiction, a move that was severely criticized in a *Miami Herald* editorial (Feb. 28, 1959, p. 6A).

16. *Keton v. City of Miami,* 14 Fla. Supp. 68 (Dade Cir. Ct. 1959).

17. *City of Miami* v. *Keton,* 115 So. 2d 547 (Fla. 1959).

18. Miami Beach had refused to allow Metro licensed contractors to do business in Miami Beach unless they were also licensed by the city. Miami Beach had also issued its own automobile inspection stickers in place of Metro's.

19. *City of Miami Beach* v. *Cowart,* No. 58C5895K (Dade Cir. Ct. Fla. 1959).

20. *City of Miami Beach* v. *Cowart,* 116 So. 2d 432 (Fla. 1959). A petition filed for rehearing was denied on January 6, 1960.

21. *Miami News,* Feb. 25, 1959, p. 14A.

22. *Miami Herald,* Feb. 25, 1959, p. 6A.

23. *Ibid.,* Feb. 21, 1959, p. 1C.

24. Mayor Robert King High and Commissioners Otis W. Shiver and George W. DuBreuil voted to fire Mr. Evans; Commissioners James W. High and B. E. Hearn voted against the motion.

25. Not a single voice of protest was raised because of the manner in which Mr. Evans had been dismissed. Yet when Melvin Reese, manager of the City of Miami was fired summarily in the summer of 1961, a hue and cry was raised by the mass media such as has not been heard in the Miami area for many years. The summary dismissal was condemned as arbitrary and undemocratic. In a dramatic televised ceremony in which tears were shed and voices broke, Mr. Reese was reinstated.

26. The late Mayor Abe Aronovitz had contested the roadblocks which were held by Circuit Court Judge Holt to be repugnant and contrary to both the United States and Florida constitutions in *Aronovitz* v. *City of Miami,* No. 59C1239A (Dade Cir. Ct. Fla. 1959). The Florida Supreme Court reversed the decision in *City of Miami* v. *Aronovitz,* 114 So. 2d 784 (Fla. 1959).

27. *Miami News,* Mar. 3, 1959, p. 1A.

28. While the newspapers referred to Mr. Willard as "a friend of Metro," the new city manager could be expected to reflect the attitudes of the City of Miami commission, as he reflected the attitudes of the Coral Gables commission when he was city manager there. The Coral Gables commissioners had objected to the transfer of violations of traffic ordinances in Coral Gables to the metropolitan courts, and Mr. Willard had supported their position. Mr. Willard remained as the City of Miami's manager until February 1, 1960, when he resigned to become a bank president. On March 21, 1960, Melvin L. Reese was appointed the new city manager.

29. *Miami News,* Mar. 4, 1959, p. 12A.

30. American Bar Association Traffic Court Program, *Preliminary Report and Recommendations for the Metropolitan Court of Dade County* (Chicago: May 12, 1959. Mimeographed).

31. The franchise granted to the Miami Transit Company by the city includes a complex formula under which franchise taxes are paid by the bus company only if it makes a profit. For instance, the City of Miami

received over $100,000 in taxes from the company in the 1957–1958 fiscal year but none in the 1958–1959 fiscal year. Under the franchise the city also reserved the right to purchase the company for $1.5 million and take over liabilities and obligations at the time of purchase.

32. The City of Miami Water and Sewer Board balked at being taken over by Metro and suggested that Metro build its own water distribution system and buy water wholesale from the city.

33. The Better Business Division of the Miami-Dade Chamber of Commerce and the City of Miami Division of Trade Standards had proposed that Metro take over weights and measures for the entire county.

34. Under the home rule charter, tax assessing and tax collecting were to be taken over by Metro in 1961 (Sec. 4.04; see Appendix G). However, Section 9.03 D allows the Metro Commission, upon the request of a municipality, to postpone these requirements on a year-to-year basis until January 1, 1966. As of 1962 the municipalities were still performing both the tax assessing and collecting functions.

35. County Attorney Davis pointed out that the City of Miami could not compel the county to consolidate if Metro did not choose to do so; City Attorney Pallot concurred.

36. *Miami Herald*, June 2, 1959, p. 6A.

37. Metropolitan Dade County Planning Department, *Planning Review Report of the Miami Seaport Location* (Miami: July, 1959. Mimeographed), p. 65.

38. Officials of Miami Beach maintained to the bitter end that the location of the port would destroy the beauty of the city, pollute Biscayne Bay, and reduce values of expensive island homes.

39. General Acts of Florida (1951), c. 26614.

40. Metro (Dade County, Florida) Resolution No. 4830.

41. Metro (Dade County, Florida) Resolution No. 2521.

42. Metro (Dade County, Florida) Resolution No. 7047.

43. A survey of all Dade County police departments by the International Police Chiefs Associations was approved by Metro on March 14, 1962. The transfer of the stockade had long been a bone of contention between Metro and the City of Miami and it was hoped the findings of the survey would lead to a recommendation by the association that Metro take over this facility.

44. *Miami Herald*, Oct. 27, 1960, p. 1B. Subsequently, citizen groups in Homestead and Florida City also began to talk secession.

45. *Ibid.*, Oct. 28, 1960, p. 4A.

46. *City of Miami Beach* v. *County of Dade*, 122 So. 2d 84 (Fla. 1960), *rehearing denied*, 129 So. 2d 413 (Fla.), *cert. denied*, 82 Sup. Ct. 45, *rehearing denied*, 82 Sup. Ct. 192 (1961).

47. See below, Chapter 16.

48. The information was obtained from Joseph W. Curtin of Metro's Personnel Department on March 20, 1962.

49. The Charter Review Board hearings are discussed in more detail at the close of Chapter 16.

50. Mr. Campbell was fired on February 14, 1961, and was succeeded by Irving C. McNayr, who was appointed on April 7, 1961.

## 16  The McLeod Amendment and Its Aftermath

1. The three cities were Miami, Hialeah, and Miami Beach.

2. University of Miami poll No. 14 elicited responses on the McLeod amendment and related issues from a random sampling of more than 500 registered voters. The poll, taken 10 days before the election, permitted the outcome of the election to be predicted within 4 per cent. The survey was conducted by the Government Department under the supervision of Professor Thomas J. Wood, assisted by Professors Gustave R. Serino and Edward Sofen. All subsequent references to poll findings in this chapter will be based on the findings of University of Miami poll No. 14.

3. Florida, *Statutes* (1961), sec. 193.11; General Acts of Florida (1941), c. 20722.

4. Metro (Dade County, Florida), *Commission Minutes,* May 16, 1961, pp. 12-13.

5. Florida *ex rel.* Glynn v. McNayr, No. 61L2784 (Dade Cir. Ct. Fla. 1961), p. 10.

6. Metro (Dade County, Florida) Resolution No. 6639.

7. Florida *ex rel.* Glynn v. McNayr No. 61L2784 (Dade Cir. Ct. Fla. 1961).

8. *Id.* at 9.

9. *Id.* at 4.

10. Florida *ex rel.* Glynn v. McNayr, 133 So. 2d 312, 316 (Fla. 1961).

11. *Miami Herald,* Aug. 14, 1961, p. 6A.

12. *Miami News,* Aug. 14, 1961, p. 12A.

13. *Miami Herald,* Oct. 12, 1961, p. 11B.

14. "Important," television station WSPT (Channel 10, Miami), a special pre-election program, October 16, 1961.

15. *Miami Herald,* Sept. 20 to Oct. 13, 1961, *passim.* Of some 95 debates, 65 were attended by McLeod speakers. Yet only a handful of respondents in the University of Miami poll were able to name any persons or groups other than McLeod who had campaigned for the McLeod amendment.

16. The University of Miami poll revealed that of those who expressed a definite reaction, 60 per cent opposed the court and 40 per cent favored it. Of the persons who responded unfavorably to the Metro courts, the largest categories included 37 per cent who took issue with compulsory court appearances for all moving violations, 16 per cent who

were critical of the court's operations, 11 per cent who complained of the excessive fines, and 8 per cent who were unhappy due to personal experiences. The purists maintain that the inconvenience and suffering are good for the motorist's soul but pragmatists are somewhat fearful of the political consequences.

17. 1313 East 60th Street, Chicago, Illinois, is the home of some of the leading state and local governmental professional organizations in the nation, including the American Municipal Association, the International City Managers' Association, the American Society of Planning Officials, the American Society for Public Administration, the Municipal Finance Officers Association, and Public Administration Service. The latter organization was responsible for the study, *The Government of Metropolitan Miami*, in 1954 and for submitting recommendations which formed the framework for the home rule charter. The PAS study was conducted under the general supervision of John D. Corcoran. In recent years PAS has been attacked by ultra-right organizations as a symbol of one-world government, as a Communist conspiracy, and the like.

18. *North Miami Beach News Post* and *South Miami Reporter*. The latter newspaper stressed the fact that metropolitan government is centralization—"subsequently socialism"—and that socialism was the advance agent of communism (Oct. 5, 1961, p. 2).

19. *Miami News*, Oct. 6, 1961, p. 1C.

20. *Ibid.*, Oct. 5, 1961, p. 18A.

21. *Miami Herald*, Oct. 13, 1961, p. 6A.

22. Ralph Renick, television station WTVJ (Channel 4, Miami), 6:30 P.M., "Tonight's Editorial," October 2, 1961.

23. All of the better public service organizations were opposed. Among those opposing the amendment were the Miami-Dade Chamber of Commerce; the League of Women Voters; the American Institute of Architects; the Miami Beach Resort Hotel Association; the Hialeah-Miami Springs Chamber of Commerce; the West Dade Democratic Club; the Opa-locka Chamber of Commerce; the Coral Gables Citizens Committee; the Miami Beach Citizens Committee for Good Government; the Miami Beach Junior Chamber of Commerce; the Air-Conditioning, Refrigerating, and Heating, and Pipe-Fitting Association; the Better Government Association; the Miami Board of Realtors, the Surfside-Bal Harbour and Bay Harbor Chamber of Commerce; the Surfside Civic Association; the West Dade Junior Chamber of Commerce; the Dade County Young Democrats Association; the Coral Gables Chamber of Commerce; the Coral Gables Junior Chamber of Commerce; the Associated General Contractors; the North Miami Beach Junior Chamber of Commerce; the Business and Professional Women's Club of Miami; the North Shore Kiwanis Club; the Transport Workers Local 500; the West Miami Town Council; the Coral Gables City Commission; and the City of Miami Commission.

24. Those designated by the respondents were the *Miami Herald* (76), the county manager (55), the League of Women Voters (54), the

Miami-Dade Chamber of Commerce (45), the *Miami News* (42), city spokesmen (17), Jaycees (6), and University of Miami personnel (3).

25. TV station WPST (Channel 10) carried "Important," a weekly Sunday evening "Meet the Press" type of program, which dealt with the McLeod amendment on a number of occasions.

26. The population of Dade County is presently distributed so that 38 per cent reside in the unincorporated areas, 31 per cent in the city of Miami, and 31 per cent in the remaining municipalities.

27. The Metropolitan Charter Review Board was composed of James I. Keller, Jr., chairman; J. Abney Cox, vice chairman; Harold Rand, M.D., secretary; J. H. Brock; George A. Frix; and William A. Graham.

28. Others on the committee were Robert Morgan, Leonard Usina, Jack Baldwin, George Cooper, and McGregor Smith.

29. Robert Morgan, certified public accountant and civic leader, and McGregor Smith, chairman of the board of Florida Power and Light Company, announced their resignation from the Crandon Committee on June 18, 1962. *Miami Herald*, June 19, 1962, p. 1B.


## 17  Finance

1. Florida, *Constitution* (1885), Art. X, sec. 7, provides that "Every person who has the legal title or beneficial title in equity to real property in this state and who resides thereon and in good faith makes the same his or her permanent home, or the permanent home of another or others legally or naturally dependent upon said person, shall be entitled to an exemption from all taxation, except for assessments for special benefits, up to the assessed valuation of Five Thousand Dollars on the said home and contiguous real property . . . but no such exemption of more than Five Thousand Dollars shall be allowed to any one person or on any one dwelling house. . . ."

2. Thomas J. Wood and Edward Sofen, *Municipal Finance in Dade County for the Fiscal Year 1960* (Coral Gables: Committee on Municipal Research, Government Department, University of Miami, 1961. Mimeographed). See also Edward Sofen, "Financial Dilemma Miami-Dade Style," *National Civic Review* (April, 1962), pp. 220–222.

3. See below, p. 188.

4. Metro took possession of the buses on February 9, 1962.

5. Florida, *Statutes* (1959), sec. 205.02. See also W. G. Heuson, M. F. Slotta, Reinhold P. Wolff, *A Study of Florida's Miscellaneous Taxes, Licenses and Fees Prepared for the Florida Legislative Interim Committee on Finance and Taxation* (University of Miami: 1960. Mimeographed), sec. X, pp. 11–12.

6. Municipal residents were contributing on the average of $4.58 per capita for services rendered exclusively to the unincorporated area.

7. Reinhold P. Wolff, *Miami Metro: The Road to Urban Unity* (Coral Gables: Bureau of Business and Economic Research, University of Miami, 1960), p. 145.

8. Assessment increases on commercial property and homes of $30,000 and more were generally much less than the average.

9. See Chapter 16.

10. Florida, *Constitution* (1885), Art. VIII, sec. 11 (1) (b). (See Appendix E.)

11. This action was motivated by Metro's intention to institute legal action to obtain its claimed share of the cigarette tax rebate in the unincorporated areas. Such a suit never materialized.

12. Urban areas are under-represented in Florida even more than in most states. Dade County has 20 per cent of the state's population and only 3 per cent of its representation. A suit brought in the Federal courts in March 1962 charged the Florida legislature with failure to apportion fairly and sought appropriate relief. A three-judge Federal court on July 23, 1962, held that the existing provisions of the constitution and statutes of Florida relating to reapportionment for the nomination and election of the members of the Senate and House of Representatives were invidiously discriminatory and in violation of the Constitution of the United States. The Florida legislature was directed to reapportion in accordance with constitutional requirements. A special legislative session convened by Governor Farris Bryant provided for a 135-member House of Representatives and a 46-member Senate. The proposal was accepted by the court as a "rational plan of reapportionment free from invidious discrimination," and was to be submitted to the voters of Florida in the November, 1962, elections.

13. Section 1(e) of the home rule amendment reads: "[The Dade County Home Rule Charter] may provide a method for establishing new municipal corporations, special taxing districts, and other governmental units in Dade County from time to time and provide for their government and prescribe their jurisdiction and powers."

14. *Fisher v. Board of Commissioners of Dade County*, 84 So. 2d 572 (Fla. 1956); the logic of the Fisher case was reaffirmed in *St. Lucie County—Ft. Pierce Fire Prevention Control District v. Higgs*, 141 So. 2d 744 (Fla. 1962).

15. *City of Fort Lauderdale v. Carter*, 71 So. 2d 260 (Fla. 1954); *Whisnant v. Stringfellow*, 50 So. 2d 885 (Fla. 1951).

16. Metro (Dade County, Florida) Ordinance Nos. 58–46, 59–8.

17. Metro (Dade County, Florida) Ordinance No. 60–7.

18. See above, note 13.

19. Section 1.01 A(11) of the home rule charter which covers "special purpose districts within which may be provided police and fire protection, beach erosion control, recreation facilities, water, streets, sidewalks, street lighting, waste and sewage collection, and disposal drainage and other essential facilities and services."

20. Section 5.05 provides that "the Board of County Commissioners and only the Board may authorize the creation of new municipalities in the unincorporated areas of the county after hearing the recommendations of the Planning Advisory Board, after a public hearing, and after an affirmative vote of the majority of the electors voting and residing within the proposed boundaries." For example, on December 6, 1960, Metro (Dade County, Florida) Ordinance No. 60–46 created a new municipality in Dade County, subject to the approval of the municipal charter by qualified electors, to be known as Islandia.

21. It has been suggested that Metro create a "paper" city for all the unincorporated areas so as to at least receive the $2 million in cigarette tax rebates which are presently going to the state. However, here, too, Section 5.05 might be interpreted to mean "real" cities rather than make-believe cities.

22. O. W. Campbell, Memorandum to County Commission: Financing Neighborhood Services (Miami: Feb., 1959. Mimeographed), p. 3.

23. One must not overlook the fact that no city would favor an annexation proposal unless the city itself believed it would benefit from such a transaction. For example, a high socio-economic community would welcome annexation of a similarly constituted area, but would be disinclined to annex a less desirable area.


18   Leadership

1. Dennis O'Harrow, Metropolitan Planning for Dade County: A Summary Report (Miami: Dec., 1958. Mimeographed), p. 51.

2. Robert C. Wood, Suburbia: Its People and their Politics (Boston: Houghton Mifflin, 1959), p. 184.

3. See above, p. 137.

4. Miami Herald, May 17, 1959, p. 1B.

5. Ibid.

6. A small group of the area's most influential and ardent consolidationists failed in 1959 to gain support from the Ford Foundation to establish a business-civic type research organization.

7. See above, pp. 143–144.

8. See Chapter 16.

9. The "leadership" survey was conducted by Dr. Ross C. Beiler, Professor of Government, University of Miami, in November and December, 1959 (University of Miami Survey No. 13). The survey was confined essentially to business and professional persons with actual or potential influence. Respondents to the survey fell into the following categories: business, 154; professions, 78; appointed officials, 11; mass media, 10; labor, 5; clergy, 3; elected officials, 2; and club women, 1.

10. Other organizations listed were League of Women Voters (20);

the University of Miami (15); television station WTVJ (13); the Florida Power and Light Company (11); the Dade County Development Council (8); the Government Research Council of the Miami-Dade Chamber of Commerce (8); the Miami Beach Taxpayers Association (5); and the Junior Chamber of Commerce (4). It is interesting to note that about 36 per cent of the interviewees did not list any organizations.

11. The list of the influentials and the number of times they were mentioned was as follows: Campbell (64); Pennekamp (61); Robert M. Morgan, special Metro auditor (41); County Attorney Darrey A. Davis (39); Abe Aronovitz, former mayor of the City of Miami (34); Mitchell Wolfson, owner of TV station WTVJ (26); Ben C. McGahey, then chairman of the Metro Commission (23); John S. Knight, editor and publisher of the *Miami Herald* (16); John McLeod, then a county commissioner (15); Winston W. Wynne, then a Coral Gables councilman and chairman of the Government Research Council (14); William C. Baggs, editor of the *Miami News* (13); Ralph Renick, WTVJ television newscaster (12); and Daniel J. Mahoney, publisher of the *Miami News* (12). It is significant that, with the exception of the former mayor of the City of Miami, every one of the persons listed as most influential was associated either with a government organization or with some facet of the mass media.

12. *Miami Herald,* May 24, 1959, p. 1B.

13. Professor Wallace S. Sayre of Columbia University points to a possible solution to this problem in the office of a "general manager" who is a professional administrator appointed to assist an elected chief executive, such as the mayor or county president. (See Wallace S. Sayre, "The General Manager Idea for Large Cities," 14 *Public Administration Review* 253–58 (Autumn, 1954). Such an arrangement is being tried in New York, San Francisco, New Orleans, Newark, and Philadelphia. Most scholars believe that it is still too early to evaluate the idea.

14. *Miami Herald,* Oct. 14, 1960, p. 1B.

15. *Miami News,* Oct. 14, 1960, p. 1C.

16. *Miami Herald,* Oct. 15, 1960, p. 6A.

17. County Attorney Darrey A. Davis and his staff should be given credit for the legal victories.

18. James K. Sours, "Some Observations on Management of Large Cities," *University of Wichita Bulletin,* Wichita, Kansas (Aug., 1957).

19. Charles R. Adrian, "Leadership and Decision-Making in Manager Cities: A Study of Three Communities," 18 *Public Administration Review* 211–12 (Summer, 1958).

20. Edward Sofen, "Problems of Metropolitan Leadership: The Miami Experience," *Midwest Journal of Political Science,* V (Feb., 1961), 18–38.

21. Aphorism of Professor Vergil Shipley, Government Department, University of Miami.

## 19   Metropolitan Miami in Perspective

1. Robert C. Wood, *Suburbia: Its People and Their Politics* (Boston: Houghton Mifflin, 1959), p. 300.

2. Scott Greer, *Governing the Metropolis* (New York: John Wiley, 1962), pp. 119–128.

3. Webb S. Fiser, *Mastery of the Metropolis* (Englewood Cliffs, N. J.: Prentice-Hall, 1962), p. 128.

4. Norton Long, Memorandum on Dade County, submitted to the Miami-Dade Chamber of Commerce and the Dade League of Muncipalities, September, 1961 (Typed).

5. Robert C. Wood, "A Division of Powers in Metropolitan Areas," in Arthur Maas (ed.), *Area and Power: A Theory of Local Government* (Glencoe, Ill.: The Free Press, 1959), p. 63.

6. Arthur W. MacMahon, *Federalism: Mature and Emergent* (New York: Doubleday, 1955).

7. Paul Ylvisaker, "Criteria for a 'Proper' Areal Division of Powers," in Arthur Maas (ed.), *Area and Power: A Theory of Local Government*, p. 28.

8. *Ibid.*, pp. 37–44.

# Index

transfer of City of Miami functions to Metro, 157–158; on lack of Metro community leadership, 199 ff; on his own resignation, 202; see also county manager

Cannon, Judge Pat, opinion on case of *Miami Shores* v. *Metro,* and city's cross complaint, 130–132

chambers of commerce, and autonomy amendment, 107, 112; see also home rule; Metro

charter, see home rule

Charter Boards, and home rule, 39 ff; decisions, notes, 279–280; see also First Charter Board; Second Charter Board; names and occupations of members—Appendix F

Charter Review Board, 181 ff; and Crandon Committee amendments, 182–184

cities, see home rule; Metro-division of powers; individual cities by name; area-topics (*e.g.,* fire protection, police protection, etc.)

City of Miami, transferal of Jackson Memorial Hospital to Dade County, 24 ff; city provisions of home rule, 41 ff; "yes" vote for home rule, 69; relationship to remainder of Dade County, 71 ff; opposition to "parasite" communities, 72; role of businessmen in consolidation movement, 72 f; political difficulties and dissatisfaction with county commission, 72–73; abolition proposal, 101 ff; dispute with Metro over zoning and building, 122–123; opposition to traffic control by Metro, 153–154; opposition to Metro, 155 ff; acquiescence in Metro court system, 157; referendum on transferal of charter rights to Metro, 157; see also Dade County; home rule; Metro (various headings); Miami; *Miami Herald;* membership on City of Miami Commission—Appendix B

City of Miami Commission, membership, see Appendix B

civil service, under Metro, 62

Committee to Stop Double Taxation, 102

communications, see consolidation; police protection

compromise proposal, 104–106; see also abolition proposal; autonomy amendment

confederation, and Metro, 58

conservatism, wealth a factor, 3 ff

consolidation, 25 f, 28 ff, 73–74; bill to consolidate tax-collecting agencies, 30; amendment to consolidate Dade County, City of Miami, and four municipalities of North Bay Village, Virginia Gardens, West Miami, and Flagler City, 30; lack of concern of electorate, 32; consolidation attempt of 1953, 33 ff; referendum demand of *Miami Herald* and *Miami News,* 34; approval of city referendum by legislature, 34; forces for and against, 34–35; defeat of referendum by City of Miami voters, 35; consolidation and Metro, 57; consolidationists and proposed transfer of City of Miami functions to Metro, 158; notes, 269 ff

constitution, of Florida, 6 ff; executive branch of government, 6 ff

contracts, power of municipalities under home rule, 56; see also home rule charter—Appendix G

Coral Gables, 13; center of opposition to consolidation, 30–31; "yes" vote on home rule, 69; opposition to Metro-ordinances, 94 ff; for and against autonomy, 111–112; analysis of anti-autonomy vote, 120; violation of Metro licensing ordinance, 124–125

Corcoran, John D., PAS consultant, on division of powers, 49; evaluation of final charter for Metro, 83

council-manager government, under Metro, 61

county, 8; see also home rule; Metro (various headings); area-topics (*e.g.,* fire protection, licensing, etc.)